Brian Pinnola

12/1/92 Ordered this book from The Center for Urban Policy Research, Rutgers University New Jersey. Book was not available for shipping until 11/29/93. Received book 11/30/93 and started reading.

5/26/94 Finished reading.

PLANNING AND ZONING NEW YORK CITY

SPONSORED BY

THE NEW YORK CITY PLANNING COMMISSION

Richard L. Schaffer, Chairman

Victor G. Alicea, Vice Chairman
Eugenie L. Birch, AICP
Amanda M. Burden
Anthony I. Giacobbe
Maxine Griffith
James C. Jao, RA
Brenda Levin
Joel A. Miele, Sr., PE
Edward T. Rogowsky
Ronald Shiffman, AICP
Jacob B. Ward
Commissioners

THE NEW YORK CITY DEPARTMENT OF CITY PLANNING

THE AMERICAN PLANNING ASSOCIATION

NEW YORK METRO CHAPTER
Sigurd Grava, President

PLANNING AND ZONING NEW YORK CITY

YESTERDAY, TODAY AND TOMORROW

Edited by TODD W. BRESSI

Copyright ©1993 by Rutgers, the State University of New Jersey

Published by the Center for Urban Policy Research
Building 4161—Livingston Campus
New Brunswick, New Jersey 08903
All rights reserved

Printed in the United States of America

Book design by Helene Berinsky and Suzanne Bennett

Library of Congress Cataloging in Publication Data

Planning and zoning New York City: yesterday, today, and tomorrow /
  edited by Todd W. Bressi.
    p. cm.
    "Based on the symposium 'Planning and zoning New York City.
  Yesterday, today, and tomorrow' held on January 30, 1992, in New
  York City, New York"—Pref.
    ISBN 0-88285-143-8
    1. Zoning—New York (N.Y.)—Congresses. 2. City planning—
  New York (N.Y.)—Congresses. 3. Zoning law—New York (N.Y.)—
  Congresses. I. Bressi, Todd W.
  HT 169.73.N47P58 1993
  333.73'17'097471—dc20   92-30574
                                                                              CIP

CONTENTS

Acknowledgments   vii

Introduction   ix

PART I
THE HISTORICAL FRAMEWORK

A 3D CBD: How the 1916 Zoning Law Shaped Manhattan's Central Business Districts
    Carol Willis   3

Zoning and the New Horizontal City
    Richard A. Plunz   27

The 1961 Zoning Revision and the Template of the Ideal City
    Roy Strickland   48

Zoning from 1961 to 1991: Turning Back the Clock—But with an Up-to-the-Minute Social Agenda
    Norman Marcus   61

Commentary
    Panel Discussion Participants—Moderator: Sigurd Grava; Frances Halsband, Jerold Kayden, Norman Marcus, Richard A. Plunz, Robert A. M. Stern, Roy Strickland, Carol Willis   103

PART II
FUTURE SCENARIOS

The Zoning of Today in the City of Tomorrow
Brian Kintish and John Shapiro — **119**

Zoning for Growth and Change
Peter D. Salins — **165**

Planning and Zoning for a Mature City
Michael Kwartler — **185**

Planning the Equitable City
R. Susan Motley — **206**

Commentary
Panel Discussion Participants—Moderator: Jonathan Barnett; Michael Kwartler, R. Susan Motley, Peter D. Salins, John Shapiro, Marilyn Taylor, Robert F. Wagner, Jr. — **224**

PART III
IMPLICATIONS

Reflections on Planning and Zoning New York City
Richard L. Schaffer — **239**

APPENDIX

A Brief Profile of Today's City and Trends for the Future
compiled by Eric Kober, with Larry Littlefield — **252**

Contributors — **262**

Credits — **265**

ACKNOWLEDGMENTS

This book, as was the symposium on which it is based—"Planning and Zoning New York City: Yesterday, Today, and Tomorrow," held on January 30, 1992, in New York City—is the result of the hard work of many individuals. Carol Clark, deputy executive director for Intergovernmental Relations of the New York City Department of City Planning, assumed responsibility for this project and managed it with her usual high degree of energy and talent. Her assistant, Suzanne Beilenson, also worked enormously hard on the project, as did my special assistant, Andrea Katz, and many other dedicated staff members.

My thanks to Sigurd Grava, president of the New York Metro Chapter of the American Planning Association, for his support and encouragement and to the members of the New York City Planning Commission for their valuable suggestions. Of course, my thanks to the authors of the papers comprising this book, as well as to the moderators and the respondents participating in the panel discussions.

Finally, I wish to express my gratitude to the organizations that funded the symposium and the editing of *Planning and Zoning New York City: Yesterday, Today, and Tomorrow:* the Vincent Astor Foundation, the J. M. Kaplan Fund, the New York City Community Trust, and the Charles H. Revson Foundation. These are foundations that have long appreciated the importance of sound planning and zoning for the future of our city, and I very much appreciate their support for this effort. I am especially grateful to Linda Gilles of the Vincent Astor Foundation; Joan Davidson, Suzanne Davis, and Anthony C. Wood of the J. M. Kaplan Fund; Patricia Jenny of the New York City Community Trust; and Eli Evans and Lisa Goldberg of the Revson Foundation for their support and encouragement.

Richard L. Schaffer
Chairman
New York City Planning Commission

ACKNOWLEDGMENTS

At the outset, I must thank the authors of the papers in this book and the panel discussion participants in the Commentary sections, who made this an extraordinary project to edit. All of us will benefit from their spirited efforts to revise their papers, which had already been polished for public presentation, in response to comments that were raised at the symposium on which this book is based, "Planning and Zoning New York City: Yesterday, Today, and Tomorrow," and within the extremely tight deadlines required to complete this book.

Eugenie L. Birch and Norman Marcus were instrumental in shaping the symposium and this book, *Planning and Zoning New York City: Yesterday, Today, and Tomorrow*. I must thank them, as well as Hilda Blanco, Sigurd Grava, Frances Halsband, Peter Mahoney, Peter D. Salins, Richard Scherr, John Shapiro, and Ayse Yonder for the advice, encouragement, and support they have given me.

I am indebted to the Design History Foundation, which afforded me the flexibility to undertake this project, and the Pratt Institute School of Architecture for providing me space to work. Also, I am grateful to my research assistants, Pankaj and Shalini Vaid, and to Tricia Solsaa, my office assistant at Pratt, who kept my correspondence flowing smoothly.

I, too, must acknowledge the many staff members of the New York City Department of City Planning who provided assistance, especially Carol Clark, whose energy drove this project; Suzanne Beilenson, for searching out and collecting most of the illustrations credited to the Department of City Planning; Sandy Hornick, for providing insight into the history of zoning and the planning challenges New York City faces; and Joan Squeri, secretary to Chairman Richard L. Schaffer. Ellen Reach, whose reporting service prepared the transcripts upon which the Commentary sections are based, provided drafts and discs efficiently.

Finally, I thank my wife, Amy B. Lempert, whose patience and support helped me keep this project moving.

Todd W. Bressi
Editor

INTRODUCTION

This book—*Planning and Zoning New York City: Yesterday, Today, and Tomorrow*—came about for two reasons. The first reason is that the year 1991 marked two very important anniversaries: It was the seventy-fifth anniversary of New York City's pioneering municipal planning document, the 1916 zoning resolution, which was the nation's first comprehensive zoning ordinance; and 1991 also was the thirtieth anniversary of the 1961 comprehensive revision of the zoning resolution, perhaps the most ambitious citywide land use strategy ever adopted in New York City.

The second reason is that New York City's revised charter mandates, I believe quite appropriately, that the City Planning Commission issue a planning and zoning report. The first one is required by December 1992, with a subsequent report due every four years thereafter. The planning and zoning report must include four sections: The first is a statement of the commission's planning policy; the second is a summary of the significant studies undertaken in the past four years; the third is an analysis of those portions of the zoning resolution that merit reconsideration in light of the stated planning policy of the commission; and the fourth is proposals for implementing the planning policy of the commission.

These milestones and the planning requirements of the revised city charter underscored the importance of analyzing the history of planning and zoning in New York City and of considering alternative scenarios for the twenty-first century. In particular, we felt it was important to reflect on the respective zoning resolutions of 1916 and 1961 and to ask such questions as: What were the planning visions and critical zoning concepts of the two resolutions? What impacts did they have on the land use, built form, and functioning of the city? What are the lessons we have learned and should keep in mind as we plan and zone for our city's future?

We commissioned the papers that form the bulk of this book from an experienced, independent, and diverse group of academics and practitioners. We also assembled an equally talented group of respondents to comment and offer their perspectives on these papers in the form of a panel discussion in the Commentary sections.

In part 1, the first group of papers sets the stage by telling us how zoning came to be in the form that we know it today. Carol Willis, an architectural historian who has provided invaluable scholarship about building early-twentieth-century New York City, describes the political and planning forces that came together in the 1916 ordinance and the effect of that ordinance on the city's physical form. Richard A. Plunz, an architectural historian who has written in depth on the history of housing in New York City, turns our attention to the impact of the 1916 zoning resolution on northern Manhattan and the other boroughs, where much of the growth since 1916 has been directed. Roy Strickland, an architect and historian, describes how planners, at midcentury, struggled to adapt prewar ideas about planning to a city that already was gaining a postindustrial footing. Norman Marcus, former general counsel to the New York City Planning Commission, details how fundamental changes in values, priorities, and planning goals have led to vast revisions in the 1961 zoning resolution.

In part 2, the second group of papers suggests where the city might go from here. The authors offer alternative perspectives with regard to planning visions, zoning, and regulatory regimes. They discuss the role of zoning as a tool to implement planning policies, recognizing that the zoning resolution, although the most powerful planning tool under the direct control of the City Planning Commission—the New York City Council willing, of course—is but one of a number of planning tools that the commission and the city planning department have available to them. Brian Kintish and John Shapiro, planning consultants who are experts in zoning, explore how well today's zoning resolution would respond to tomorrow's planning challenges and chart a course for revising the zoning resolution one land use at a time. Urban planning professor Peter D. Salins argues that the goals and structure of zoning must be less ambitious and more in line with the 1916 resolution. He foresees a more adaptable, efficient, and market-driven city, in which change is accommodated by a more coarse-grained, minimalist system of zoning regulation than the one we now have in place. Michael Kwartler, an architect and urban designer, describes a "place-based" planning approach that recognizes the importance of allowing appropriate change in manageable increments. He envisions a mature city of highly imaginable places and neighborhoods shaped by a more fine-grained zoning regime than the one we now operate under. R. Susan Motley, president of a community development firm and a former New York City planning commissioner, argues that the first priority should be creating an inclusive planning and zoning process, from which would emerge a more equitable city.

INTRODUCTION

After each of these two groups of papers, we present edited versions of the panel discussions that took place after drafts of these papers were presented at the symposium in January 1992. In part 3, I offer reflections on how we are addressing the planning and zoning issues that will shape New York City for decades to come. Finally, an appendix, compiled by city planning department staff Eric Kober and Larry Littlefield, includes a statistical profile of today's city and trends for the future.

Richard L. Schaffer
Chairman
New York City Planning Commission

PART I
THE HISTORICAL FRAMEWORK

A 3-D CBD:
HOW THE 1916 ZONING LAW SHAPED MANHATTAN'S CENTRAL BUSINESS DISTRICTS

CAROL WILLIS

Of the human acts that have shaped the magnificently *unnatural* geography of the city and created its unique sense of place, two stand out: the Commissioners' Plan of 1811 and the zoning resolution of 1916, with its later revisions. The first imprinted Manhattan with a two-dimensional plan, a rectangular grid defined by broad north-south avenues and multiple east-west cross streets and by its standard units, blocks of two hundred feet by six hundred to eight hundred feet. The second—zoning—determined the city's three-dimensional form by restricting uses by district and, especially, by limiting the maximum mass of a building allowed on a given site.[1]

The early-nineteenth-century Commissioners' Plan was a simple blueprint for the expansion of the city that delineated a separation between two types of space: public and private.[2] An illustration of the 1811 grid makes clear this binary condition; the white areas, which represented streets and an occasional park, were public space while the dark blocks were private. Ownership of property extended from the lot lines straight up into the stratosphere. Thus, a black-and-white diagram of private property versus public space cut horizontally through the city at the level of one hundred or five hundred or one thousand feet would look exactly the same as the commissioners' grid.

This situation changed dramatically with the passage of zoning in 1916. The ordinance introduced the concept of the zoning envelope, which defined the maximum mass allowed a building—that is, the limits of a spatial envelope beyond which a developer could not build (though a structure could, and often did, fill less than its maximum envelope). Although there were a number of different formulas, in general terms, the law required that after a prescribed vertical height above the sidewalk (usually ninety feet for

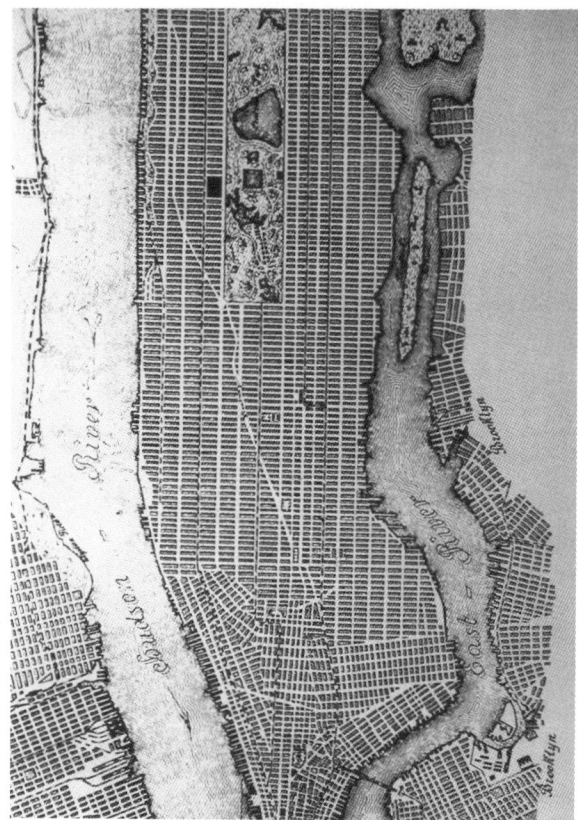

FIGURE 1
Commissioners' grid in lower Manhattan.

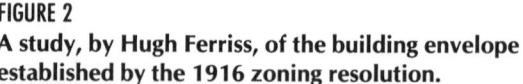

cross streets or one hundred fifty to two hundred feet for avenues), a building had to be stepped back within a diagonal plane projected from the center of the street. A tower of unlimited height was permitted over one-quarter of the area of the lot.

The resulting stepped-pyramid or "wedding cake" massing typified New York City high rises from 1916 until 1961, when the zoning law was revised. Whole ranges of masonry cliffs and mountains shaped by the zoning law sprang up in areas of intensive development, such as the East Forties and the garment district. Downtown, more than thirty-five new setback buildings squeezed into the already dense quarter and several lifted slender towers sixty or more stories into the sky.

In addition to prescribing the distinctive skyscraper massing, the 1916 ordinance created a new dimension of space *above and around* buildings. This "gray space" (since it was neither precisely public nor private) can be

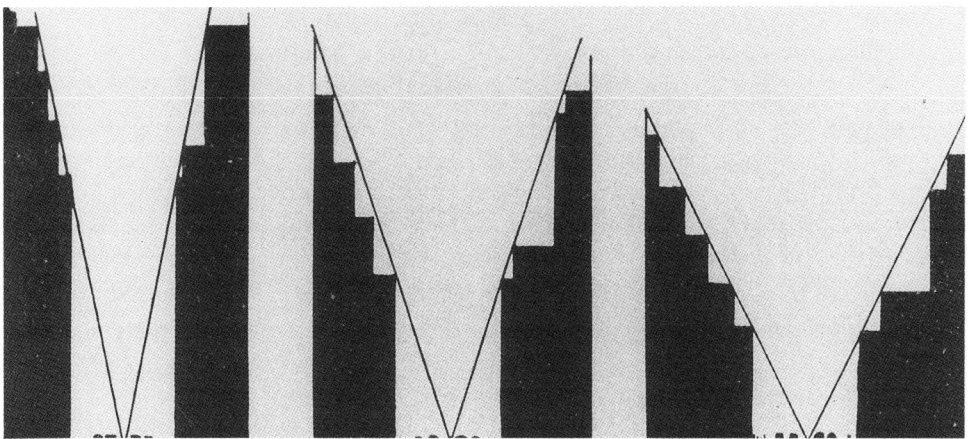

FIGURE 3
The setback line established in the 1916 zoning resolution helped control the maximum mass of buildings.

thought of as the negative of the zoning envelope; it comprised the three-quarters of the shaft of air directly above the property lines that the owner was prohibited from enclosing within walls. A hypothetical horizontal section cut through Midtown blocks at the level of five hundred feet would thus look quite different from the two-color diagram of the commissioners' grid; it would show white streets and gray blocks, with only 25 percent blackened to designate completely private space.

The concept of gray space can also be applied to the 1961 zoning ordinance and later revisions, which encouraged plazas, vest-pocket parks, indoor atria, and other amenities. These street-level spaces, which were traded by developers for bonus floors under the incentive provisions, were, in effect, privately financed public access areas. One way to view the history of zoning in New York City is as an effort to reclaim for the public a measure of open space, both on the ground and in the air, that was defined as private under the Commissioners' Plan.[3]

CONDITIONS LEADING TO THE ENACTMENT OF THE 1916 ORDINANCE

The distance of three-quarters of a century and the subsequent revisions of the first zoning law make it difficult today to comprehend how radical and innovative the concept was in 1916—radical in the sense that there were few legal precedents for such drastic restrictions on property rights and innovative in the way that it created formulas that limited height and bulk while still allowing the construction of tall and profitable towers.

New York was the first American city to combine in one ordinance the established precedent of districting by use with restrictions on the maximum mass allowed individual buildings. The 1916 zoning resolution is thus often referred to by historians as the nation's first *comprehensive* zoning law. Because of New York City's national dominance, the publicity given its legislation helped to propel a wave of zoning that spread across the country in the 1920s.[4] As planning historian Marc Weiss has demonstrated, the experience and legislation in New York City were unique because they originated in a movement to regulate *commercial* property rather than from a desire to protect residential uses.[5]

In the laissez-faire years before 1916, there were no restrictions on the height or lot coverage of structures other than tenements. After the introduction of elevators in the 1850s, which made it possible to rent space above the fifth or sixth floor, and with the spread of steel-cage construction in the 1880s and 1890s, towers soared to unprecedented heights. In 1898, 15 Park Row rose 387 feet above the sidewalk to become the world's tallest office building. By 1913, Manhattan boasted 997 buildings of eleven to twenty stories and fifty-one buildings of twenty-one to sixty stories.[6]

Typically, these early skyscrapers had the appearance of solid blocks extruded straight up above their lot lines. The Flatiron, Adams Express, and Equitable buildings are well-known examples of this type, but there were many other big, bulky office and loft buildings of about sixteen to twenty stories that began to transform areas like Park Avenue South, Union Square, and Fifth Avenue near Madison Square around 1910. In prestigious central locations, such as Wall Street and lower Broadway, high land costs and the potential for high rents produced even taller towers, often on very small sites. For its new home office, Bankers Trust purchased 4,900 square feet at the corner of Nassau and Wall streets for $820 a square foot (a record rate) and shoehorned a thirty-nine-story tower onto the lot. On Exchange Place, really an alley some forty feet wide, buildings of twenty and more stories walled the street, casting it into permanent shadow.

Such densities contributed to conditions that threatened public safety and greatly depressed rents for lower floors. Skyscrapers added to congestion on the streets, bred disease by inhibiting sunlight and ventilation in offices, and presented difficulties for fire control. Nevertheless, many believed there were few alternatives for the urban future. Popular prophecies in cartoons and magazines typically exaggerated current conditions, as in the famous illustration for *King's Views,* which depicted a city of towers that would be congested, chaotic, and incredibly dense.[7]

For several decades before 1916, government officials and urban reformers proposed legislation to curb rampant growth—without success. Calls for

FIGURE 4
The massive Equitable Building, seen here from Rector Street and Trinity Place, helped galvanize support for the zoning ordinance.

FIGURE 5
Rendering by Harry M. Pettit, from *King's Dream of New York* (1911), prophesied the outcome of overbuilding.

limits on heights were frequent from the 1870s on, when commercial buildings first began to challenge the dominance of church spires on the skyline. In 1884, a bill introduced to the New York State Legislature proposed a maximum building height of eighty feet throughout the city; although that bill failed to pass, a law was adopted in 1885 that restricted multifamily dwellings to seventy or eighty feet in height, depending on the width of the street.[8]

Proponents of the City Beautiful movement advanced aesthetic arguments for limiting building heights. In 1894, architect Thomas Hastings told the convention of the American Institute of Architects: "From the artistic point of view... there is nothing more unfortunate in the general aspect of the city than the necessarily broken sky-lines of our streets, because of there being no legal limitation as to the height of buildings."[9] Hastings favored a maximum of eight or ten stories, and he continued to argue for that limit in testimony to the 1913 Heights of Buildings Commission and even into the 1920s.[10]

In 1896, architects Ernest Flagg and George B. Post also spoke out against the rampant rise of commercial towers. Reporting their efforts, the *American Architect and Building News* noted: "The campaign, begun this year by the more thoughtful part of the public and the profession, against the fashion of high building is proceeding with much vigor, and, apparently, with a good deal of success."[11] Although Flagg would have preferred an absolute limit

FIGURE 6
A proposal for extending Madison Avenue south to Union Square reflected the influence of Baron Georges-Eugène Haussmann's improvements to Paris, including the ordered development along its avenues.

on heights, he recognized that in some areas real estate pressures made such an approach unrealistic. Therefore, he proposed that the height of buildings be geared to the width of the street (or a maximum of one hundred feet) but also be allowed a tower of infinite height to rise on one-quarter of the lot. Having first outlined this plan in 1896, he continued to promote it through the debates of the next twenty years, including in 1907, when he became the architect of the world's tallest office building; indeed, his Singer Building illustrated his proposed reforms by voluntarily limiting the coverage of its slender tower to 25 percent of the lot.[12]

Despite his readiness to accommodate the clamoring of capitalism for a presence on the skyline, Flagg dreamed of a harmonious and *horizontal* urbanity. As he professed to the 1913 Heights of Buildings Commission:

> To me it is absolutely incomprehensible how anyone can prefer the wild disorder of the American city to the dignified, restrained, and artistic arrangement of the European one, where uniform sky lines of the ordinary buildings give an appearance of refinement and civilization to the streets and afford a suitable setting and a proper background for the public buildings, churches and monuments that rise above them.[13]

Architects like Hastings, Flagg, and Daniel H. Burnham were leaders of the profession in the early 1900s, but these architects, rather than offering a conception of urbanism that responded to the needs of the expanding corporate and commercial city, continued nineteenth-century values. Their paradigm was Paris, especially the Second Empire capital as it was refashioned from 1852 to 1870 by Emperor Napoléon III and Baron Georges-Eugène Haussmann, the French administrator. The elegant avenues of five- and six-story apartment houses, characterized by continuous cornice lines and mansard roofs, were produced by strict building codes.[14]

The French laws were explained frequently in American architectural journals, and many American cities aspired to the Parisian model. In 1903, a group of architects and civic leaders serving on the City Improvement Commission recommended height controls for New York, envisioning new tree-lined boulevards and parks, such as Madison Square, ringed by ten-story buildings. Similarly, the 1909 *Plan of Chicago*, developed by Burnham for his colleagues at the Commercial Club, banished the skyscraper from its idealized "Paris by the Lake."[15]

At the time that New York City was debating zoning, height controls were, in fact, fairly common in American cities. The other major skyscraper metropolis, Chicago, set a 130-foot maximum in 1893 (which was raised to 260 feet in 1902 then lowered to 200 feet in 1910).[16] A table in the 1913 *Report of the Heights of Buildings Commission* listed twenty-one U.S. cities with height restrictions; many of these were set at 125 feet (as in Boston, where the law dated to 1891) while others ranged from 150 feet, as in Los Angeles, to 225 feet, as in Milwaukee.[17] That same year, 1913, the Woolworth Building topped off at 792 feet.

In New York City, for whatever reasons—the vitality of its capitalist environment, the desire of corporations for a symbol on the skyline, or the water-bound confines of lower Manhattan—the pressures to multiply the value of land by stacking story upon story were enormous. Although there was another attempt from 1906 to 1908 to control heights by revising the building code, again the proposals of Flagg and other advisers failed to be implemented.[18] Urban reformers and others who continued to campaign for controls found greater sympathy at city hall after Fusion party Mayor William J. Gaynor and Manhattan Borough President George P. McAneny took office in 1909, but they still could not force legislation without the support of business and real estate interests.

That support finally began to materialize between 1911 and 1913 and led directly to the passage of the 1916 zoning law. There were two major causes for this shift, both rooted in the drive to stabilize real estate values. The first was the concern about overbuilding in lower Manhattan, both in the increased scale of such mammoth new structures as the Equitable Building at 120 Broadway and in the rate of vacant office space. The second was the lobbying of the Fifth Avenue Association, a powerful group of merchants, hotel operators, and business interests that was organized in 1907 to fight the spread of loft buildings into the fashionable retail district north of Thirty-fourth Street.

The Equitable Building, completed in 1915 as the proposed guidelines for the zoning ordinance were being debated, was one of the last, but most egregious, examples of the problems of unregulated development. The largest office building in the world (in terms of volume: 1.2 million square feet), it covered an entire block of just under an acre and housed thirteen thousand workers.[19] At 542 feet tall, the enormous limestone-clad slab cast shadows across several blocks of prime rental space to the north, including much of the Singer Tower. The Equitable stole light and clients from surrounding buildings. Many owners requested and were granted reductions in tax assessments due to the decline in the value of their properties.[20] Although the rampant growth represented by the Equitable was hardly new, it dramatized the vulnerability of real estate values to actions of not only immediate neighbors but also greedy developers blocks away.

Unstable property values also were a problem uptown, where retailers on Fifth Avenue were fighting the proliferation of manufacturing lofts on side streets.[21] In the early 1900s, many of the same merchants had abandoned the Ladies' Mile shopping district south of Twenty-third Street after that area had been flooded with lofts used by the garment industry. The immigrant

FIGURE 7
Merchants and hoteliers along Fifth Avenue north of Thirty-fourth Street worried that loft factories would cluster nearby. Fears of unstable property values also led to support for zoning.

workers who spilled out onto the avenue during lunch hour and other breaks discomforted the upper-class shoppers and the area lost its chic. Store owners relocated farther north among the mansions and high-priced hotels in the area between Thirty-fourth and Fifty-ninth streets—but again, new loft buildings began to cluster near their markets. Property values in the old and largely vacant district south of Twenty-third Street declined sharply, and many people feared that lofts would invade the new area. The *Real Estate Record and Guide* warned: "People living there would have to move out, abandoning their homes; the principal retail section would be ruined; the hotels would lose their guests, and New York City as a whole would receive a death blow."[22]

In 1911, the Fifth Avenue Association appealed for action to a sympathetic McAneny, then Manhattan borough president and, after November 1913, president of the Board of Aldermen.[23] A commission was established and a report prepared that recommended that buildings on Fifth Avenue be limited to 125 feet. Although the merchants would have preferred to prohibit manufacturing entirely, the legal grounds for such an action were uncertain. Since the police power of municipal governments to limit heights by districts had been upheld in the courts, the 125-foot cap seemed the better solution, as it would have the effect of making loft construction uneconomical without adversely affecting retail stores.

The initiative of the powerful Fifth Avenue Association opened the door for a broader view of planning that had been the goal of reform-oriented officials, such as McAneny and his close colleagues Edward M. Bassett, Lawson Purdy, the city tax assessor, and Nelson P. Lewis, the chief engineer of the Board of Estimate. All four men were key figures in drafting the 1916 ordinance and were active in the planning movement nationally.

On February 27, 1913, the Board of Estimate adopted a resolution proposed by McAneny to establish a Committee on City Planning that would investigate the feasibility of regulating the heights of buildings and dividing the city into separate use districts. This committee appointed several advisory groups, which held a succession of conferences, prepared a report with specific guidelines, and drafted a bill to be sent to the state legislature that would amend the city's charter to give the Board of Estimate the power to regulate the heights and uses of buildings.[24]

After that bill was signed into law on April 14, 1914, a second body was formed to hash out the specifics of the code and to win it wide public support. Officially appointed on June 26, 1914, the Commission on Building Districts and Restrictions methodically began the task of accumulating data, holding public hearings, sounding out the business community, and considering neighborhood requests for changes in the proposed boundaries of districts. The commission's progress was slow, and by January 1916, when the promised report was not forthcoming, the frustrated Fifth Avenue Association threatened independent action—a boycott against suppliers who operated factories within the area between Thirty-third and Fifty-ninth streets and Fourth and Seventh avenues. Greater attention from the commission convinced the merchants to drop the boycott, and on March 10, 1916, a tentative report was submitted to the Board of Estimate and public hearings were scheduled.[25]

After the series of required hearings and yet another round of informal public hearings, modifications were made and subcommittee reports issued in order to ensure the cooperation of various city agencies and officials.[26] Nearly two years later, after considerable politicking and revisions, the zoning resolution came to a vote on July 25, 1916, and passed the Board of Estimate by a vote of fifteen to one, with the borough president of Staten Island as the lone dissenter.[27]

Why did the ordinance written from 1913 to 1916 succeed when so many earlier efforts had failed? In one sense, New York City was simply catching up to national changes. These years represented the last gasp of

Progressive Era reforms and a time of growing professionalism in city planning. At annual meetings of the National Conference on City Planning, which began in 1909, planners enthusiastically promoted the concept of zoning, especially as practiced in some German cities, as part of a program of comprehensive planning. By this time, advocates of zoning also were beginning to feel confident that there were sufficient legal precedents to defend zoning's constitutionality. In 1908, Los Angeles had enacted the country's first citywide use zoning and successfully defended it in court under the principle of the municipal police power. In 1909, the U.S. Supreme Court upheld Boston's height controls.[28]

The key factor in the enactment of zoning, however, was the depressed state of the real estate industry. The city had experienced record activity in conveyances and construction in 1905 and 1906, then a sharp decline during the financial panic of 1907. Another banner year in 1909 saw the largest number of building plans ever filed in the Borough of Manhattan. Then a slow, but steady, decline began. In January 1915, the *Real Estate Record and Guide* reported that the previous two years had been a time of "unprecedented stagnation" and that prospects for recovery were uncertain.[29] Vacancies in high-rise buildings south of Chambers Street in 1913 averaged 12.5 percent, with rates for the second through sixth floors running from 15.0 to 17.0 percent.[30] Given these conditions of oversupply, the real estate industry began to perceive regulation as working in its interest and to support the proposed zoning resolution.[31]

The 1916 zoning resolution was thus the product of more than twenty years of debate over the perennial problem of overbuilding, as well as a response to the exigencies of real estate cycles well beyond the control of planners. The alliance that supported zoning included city officials, civic reformers, architects and engineers, real estate and business interests, and their financial institutions. Although owners of residential property in all of the boroughs also figured in the support, they were not a catalyst.[32] Each group had somewhat different interests and goals, but the decisive factor in the passage of legislation in 1916 was the desire to protect property values, especially the high and extremely vulnerable values of commercial land in Manhattan.[33]

THE REGULATIONS AND THEIR IMPACT ON THE CENTRAL BUSINESS DISTRICTS

The 1916 zoning resolution established two types of regulation: the separation of *uses* by districts and restrictions on the *height, bulk, and area* of buildings. Maps of the entire city were prepared that indicated which regulations governed development at any specific location. The resolution also outlined an administrative procedure for enforcing and amending the code through the Board of Standards and Appeals.[34]

There were three categories of uses: residence, business, and unrestricted. Divisions were quite straightforward. Unrestricted districts meant exactly that. Residential districts permitted houses, apartments, hotels, clubs, schools, churches, and other cultural and institutional uses. Small-scale businesses, such as doctors' offices, dressmakers, and artists' studios, also were allowed. Business districts encompassed a broad range of commercial functions but excluded any industry that was "noxious or offensive by reason of the emission of odor, dust, smoke, gas, or noise."[35] Among the many uses expressly forbidden were brewing and distilling, fat rendering, fertilizer manufacture, garages for more than five vehicles, sawmills, and stockyards. Other types of light manufacturing, such as the garment trades, were permitted but limited to no more than 25 percent of the total floor space of the building.

In general, the mapping of use districts tended to reinforce rather than alter existing patterns. Most of the east side of Manhattan was zoned either as business or unrestricted, except for Fifth and Park avenues and their crosstown streets near Central Park. The Upper West Side was solidly residential, save for Broadway and Amsterdam and Columbus avenues. The majority of sites below Twenty-third Street were unrestricted, but the financial district was designated for business, as were the principally residential areas of Greenwich Village and the tenement districts of the Lower East Side. Midtown above Twenty-third Street and between Second and Tenth avenues was almost entirely a business zone, except for the area west of Seventh Avenue from Thirty-fourth to Forty-second streets (which became the garment district in the 1920s). Consequently, the expansion of the lofts and activities that had precipitated the protests of the Fifth Avenue Association was limited, although light manufacturing activities were still possible in 25 percent of a mixed-use building.

The zoning envelope was the most innovative aspect of the ordinance. Although the concept of regulating bulk had precedents in Parisian building codes, at the scale introduced in New York City, the formula for a maximum spatial envelope was entirely new. The idea of stepping back the upper floors to allow more light to reach the street had first been suggested in the 1890s, and in 1907 and 1908, several prominent architects, including David K. Boyd, had proposed a formula for setback massing.[36] That idea, combined with Flagg's plan for allowing a tower on one-quarter of the site, became the basis of the zoning envelope.

There were five formulas regulating the height and bulk of buildings. All were based on the width of the street and the setback principle, but each resulted in a slightly different spatial envelope. For example, in a "one-and-

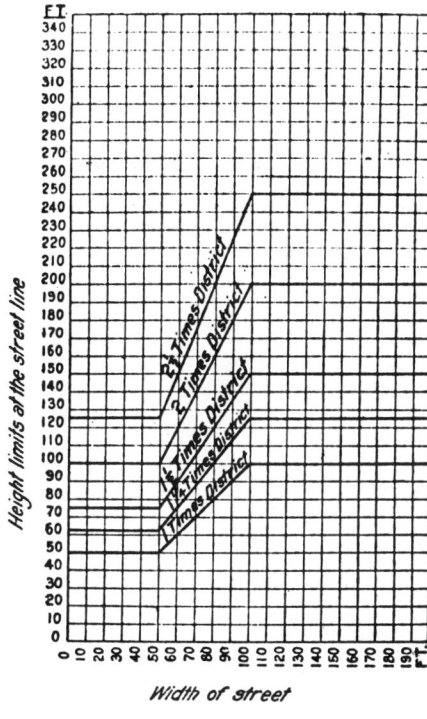

Width of street

FIGURE 8
Chart showing height limits at the street line for all street widths in all height districts.

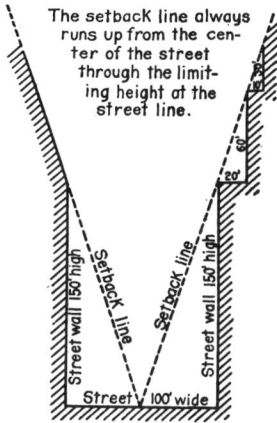

FIGURE 9
Typical example of the setback principle in a "one and one-half times" district for a one hundred-foot-wide street.

one-half-times district," if the street were one hundred feet wide, the facade could rise sheer to one hundred fifty feet before the first setback. Above that level, the mass had to step back in a ratio of 1:3—that is, a one-foot setback for each three feet of additional height. In a "two-times district," if the width of the street were one hundred feet, the building could reach two hundred feet before it had to begin stepping back at the rate of one foot for each four feet of additional height.[37]

All of Manhattan was liberally zoned as one-and-one-half-, two-, or two-and-one-half-times districts, except for the corridor of Fifth Avenue between Thirty-second and Fifty-ninth streets and two principally residential areas in the northwest corner of the island, Washington Heights and Inwood, which were designated one-and-one-quarter-times districts. The different formulas produced many permutations because both the width of streets and avenues and the factor of multiplication varied. In general, buildings on avenues could rise sheer for about fourteen to eighteen floors; on side streets, they were generally nine to twelve stories before the first setback.

The specific guidelines were drafted by George B. Ford, an architect and engineer who had worked in the office of George B. Post and who had served as the secretary for the Heights of Buildings Commission as well as a consultant to the Commission on Building Districts and Restrictions and the

Planning Committee. Precisely how Ford developed the formulas and to what extent he consulted and compromised with the real estate community are questions that deserve further research. Ford's envelopes were generous; the volume in the setbacks, together with the area allotted for a tower, added up to very high densities, especially for buildings on large sites. Yet the liberality of formulas ensured their success. Unlike other cities, such as Chicago, which capped heights but then kept raising and lowering them under pressures from real estate interests, New York City maintained its standards for forty-five years before it *reduced* the permissible bulk.

Another system, area districts, controlled the lot coverage, or the portion of the rear or sides of the lot that was kept open in yards or courts. There were five area districts, A through E. All of Manhattan was designated either A (for waterfront areas, in which coverage of 100 percent of the lot was allowed) or B (which called for either courts or rear yards approximately the same as those required by the Tenement House Law).[38]

The zoning ordinance had several important effects on skyscraper design and city building. First, if an owner wanted to exploit the maximum volume allowed for his lot, the shape of the building was, in effect, predesigned by the code. The zigguratlike forms of the Paramount Building at Times Square

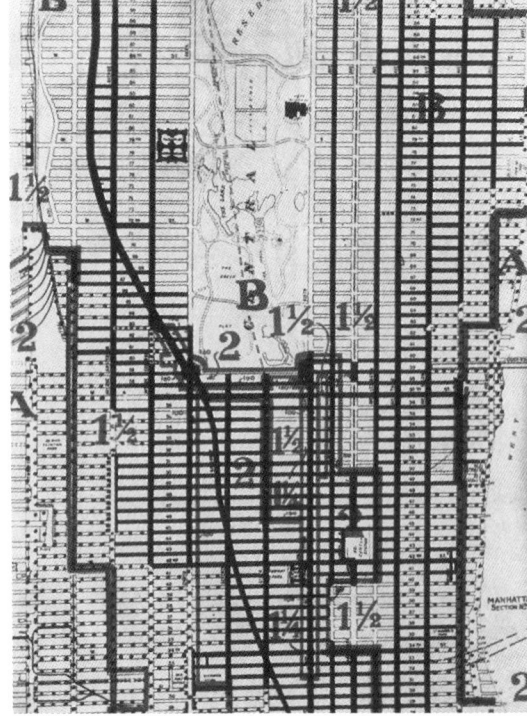

FIGURE 10
Map of height and bulk regulations for Midtown Manhattan.

THE 1916 ZONING LAW AND THE CBD

FIGURE 11
Hotel New Yorker.

FIGURE 12
Empire State Building.

or the Insurance Center at 80 John Street illustrate how owners and architects learned to press their structures to the boundaries of the zoning envelope. In fact, after about 1923 or 1924, many designers began to treat the setback as an aesthetic. Buildings were conceived as simple sculptural forms, a diminishing series of stacked boxes with their edges often emphasized with ornamental banding. Today, we associate this treatment with the Art Deco style, but in the twenties numerous other terms were used, including the "setback style," "New York style," or simply "modern."[39]

FIGURE 13
Hugh Ferriss, "Looking West from the Business Center."

FIGURE 14
Francisco Mujica, "Hundred-Story City in the Neo-American Style."

The limitation of the tower to one-quarter of the lot encouraged the assemblage of smaller parcels of land into large lots. Because much of the space inside a tall tower is consumed by elevator shafts and other service areas, lots had to be at least one hundred fifty by two hundred feet in order for the tower to contain enough office space to be profitable. The enormous size of the Empire State Building's site, 197 by 425 feet, meant that its shaft could expand to 100 by 212 feet. This was large enough for the fifty-eight elevators necessary to deliver first-class service to the building's eighty-five stories while allowing each of the tower floors to offer about fifteen thousand square feet of rentable space. Thus, the zoning formula, together with the economics of maximizing rental space, made larger buildings logical. However, such large sites were rare, principally because of the divided ownership of the standard twenty-five- by one hundred-foot parcels that were the legacy of the Commissioners' Plan of 1811 and because of generally high land prices.[40]

Nevertheless, many observers predicted that by 1960 or 1980, Manhattan would evolve into a metropolis of huge setback structures covering one or more full city blocks. Each superblock would be an autonomous "city within a city" linked by efficient mass transit and multilevel highways. The most famous designer of such prophecies was Hugh Ferriss, whose romantic charcoal renderings, especially in his 1929 book *The Metropolis of Tomorrow*, imagined a new urban topography of mountainous towers set at half-mile intervals and surrounded by abundant light, air, and open space.[41] Perhaps the most regimented vision of an urban vista extrapolated from the setback formula was the 1929 image created by Chilean architect Francisco Mujica, entitled "Hundred-Story City in the Neo-American Style."[42] Other prominent New York City architects, such as Harvey Wiley Corbett and Raymond Hood, offered what were intended as serious, if still somewhat unrealistic, proposals for a rationalized skyscraper city that were inspired by their thinking about future manipulations of the zoning law.

In the 1920s, zoning became a form-giving principle behind both a new approach to skyscraper design and a new vision of the modern metropolis. The idea that the *whole city*—private property as well as public space—could be subject to public controls inspired a new sense of power and optimism. Hood called zoning "the first great step forward into community planning under which the individual owner submits to the public welfare," and Ferriss proclaimed the law regarded building operations "not from the point of view of the individual plot, or owner, or designer, but from the argus-eyed view of the city itself."[43] These men saw zoning as a democratic dimension in city building because it protected the public good over the formerly unrestricted rights of property. In the unprecedented control that zoning afforded to shape both the individual building and the city plan, they perceived the possibility of not only regulating further urban growth but also rationalizing it.

No such monumental order had been intended, or even foreseen, by those who drafted the law. In 1929, Ford recalled how in developing the different formulas for the zoning envelope, in addition to studying how to bring the most light and air into the street, he and his staff had worked to achieve a variety of architectural effects, including towers, terraces, and gables that "would permit all the variety and spontaneity of treatment that we are revelling in today."[44] Ford made the realistic assumption that, for the most part, new buildings would replace older ones lot by lot rather than block by block.

The zoning ordinance was a practical, not a visionary, document. No particular ideal of urbanity or architectural aesthetic motivated it, as had been the case with the City Beautiful movement, and as a result, it offered no inspiring visual imagery—no "big plans" with the "magic to stir men's blood," as in Burnham's famous phrase, nor was it a philosophical critique of the skyscraper and its place in civic life. Such concerns were considered insufficient legal grounds for the municipal government to exercise police power over private property. Crafted in compromise by a broad coalition of interests, zoning had to be fairly modest in its restrictions and readily amendable.

Indeed, the major criticism of zoning in the mid-1920s by many of the original reformers, such as Bassett, Purdy, and Ford, was that it was far too liberal. In the years immediately after its passage and during the postwar period, support for zoning had been nearly unanimous; but the extraordinary building boom that began in New York City in late 1921 and that lasted into 1930 and 1931 (during which time the city nearly doubled its total office space) clearly demonstrated the extreme densities that could occur within the regulations. Variances were easily won, and height districts were increased in a number of areas, including Eighth Avenue from Thirty-third to Fifty-sixth streets.[45] As construction broke records in 1925 and 1926, calls for stricter regulations became more insistent, and a major debate over how to curb the skyscraper was waged in both professional circles and in public forums. In 1926, Mayor Jimmy Walker appointed the City Commission on Plan and Survey, a forerunner of the City Planning Commission, to recommend changes in the resolution. However, no major actions to reduce building heights or bulk were passed during the boom.

Was the 1916 zoning resolution a success or a failure? The answer is different for idealists and realists. Some of the disparity is suggested in the comments of Bassett in a discussion of the revisions he proposed for his own legislation in 1931:

> New York City did not advance very far when it adopted the two and two and one-half times limit with setbacks and 25 percent towers, and there may be many who say that with this limit the skyscraper problem

THE 1916 ZONING LAW AND THE CBD

FIGURE 15
At sunset, the buildings on Manhattan's cross streets are turned into a silhouette that resembles the building envelopes instituted by the 1916 zoning.

was hardly touched, that skyscrapers are being erected as high as they probably would have been without zoning, that the total rentable floor space in the high building blocks has not been affected, and that street congestion is as great as if buildings had been left unregulated. These criticisms are partly true. On the whole, however, the results of zoning have been to give greater access of light and air to separate buildings and to the street. The opportunity of blanketing one building by another has been lessened. Architecturally New York has been greatly improved by zoning. What more can be done? Nearly all will admit that something ought to be done. But to say what ought to be done and to say what can be done are two quite different things.[46]

The temptation to measure the 1916 ordinance in 1990s' terms—for example, to criticize its restrictions on development as weak or as lacking a "vision" of the city—should be avoided. Zoning was (and is) not planning, and viewed in its proper historical context, the first ordinance was a tremendous, not a timid, step. For the first time, there existed a real tool that could shape actual masses and spaces and that applied to the *entire* city. Zoning thus changed the mind-set of many who speculated on the urban future, infusing them with a new sense of efficacy.[47]

Not the least of the law's legacy was its influence on the visual experience of being in Manhattan's most densely developed commercial districts. One of the most extraordinary effects in any modern city occurs on Midtown cross streets, where the constructed canyon walls shave back like eroded cliffs and frame a sliver of open space that seems a "slice of sky." Because these streets typically end at water and there is often nothing visible on the distant shore, one has the sense that the road and sky meet without mediation, like the vanishing point of a one-point perspective drawing. The narrowness of this space makes it read as a *positive* shape rather than as a void. The slice of sky is often radiant with light, as in early summer, when, around eight in the evening, the sun sets precisely on the axis of the cross streets. There is hardly a more thrilling experience in architecture than to walk along an avenue during these minutes and to look west at each intersection to see the raking light across masonry facades and the pastel colors of the sunset.

These effects are produced by the rigid rectilinearity of the nineteenth-century commissioners' grid and the richly plastic massing formulas of the 1916 zoning ordinance. Both artificial systems were imposed on the island with the purpose of turning land into property; in doing so, they created Manhattan's magnificent morphology.

NOTES

1. The published reports of the two city-sponsored zoning commissions are extremely rich documents, packed with research data, tables, illustrations, and testimony, as well as the specifics of the proposed regulations and the final legislation. See *Report of the Heights of Buildings Commission* (New York: Board of Estimate and Apportionment, 1913) and Committee on the City Plan, *Final Report of the Commission on Building Districts and Restrictions* (New York: Board of Estimate and Apportionment, 1916), hereafter referred to as *Final Report*.

There are two outstanding historical discussions of the zoning resolution. S. J. Makielski, Jr., in *The Politics of Zoning* (New York: Columbia University Press, 1966), concentrates on the politics of reform that promoted zoning and the compromises among various interests that created the final legislation. Seymour I. Toll, in *Zoned American* (New York: Grossman, 1969), details the legal history of zoning.

THE 1916 ZONING LAW AND THE CBD

Useful sources that include critiques of zoning that were made in the 1920s are Thomas Adams, *Buildings: Their Uses and the Spaces About Them,* Vol. 6: *Regional Survey of New York and Its Environs* (New York: Regional Plan Association, 1931), and George B. Ford, *Building Height, Bulk, and Form* (Cambridge: Harvard University Press, 1931).

For more recent analysis, see Michael Kwartler, "Zoning as Architect and Urban Designer," *New York Affairs* 8 (Winter 1985): 104–119; and two essays, Marc A. Weiss, "Density and Intervention: New York's Planning Traditions," and Keith D. Revell, "Regulating the Landscape in New York City: Real Estate Values, City Planning, and the 1916 Zoning Ordinance," in David Ward and Oliver Zunz, eds., *The Landscape of Modernity* (New York: Russell Sage, 1992).

2. On the Commissioners' Plan, see Edward K. Spann, "The Greatest Grid: The New York Plan of 1811," in Daniel Schaffer, ed., *Two Centuries of American Planning* (Baltimore: Johns Hopkins University Press, 1988), pp. 11–39.

3. Norman Marcus takes up this point, in regard to the 1961 comprehensive revision, in his paper in this book, "Zoning from 1961 to 1991."

4. By the end of the decade, nearly eight hundred municipalities had enacted such laws, which affected about three-fifths of the nation's urban population, nearly thirty-seven million people. See Toll, *Zoned American,* p. 188.

5. Marc A. Weiss, "Skyscraper Zoning: New York's Pioneering Role," *Journal of the American Planning Association* 58 (Spring 1992).

6. *Report of the Heights of Buildings Commission,* p. 15.

7. A compilation of such illustrations can be found in Moses King, ed., *King's Views of New York, 1886–1915* (New York: Arno, 1974).

8. *American Architect and Building News* (15 March 1884): 121, and (20 June 1885): 289. Hotels and other large residential buildings without individual kitchens were exempted.

9. Thomas Hastings, "High Buildings and Good Architecture," *American Architect and Building News* (17 November 1894): 67–68.

10. *Report of the Heights of Buildings Commission,* pp. 234–235.

11. The article discusses the proposals of Flagg that were published in *Cosmopolitan* (see note 12) and refers to Post's speech; see *American Architect and Building News* (16 May 1896): 61.

12. See Ernest Flagg, "The Dangers of High Buildings," *Cosmopolitan* (May 1896); and Ernest Flagg, "The Limitation of Height and Area of Buildings in New York," *American Architect and Building News* (15 April 1908): 125–127.

In the latter article, Flagg wrote: "I think the [height] limit proposed here of one and one-half the width of the street is more than it ought to be, but I don't believe that any less would be acceptable [to property owners]." With some changes, his idea for the 25 percent tower was incorporated into the 1916 ordinance.

For an assessment of Flagg's career, see Mardges Bacon, *Ernest Flagg: Beaux Arts Architect and Urban Reformer* (Cambridge: MIT Press, 1986).

13. *Report of the Heights of Buildings Commission,* p. 224.

14. In Paris, the height that buildings were allowed to rise from the street line generally was equal to the width of the street; additional stories, tucked under mansard roofs, were set back within an arc that allowed sunlight to reach the pavements. For a discussion of the French regulations, see the *Report of the Heights of Buildings Commission.*

15. For the Parisian precedents for the *Plan of Chicago,* see Joan Draper, "Paris by the Lake," in John Zukowsky, ed., *Chicago Architecture, 1872–1922* (Munich: Prestel, 1987), pp. 107–119.

16. For the dates of Chicago's vacillating height limits, see *Studies on Building Height Limitations in Large Cities* (Chicago: Chicago Real Estate Board, 1923).

17. *Report of the Heights of Buildings Commission*, p. 23. Of course, every city save Washington, D.C., eventually lifted the caps when real estate pressures became too great.

18. See, for example, the recommendations of the committees of the American Institute of Architects and the Society of Beaux Arts Architects as reported in *American Architect and Building News* (17 June 1908): 15–16.

19. Sally K. Chappell, "A Reconsideration of the Equitable Building in New York," *Journal of the Society of Architectural Historians* 49 (March 1990): 92.

20. Toll, *Zoned American*, p. 71.

21. The most vivid account of this influence on the passage of zoning is given by Toll in chapters 3 and 6 of *Zoned American;* also see Makielski, *Politics of Zoning,* pp. 11–18.

22. As quoted in Robert A. M. Stern, Gregory Gilmartin, and John Massengale, *New York 1900* (New York: Rizzoli, 1983), p. 33.

23. Makielski, *Politics of Zoning,* pp. 11–18 passim. Much of the following discussion of the political actions that led to the passage of the zoning resolution is based on Makielski's research.

24. Makielski, *Politics of Zoning,* pp. 14–23.

25. Makielski, *Politics of Zoning,* pp. 23–28, 30–32.

26. As described by Makielski, the views expressed in the hearings have a familiar ring that transcends the decades: "The local civic organizations were eager to endorse the plan, but they were also eager to ask for larger and larger restrictive areas—to protect their neighborhoods, playgrounds, and parks. The business and real estate groups, whose support had obviously been won, struggled for room. Their chief concern was the boundaries of the unrestricted districts—do not limit the area available for growth, they argued." Makielski, *Politics of Zoning,* p. 33.

27. Ibid., pp. 39–40.

28. Marc Weiss, *The Rise of the Community Builders: The American Real Estate Industry and Urban Land Planning* (New York: Columbia University Press, 1987), pp. 79–106.

29. For data about the building industry, see "A Review and a Prospect," *Real Estate Record and Guide* (6 January 1912): 5–6; and "Real Estate Review and Prospect," *Real Estate Record and Guide* (2 January 1915): 3–4.

30. *Report of the Heights of Buildings Commission,* appendix 3.

31. For official statements by members of the real estate industry in support of zoning, see the "Record of Testimony and Statements in Relation to the Necessity for Districting Plan" in the *Final Report.* Marc Weiss has analyzed the support given zoning by the real estate and financial communities in "Density and Intervention" (see note 1). Also relevant is another Weiss article in which he argues that there is a pattern to efforts to regulate the building industry that relates directly to the cycles of boom and bust—that is, that government initiatives are successful only in a downturn or the early phases of an upturn but never during the boom. The situation in New York City from 1913 to 1916 sustains that argument. See Marc Weiss, "The Politics of Real Estate Cycles," *Business and Economic History* 20 (1991): 1–8.

32. As with commercial land, the ordinance as framed tended simply to follow and reinforce existing residential patterns. See Richard A. Plunz's paper in this book, "Zoning and the New Horizontal City."

33. Although owners of residential property in all of the boroughs also provided support for zoning, they were not a catalyst. As with commercial land, the ordinance as framed tended simply to follow and reinforce existing residential patterns.

THE 1916 ZONING LAW AND THE CBD

34. The Building Zone Resolution, passed on July 25, 1916, was reprinted many times in a practical format. I have used one of the pamphlets prepared by George B. Ford for the New York Title and Mortgage Company that included the amendments in the code made on January 1, 1920, and published that year: *New York City Building Zone Resolution: Restricting the Height and Uses of Buildings and Prescribing the Minimum Sizes of Their Yards and Courts.*

35. Ibid., p. 7.

36. Articles in architectural journals in the 1890s and early 1900s discussed the "ancient law of lights" as a precedent for the idea of containing the upper floors of a building within an angle drawn from the street; today, the concept is known as the sky-exposure plane.

There were a number of architects who proposed a setback massing for tall buildings. In Chicago in 1891, Louis H. Sullivan published his well-known, but never executed, design for the "Fraternity Temple," also known as the Odd Fellows' Hall. Similar projects were suggested by New York City architects. In *Municipal Affairs* (New York: The Reform Club, 1898), Charles R. Lamb published drawings of a proposed system of setback skyscrapers with bridges that connected pedestrian walkways on upper terraces, an idea that he continued to promote in newspaper articles for the next ten years. Another supporter of the setback solution was David Knickerbacker Boyd, president of the Philadelphia chapter of the American Institute of Architects, who described the idea in his article, "The Skyscraper and the Street," in *American Architect and Building News* (18 November 1908): 281–383; Boyd repeated his proposals to the 1913 commission; see *Report of the Heights of Buildings Commission,* pp. 188–190.

37. The five basic formulas were:

- 1 times width of street = 1-foot setback : 2-foot rise
- 1¼ times width of street = 1-foot setback : 2½-foot rise
- 1½ times width of street = 1-foot setback : 3-foot rise
- 2 times width of street = 1-foot setback : 4-foot rise
- 2½ times width of street = 1-foot setback : 5-foot rise

38. Ford, *New York City Building Zone Resolution,* p. 13.

39. For example, one of the most prolific setback skyscraper designers, Ely Jacques Kahn, wrote in 1926: "Almost unknown to the New Yorker himself, a new style of architecture is being created that is so characteristic of New York that it would be more logical by far to call it a New York style, although it is also something essentially American." I discuss and document the positive reactions to zoning by the architectural profession; see Carol Willis, "Zoning and Zeitgeist: The Skyscraper City in the 1920s," *Journal of the Society of Architectural Historians* 45 (March 1986): 47–59.

40. A recent *New York Times* article demonstrated the persistent difficulty in assembling multiple sites by noting that "17 years after abandoning its vision of a second Rockefeller Center east of Times Square, the Durst Organization has apparently given up trying to assemble one last major parcel on the Avenue of the Americas, and will content itself with building one-story shops." David Dunlap, "Commercial Property: Holdouts," *New York Times* (28 February 1990): sec. 10, p. 7.

Several full-block buildings were erected around 1930, including the Waldorf-Astoria Hotel, the Starrett-Lehigh warehouse, the London Terrace apartments, the office buildings on Madison Square for New York Life and Metropolitan Life Insurance, as well as the renowned three-block development of Rockefeller Center.

41. Hugh Ferriss, *The Metropolis of Tomorrow* (New York: Ives Washburn, 1929; republished by Princeton Architectural Press, 1986). Also, see my comments in an essay on the inspiration Ferriss derived from the zoning law in Carol Willis, "Drawing Towards Metropolis," in the 1986 edition.

42. Francisco Mujica, *The History of the Skyscraper* (Paris and New York: Architectural Press, 1929), Plate CXXIV.

43. Raymond Hood in "The Future of the Skyscraper," *New York Times* (13 September 1931): 2; Hugh Ferriss, "Civic Architecture," *Arts and Decoration* 18 (November 1922): 12–13.

44. George B. Ford, "What Makes 'The City Beautiful'?" in *Planning Problems of Town, City and Region: Papers and Discussions at the 21st Conference on City Planning* (Philadelphia: William F. Fell, 1929), p. 174; quoted in Revell, "Regulating the Landscape in New York City" (see note 1).

45. For a thorough discussion of the implementation of zoning in the 1920s and the reactions of the planning community and real estate interests, see Weiss, "Density and Intervention."

46. Edward M. Bassett, "Control of Building Heights, Densities and Uses by Zoning," in *Buildings: Their Uses and the Spaces About Them*, Vol. 6: *Regional Survey of New York and Its Environs* (New York: Regional Plan Association, 1931), p. 367.

47. For a further discussion of how zoning changed the way that architects perceived the urban future, see my article, Willis, "Zoning and Zeitgeist."

ZONING AND THE NEW HORIZONTAL CITY

RICHARD A. PLUNZ

The Building Zone Plan (commonly called the zoning resolution) that New York City enacted in 1916 has been universally viewed by historians as landmark legislation in relation to the issue of design control and the urban landscape.[1] Generally, this view focuses on those aspects of the resolution that pertain to tall buildings—the building setbacks that it generated became an emblem of Manhattan architecture in this century. Other aspects of the resolution, however, those related to its influence on development in the periphery of the city, have seen little discussion.

Admittedly, it is not nearly as easy to trace the resolution's direct, causal effect on the form of buildings in the city's outer neighborhoods as it is to trace the resolution's effect on center city office, loft, and residential towers. Outside Manhattan's central business and residential districts, the resolution functioned more as a catalyst than as a control. It worked in league with other forces, including the building code, the extension of mass transit routes, and the city's political economy, to produce the new development and the new forms of urbanism that emerged throughout much of the boroughs during the boom decade of the 1920s. What the resolution produced could be called a new horizontal city, a city characterized by neither the towers nor the tenements of Manhattan.[2]

Considering that the city saw more growth in the outer boroughs than it did in Manhattan after 1916, and that zoning provided a framework for this expansion, it is important to understand exactly how the resolution functioned as a control mechanism.

The direct physical intervention embodied in the "setback" portion of the Building Zone Plan leaves little doubt about the motivation of the zoning resolution. It assumed inordinate growth at the dense center of the city and took steps to provide a reasonable formal definition for it.

The lower density periphery of the city also was viewed as an area of inordinate growth; in fact, more growth than at the center. For lower density areas, then as now, the nature of the controls had to be different. For this latter context, the resolution functioned far less directly as an architectonic device. It was only one of several important tools that together acted as the final arbiter of form. The resolution's strongest presence, perhaps, lies in the arena of psychological order; it created the confidence that stimulated development while other legislative devices also contributed to physical coherence.

THE CASE FOR ZONING IN THE OUTER BOROUGHS

The report of the 1916 Commission on Building Districts and Restrictions was preceded by the report of a Heights of Buildings Commission in 1913, and it was in that report that the need for a comprehensive view of New York City development was first expressed. The building heights commission fulfilled its mandate to create the text for a law regulating the "height, size and arrangement of buildings," but the commission went further, arguing that zoning was needed throughout the city, not just in areas with concentrations of tall buildings. Its report made clear that there were pressing problems related to excessive building bulk and density outside Manhattan, noting that "there are areas in the Bronx and in Brooklyn where Lower East Side conditions of excessive congestion of population are being repeated."[3]

The need was obvious. By the turn of the century, development outside Manhattan was already significant and showed no signs of stopping. Brooklyn had long been a major city in its own right, and the Bronx was outpacing the rate of growth of Manhattan. Between 1910 and 1930, the population of Manhattan grew by only 1 percent, to 1,850,093. During the same period, Brooklyn's population surpassed Manhattan's, growing by 119 percent, to 2,560,401. The Bronx exploded, growing by 531 percent, to 1,265,258; likewise, Queens grew by 605 percent, to 1,079,129.[4]

Development in the Bronx and Queens differed drastically. By the end of the 1920s, the Bronx was a borough of apartments, with only 18.5 percent of the dwellings constructed between 1920 and 1930 built as one- or two-family houses. Queens was the opposite, with 70 percent one- and two-family houses.[5] Thus, the new building regulations would have to accommodate an unprecedented variety and scale of peripheral conditions.

The building heights commission, like its successor, made the argument that real estate values would be conserved by limiting heights of buildings, in the outer boroughs as well as in Manhattan. The report also discussed the question of the use of buildings in low-density areas:

ZONING AND THE NEW HORIZONTAL CITY

Again take the case of the man who builds a home in a district which at the time seems particularly suited for single family dwellings. In a few years the value of his property may be largely destroyed by the erection of apartment houses, shutting off light and air and completely changing the character of the neighborhood. When single family dwellings, apartment houses, stores and factories are thrown together indiscriminately, the health and comfort of home life are destroyed and property and rental values reduced.[6]

The success of this protectionist strategy would depend on isolating new, higher density growth within previously undeveloped areas. Herein lay one of the chief contradictions between the commission's ideals and the realities of urban development: much of the new growth of the 1920s involved increasing the density of already developed areas, presumably at substantial long-run increases in property and rental values.

The tendency toward making already developed areas more dense was directly in conflict with the ideological thrust of the building heights commission, which was a straightforward adherent of dispersal. Robert H. Whit-

FIGURE 16
Unimproved property in the Bronx: the borough grew tremendously from 1910 to 1930.

FIGURES 17, 18
The zoning ordinance sought to rationalize growth and protect land values by keeping apartments and stores out of single-family residence areas.

ten, the secretary of the Committee on the City Plan, described the priority of the Building Zone Plan in certain terms:

> Both the environment of the home and the home itself must be protected and safeguarded in every possible way if we would preserve under the necessarily crowded conditions of city life the physical and moral health and general well-being of the people.

He then quotes the commission:

> The necessity for reducing the stress and strain of city life is becoming more and more apparent. This is essential if the city is to be used, conserved and handed down to succeeding generations instead of being abused and exhausted.[7]

Of course, the term "home" is used pointedly here, carrying with it the ideal of "house" rather than "tenement." In this regard, the commission's outlook was consistent with the outlook of the housing reformers who had been active in New York for four decades. Housing reformers always coupled the realities of urbanization with the dream of escape—the idea that the deserving working class would be far better off in suburban cottages than in urban apartments, even though there was no practical possibility of achieving that goal.

Questions of use and density would be paramount in developing a strategy for shaping development on the city's periphery. The Commission on Building Districts and Restrictions attempted to come to grips with these issues in its final report,[8] but this turned out not to be so easy a task: mass transit held great promise for dispersing the city's population to lower densities and liberating them from density.[9] In practice, though, it tended toward the opposite.

THE BUILDING ZONE PLAN AND NEW YORK CITY'S MASS TRANSIT SYSTEM

The ideal of dispersal did not exactly result in the sanguine outcome for which reformers had hoped. In reality, the new mass transit lines tended to work against the goal of placing people in houses; rather, they generated a pattern of higher density development around station nodes and disrupted many existing lower density areas. The higher densities were necessary to pay off the infrastructure investment, a reality that the 1916 commission could not afford to overlook.

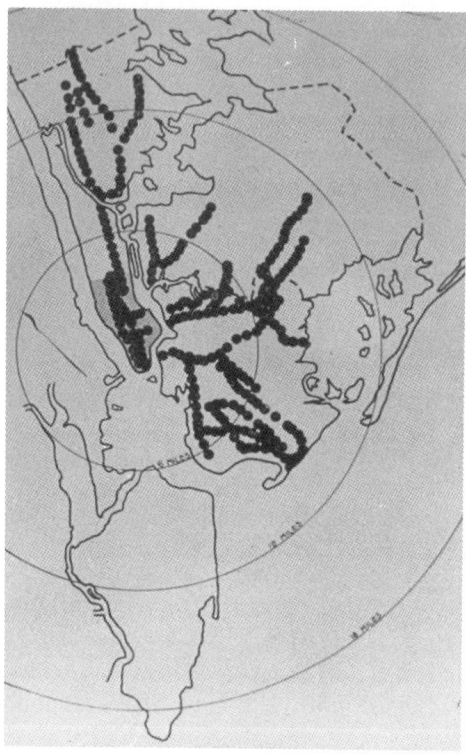

FIGURE 19
The earliest development in the outer boroughs took piace along mass transit lines. This map shows areas within a short walk of subway stations at the time zoning was passed.

This contradiction was at the core of the deficiencies of the Building Zone Plan in the boroughs. Transit worked against the dispersal ideas of the planners, yet the Building Zone Plan had to reflect the transit planning that had been in process during the previous four decades. By 1916, the previous four decades of mass transit initiatives were finally coming to substantial fruition in the boroughs. While key lines in Manhattan had been established early, most connections to the city's edges had remained primitive.[10]

The zoning resolution, in this regard, could only function to reinforce the obvious. Whitten later described this formulation in straightforward terms:

> While the location of the rail and water terminal facilities fixes the location of industry of the heavier type, the passenger transportation system is the chief factor in determining the location of business centers and sub-centers and in determining the building up and the intensity of use of various residential districts. The rapid transit system at present in operation or under construction will necessarily determine the general lines of city growth and development for many years to come.

A time zone transit map was carefully worked out showing the time from every part of the city to City Hall and to 14th Street. This time includes the time required to walk from any given location served by a transit line to the nearest station and the running time from that point to the City Hall or 14th Street. As a rule only the five-cent fare routes are considered. Areas beyond half a mile or a ten-minute walk from a transit line are not dealt with, as a half-mile belt is considered the limit of any considerable influence of a transit line. The time zone map includes lines planned and under construction as well as those now in operation and is based on estimated running time when the new dual subway system is in full operation.

This time zone map was in constant requisition to assist the judgment of the commission in its determination of the appropriate use and the appropriate intensity of use of particular areas.[11]

Thus, mass transit was the principal vehicle for projecting future growth. According to Whitten, the "main roads and thoroughfares" were also of "great importance," in that they "often fixed the location of future transit lines and local business streets."[12] Beyond that, he admits that "the entire zone plan . . . is based on a frank acceptance of existing conditions."[13]

In this sense, the plan was simply a logical reflection of the status quo, or at least of what the status quo would predictably become. Even though much of the land in the boroughs was not yet developed, and all of the transit lines were not yet in place, the development pattern was still irrevocably fixed. It was reactive rather than visionary; the real "vision" lay in the transit plan.

The question that arises, of course, is how and by whom the transit plan was implemented. The most one can say here is that it was a geopolitical evolution of considerable complexity and intrigue: from the old-money families and their large estates in the Bronx, the value of which would be enhanced by the public investment in transit; to the various entrepreneurs along the way, such as Edward A. MacDougall at Jackson Heights in Queens; to simple engineering and topographic constraints. The stakes were high. The subway subsidized land development and fueled profits. Jackson Heights was a classic example: it transformed from cornfields in 1910 to dense urban fragment less than two decades later, with the Corona Line as the elixir, carefully orchestrated by MacDougall and his Queensboro Corporation.[14]

Other existing conditions besides transit were considered in determining the configuration of the Building Zone Plan. The plan included maps of topographic features, vehicular traffic counts, population distribution, existing buildings, building use, building bulk, and land values.[15] This information was overplayed to defend the view that the density of development

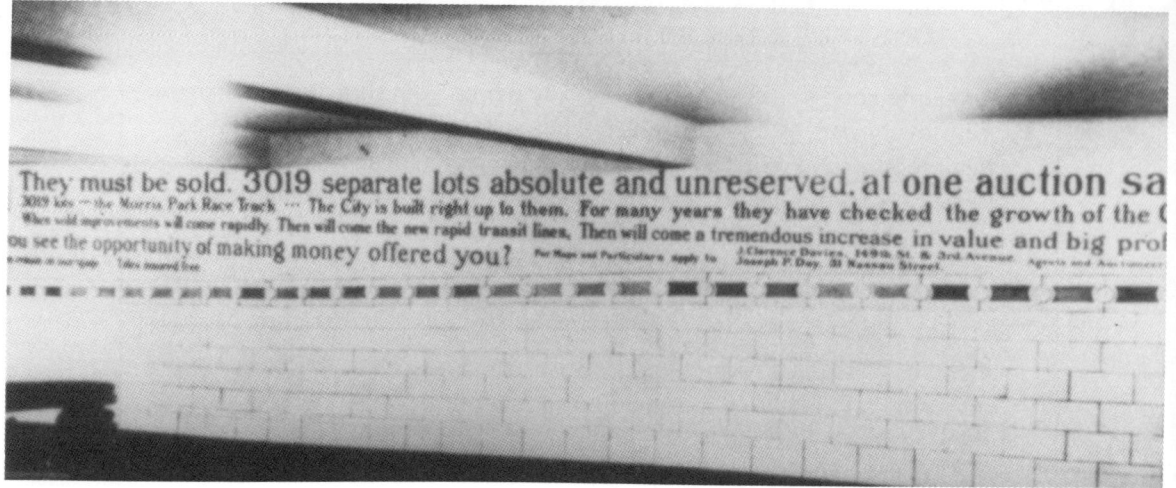

FIGURE 20
Advertisement in the Fulton Street station, 1913.

FIGURE 21
Corona Avenue subway line in 1920, showing undeveloped land.

FIGURE 22
New housing along the Liberty Avenue elevated.

should support existing and planned infrastructure. There was also an effort to control, to some extent, the mixing of incompatible uses and densities, but in this regard, from the beginning the plan was least effective in locations where maintenance of low densities was considered desirable.

THE CREATION OF THE BUILDING ZONE PLAN

The Building Zone Plan attempted to realize its mandate by controlling three dimensions of growth: use, building height, and area (or lot coverage). The dimension of use was regulated by establishing districts in which one or another type of activity might be allowed. Three such districts were mapped throughout the city: residence, business, and unrestricted. The latter was a euphemism for industrial or other undesirable uses.

Height controls related the allowable height of a building's street wall (walls along the edge of the lot that is facing the street) to the width of the street that it adjoined. The city was mapped in five districts that allowed different ratios: The lowest restriction was a maximum street wall of one times the street width; others allowed ratios of one and a quarter times, one and a half times, two times, and two and a half times. Additional height could be added through the famous setback provisions.

As far as the developing boroughs were concerned, however, height controls were by and large inapplicable. The vast majority of new construction did not exceed the four- or five-story maximum due to other kinds of building constraints, which will be examined presently. Even for the strictest one times category, exemptions were made for streets less than fifty feet wide, in effect permitting five-story buildings anywhere, including areas of detached houses.

The only real deterrent to tenement density was the third dimension—area—which controlled the portion of a lot that a building could cover. The mapping of these districts was generally related to the use that was anticipated for that district. The "A" district limited courtyard dimensions and was intended for warehouse areas and the like. The "B" district stipulated rear-yard requirements and minimum side-yard dimensions when present. It was intended to apply to all types of building. The "C" district combined requirements for yard and courts and closely reflected the Tenement House Law (New Law Tenements), except for buildings more than six stories tall, for which it became more stringent. The "D" district lowered coverage and configuration to a level appropriate for one- and two-family row houses. Finally, the "E" district was designed to reflect the coverage and configuration of detached and semidetached single-family houses. It required that buildings be detached with low coverage, ranging from 50 to 70 percent, depending on the particular context.[16] Although this district was intended to protect low-density residential areas, a freestanding apartment building could still be built among single-family houses simply by reducing coverage.

Intense opposition focused on the provisions related to low-density development. It was as obvious then as now that the zoning was wholly inadequate to discourage tenement densities from spreading to the boroughs wherever the marketplace could support them. The City Club of New York was perhaps the most vehement and vocal opponent, demanding more effective restrictions in the boroughs. It lobbied extensively before the resolution was passed, but to little avail. Specifically, the club recognized that:

> Most of the districts, particularly outside the Borough of Manhattan, in which the height of buildings is permitted to be one and one-half times the width of the street, should be reduced to once the width of the street, or less.
>
> Most of the so-called "C" districts and some of the "B" districts should be made "D" districts, with the more adequate limitations upon use of the lot area which are provided for in the "D" classification.[17]

FIGURE 23
Area "D" district lot coverage regulations.

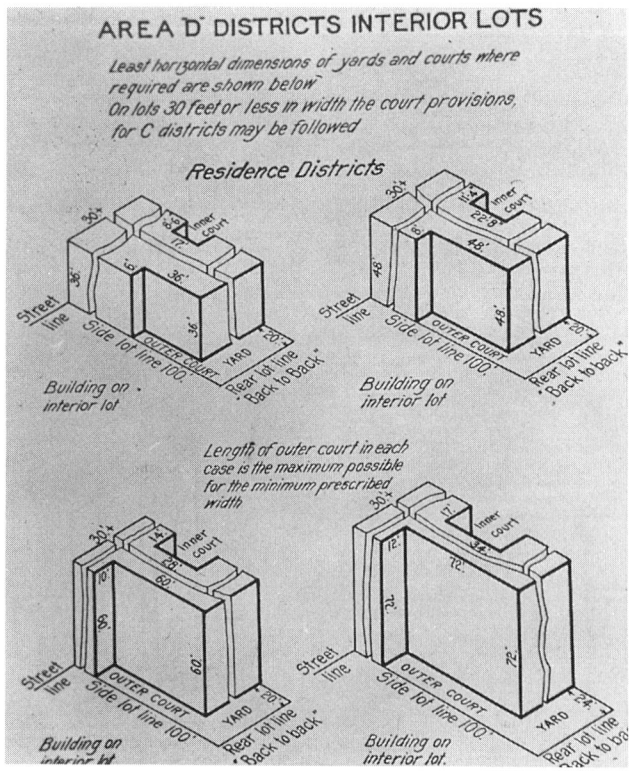

The City Club pointed out that large areas of Brooklyn, for example, were mapped at a height limitation of one and one-half times the street width; on a typical sixty-foot-wide street, this would allow buildings as high as eight or nine stories. The club also questioned area limitations. In a C district, for example, an eight-story building could have almost the same coverage as a five- or six-story building. In a D district, supposedly intended for one- and two-family houses detached or in rows, a five-story tenement could be built at 60 percent coverage. For Brooklyn, the club expressed a fear that the high densities that had developed in Brownsville, for instance, could conceivably spread throughout the borough. The Bronx, perhaps already written off as the borough of apartments, seemed to be far less a subject of concern.[18]

Among the City Club recommendations for changing the 1916 proposal were two new height districts, with limitations of fifty feet and thirty-six feet. The club also proposed an extensive reduction in density through the elimination of all C districts in Brooklyn, Queens, Staten Island, and "perhaps the Bronx." It also advocated changing the mapping of many residential areas from B districts to C and D.[19]

No comprehensive revision took place on this scale. Instead, the resolution was changed by piecemeal negotiation, instigated by various localized constituencies, before it was finally passed. Many of the requests were for down-zoning areas—down-zoning typically means rezoning a parcel and changing density, use, bulk, or other restrictions in a manner that effectively reduces the intensity of development that is allowed or the value of the parcel—that had been mapped with the C district, which was nothing more than a reflection of the standards of the Tenement House Law as it had existed since 1901. The leniency of D and E districts, areas intended to be for single-family homes, was also the cause of substantial negotiation. Developers could put up five-story buildings in either of these districts by simply adding open space around the building (in E districts, coverage was limited to 50 percent for interior lots).

All of the changes proposed between the publication of the plan on March 10, 1916, and its enactment into law on July 25 concerned the outer boroughs rather than Manhattan and down-zoning of one form or another through expansion of D or E districts.[20] Yet, as described previously, these latter districts had little protection from the same building types that the C district encouraged. Apparently, there was a great hesitation to control density by anything more than cursory means anywhere in the city. Strict controls, it seemed, represented the specter of an "antigrowth" mentality that was not at all the New York tradition, and they threatened to prevent densities adequate to repay the investment that was being made in new infrastructure.

Appeals before the Commission on Building Districts and Restrictions had to do with political adjustments: where growth should and should not happen (concerns of the "not-in-my-backyard" tenor). Pressure came from the various interests that wished to protect the elite neighborhoods of one- and two-family houses from higher density development. All manner of deal making ensued in order to protect the sanctity of the icon of the culture, the middle-class, single-family house, in a city that was expanding far beyond the realm of such politesse. However, the neighborhoods of this type that lay along the burgeoning subway lines could not escape larger economic destiny in spite of their political clout.

The newspapers provided a running record of the kind of negotiation that ensued in each borough. One of the most pressing concerns was the preservation of side streets. In Brooklyn, this goal was apparently at the heart of the planning effort; *The New York Times* described Brooklyn residential planning as an effort "to preserve the side streets whenever possible for residential use. The avenues along the ends of the block have usually been indicated as business districts."[21]

The testimony recorded in the commission's final report also documents a number of issues involving the protection of houses. For example, it records a debate about Ocean Avenue in Brooklyn. The Fiske Terrace Association was concerned that Ocean Avenue would become "one solid mass of apartment houses." It wanted the commission to classify everything behind the avenue as an E district in order to try to protect the houses there.[22] As for its fears about Ocean Avenue, the association was correct, but there was at least a certain psychological value in obtaining the restriction: property values might be expected to hold for a little longer before the apartment buildings would cause devaluation.

The Building Zone Plan also set expectations that had far greater financial implications than protecting the value of single-family homes. An important example was in Jackson Heights, where the Queensboro Corporation would never have committed the large capital needed for the enterprise without guarantees that the development would be protected from undesirable adjacent uses. The Building Zone Plan kept those uses at bay by creating twenty-two thousand acres for industrial development in Long Island City, safely away from Jackson Heights.[23]

Especially well represented in the commission negotiations were the elite, preexisting residential enclaves, which did not want to be touched by any change in status at all. For instance, there was pressure to protect Riverdale, City Island, and the area east of the Bronx River Parkway. Originally, the commission had not zoned them, assuming that they were not particularly vulnerable anyway, but that was not enough, and pressure was brought to bear. Riverdale, at least, was zoned as an E district. The others remained without jurisdiction at the time.[24]

CONTINUING CONCERNS ABOUT DENSITY

The struggle for down-zoning continued long after the passage of the resolution. The zoning amendments made during the next three decades are an indication of just how prophetic the City Club concerns were. Between July 1916 and December 1940, 1,371 amendments were made to the original resolution, most of them in the outer boroughs. The majority of these had to do with down-zoning, and as might have been expected, this activity was most intense during the boom years of the mid-1920s, when the boroughs were exploding.

Most of the modifications involved changes in use districts rather than changes in height or lot coverage.[25] The imposition of stricter use restrictions had to do, primarily, with protecting the sanctity of existing residential areas. In general, there was less imperative for changes in height districts in that little residential construction in the boroughs was more than six stories high anyway (for reasons that will be discussed subsequently). Queens and Brooklyn saw the most changes in area (or lot coverage) districts, a reflection of the concern about limiting higher densities. The Bronx seems to have been relegated to its position as the preeminent urban borough.

Between 1916 and 1940, there were also a number of modifications to types of districts that were available for mapping; the most important amendments tended toward further protection for areas with low density and, in particular, with single-family homes. These changes included the creation of a three-fourths times height district, which lowered the one times district even further, in 1921. An "F" area district was added in 1922; this district lowered maximum permitted lot coverage and added even stricter yard requirements, compared to the E district. In 1923, one-half and one-quarter times height districts were created, limiting the height of buildings in some areas even further. In 1938, the "G" area district limited for the first time the type of structure that could be built within a given residential area. Intended to give some further protection from invasion by apartment houses, it allowed only single-family houses.[26]

In spite of these efforts to protect the single-family house, much of the post-1916 city was filled out with apartments. The numbers are revealing: for the period between 1916 and 1929, the net increase in apartments within the entire city was 359,441. Only 33,363, or 9 percent, were built in Manhattan. The number of apartments in Manhattan grew by only 6 percent, compared with 54 percent for the Bronx, 33 percent for Brooklyn, and 65 percent for Queens.[27] One could argue that in spite of the acrimony over keeping densities low, the urbanism that developed was actually more dense as a result of the zoning. At least, high density was sanctioned in particular areas because of the influence of transit.

The 1920s boom in the boroughs basically rendered the New Law tenement form obsolete, at least as it had developed in Manhattan. The economic formulas that had generated the New Law tenements in 1901 were no longer operative. Cheap land, made accessible by the new mass transit, meant that maximizing density was no longer the primary factor that determined the profit that could be made from building affordable housing.

The controversial 1922 Tenement House Competition demonstrated that, indeed, higher profits could be obtained from lower density. It showed that given cheaper land, a reduction in the number of rooms could simplify construction while increasing the attractiveness of an apartment to the emerging middle class, whose numbers were swollen by the record immigration of the previous two decades.[28] This condition directly contradicted previous thinking, which always equated more rooms with more profits.

The new thinking led to all manner of hybrid apartment forms, based on the reduced densities allowed in outer borough locations. The B through E districts provided a variety of contexts within which a variety of responses developed. Because of the relative flexibility of the controls, almost anything could be built anywhere, dictated by the vagaries of the marketplace rather than strict zoning regulations. So volatile and uncharted was the marketplace that frequently five-story buildings would coexist with houses. At Jackson Heights, for example, such juxtapositions were even condoned.[29] As the low land cost removed the principal obstacle to this lower coverage, the results embodied a remarkable era of innovation. A new kind of horizontal city emerged.

OTHER FACTORS THAT INFLUENCED THE FORM OF APARTMENT BUILDINGS

The form and intensity of the higher density, outer borough development also were defined by certain advances in building technology, principally the elevator. When residential elevators were introduced in the 1870s, they could be used only in the tall structures intended for upper-income residents, primarily because the costs of the equipment and of the operators required to run it were excessive.

By 1920, this constraint had changed. Cheaper alternating-current machinery came into use, and, more important, the New York City Building Code was revised to permit automatic self-service elevators in large apartment buildings. The legalization of self-service meant that the long-term cost of elevators could be drastically reduced because operators were no longer required. A whole class of tenants who had formerly been relegated to walk-up buildings could enjoy the convenience of the elevator. In Manhattan, this development stimulated the construction of tall buildings with small

FIGURE 24
Woodrow Wilson Court, a typical Bronx apartment building on Fordham Road, was shaped not only by zoning but also by elevator technology, building codes, and the multiple dwelling law.

apartments for middle-income tenants. In the outer boroughs, it helped stimulate the evolution of housing types, the most important (in terms of its significance to middle-class New Yorkers) being the garden apartment.[30]

Other factors, though, conspired to keep outer borough, high-density development primarily in the four- to six-story range despite the introduction of elevators. Chief among them were building code requirements for fireproof construction. In buildings of five stories or less, nonfireproof construction was permitted except at the ground floor. In six-story buildings, the first two floors were required to be fireproof, making construction slightly more expensive. For buildings of seven stories or more, however, fireproof construction was required throughout, increasing the costs substantially.

These rules, in effect, reinforced the resolution's height limitation of fifty feet in outer borough residential zones. The cost of a self-service elevator, therefore, could be offset by the cheaper construction in buildings under seven stories. The intricate balance between building laws, construction cost, and land economics provided that the greatest return could be realized on four- to six-story buildings.

As a result, during the 1920s, large areas of the outer boroughs witnessed a surge in the construction of middle-income elevator buildings that were virtually no taller than New Law tenements. These buildings might coexist with single-family houses, especially in areas at the edge of the influence of transit.[31] The character of this latter new city was created obliquely by mass transit, reinforced by the zoning, and realized in concert with several other factors, most importantly the building codes. Perhaps it will never again recur, at least in the New York City experience.

THE AUTOMOBILE-ORIENTED CITY

After 1940, the most significant amendments to the zoning resolution reflected the sensibility of development to come. For example, the focus shifted to large-scale development and the desire to allow more flexibility for both residential and industrial projects. An effort was made to recognize that new, "clean" industry could coexist with residential uses. Also, the constraints on large, planned housing estates were given special recognition in that their configuration differed from small-scale, incremental initiatives.

The most significant changes, though, involved the antithesis of the transit-generated, high-density horizontal city: enter the automobile-generated, low- to medium-density city of single-family houses. For a time in the boroughs, these two typologies evolved and coexisted in a symbiotic relationship, with the automobile filling out the areas not covered by transit. This confluence could not have been achieved as little as a decade earlier in that it was not until the 1920s that the automobile began to proliferate as a form of popular transportation. The automobile created another city, apart from the possibilities that framed the discussions that shaped the 1916 Building Zone Plan.

Most fundamentally, the automobile began to shift the economics of land development that had been forged by the development of transit several decades earlier. In the Bronx, for instance, for Joseph P. Day, the real estate entrepreneur whose fortunes had depended heavily on New York City's transit extensions and whose success depended in large part on his ability to anticipate new patterns of development, the omens were clear by 1925:

> The automobile has been, perhaps, the foremost factor in the development of large areas located at a distance from the subways, elevated and trolley lines. It is no longer a question of living directly along the route of a transit line and homeseekers generally have come to realize that some of the most desirable homebuilding sites in the Bronx are those that are located some distance from the transit lines, but which, nevertheless, are easily accessible by automobile.[32]

In order to domesticate the automobile, new housing types emerged, particularly in D and E districts. Garages had to be added to traditional housing types, which themselves began to change through all manner of experimentation. Yet the house forms remained urban. For example, the row house was modified to accommodate the automobile underneath, or the garden apartment could integrate the automobile within the garden, or the garages might become the source of their own place making.[33] An extraordinary record of this innovative period can be seen in the housing stock that still exists in the boroughs.

All of these approaches were left behind in the suburban explosion of the postwar era. The city was deurbanized, together with its domestic architecture. Lower densities and automobiles were inextricably tied to detached cottages in the countryside rather than to attached formations in the boroughs. The constant tinkering with zoning in the boroughs, which continued until the citywide zoning revision in 1961, was insignificant compared to what was happening further out in the suburbs. In 1961, the "tower in the park,"[34] the ultimate in reductionist urbanism, came to dominate outer borough zoning and diminished any real possibility of further enrichment of the legacy that had matured by then. In fact, the 1961 rezoning helped thwart just about all development.

What has happened in much of the boroughs since 1961 has made many of the concerns of the original framers of the Building Zone Plan obsolete.

FIGURE 25
Elmhurst Manor, Queens.

FIGURE 26
Contrast between pre-1961 and post-1961 development along Lafayette Avenue, Brooklyn.

The destruction of the fabric by abandonment and arson in the 1960s and 1970s led to a natural down-zoning in many of the most dense areas of the Bronx and Brooklyn. These areas returned from the urbanism of the new horizontal city back to farmland within a half century.

The model for subsequent rebuilding has been the automobile-dependent city. Single-family homes have been built at densities far below what the zoning permits and quite possibly far below what the city's infrastructure requires for long-term survival (including the mass transit that generated the urbanization in the first place). This combination of building regulations, consumer preferences, land economics, housing subsidies, and technology has resulted in a curious reversal of the rules put in place by the 1916 zoning. Perhaps, in these areas, at least, the conception of zoning also must change, from limiting the maximums to limiting the minimums.

NOTES

1. Apart from the original commission reports and legislation, several general references are helpful in understanding the groundwork for the 1916 resolution and its aftermath. These include S. J. Makielski, Jr., *The Politics of Zoning* (New York: Columbia University Press, 1966); Seymour I. Toll, *Zoned American* (New York: Grossman, 1969); and Jeanette L. Evans, "NYC Zoning: A Comparison of the 1916 and 1961 Ordinances," master of science urban planning thesis, Columbia University, 1984. Also consulted were Marc A. Weiss, "Density and Intervention: New York's Planning Traditions," and Keith D. Revell, "Regulating the Landscape in New York City: Real Estate Values, City Planning, and the 1916 Zoning Ordinance," in David Ward and Oliver Zunz, eds., *The Landscape of Modernity* (New York: Russell Sage, 1992).

2. In this regard, the 1916 resolution would seem to have been more successful than the 1961 effort, which functioned as a constraint to development in the boroughs.

3. New York City Board of Estimate and Apportionment, *Report of the Heights of Buildings Commission to the Committee on the Heights, Size and Arrangement of Buildings* (31 December 1913): 56.

4. Ira Rosenwalke, *Population History of New York City* (Syracuse: Syracuse University Press, 1972), Table 64.

5. *New Dwelling Units Completed 1921–1972 in New York City* (New York: Department of City Planning, 1973).

6. Ibid., p. 67.

7. Robert H. Whitten, "The Building Zone Plan of New York City," unpublished manuscript in the collection of the Avery Architectural and Fine Arts Library, Columbia University, 1916.

8. A final report was published as *Final Report of the Commission on Building Districts and Restrictions* (New York: Board of Estimate and Apportionment, Committee on the City Plan, 1916), hereafter referred to as *Final Report*. The legislation as approved, together with notes and mapping, is found in George B. Ford, *Building Zones: A Handbook of Restrictions on the Heights, Area and Use of Buildings, with Especial Reference to New York City* (New York: Lawyers Mortgage Company, 1918). Ford gives recognition to the expansion of the goals of the Height of Buildings Committee on page 1.

9. This argument dates from the pioneering philanthropy of Alfred Treadway White. See Richard A. Plunz, *A History of Housing in New York City, Dwelling Type and Social Change in the American Metropolis* (New York: Columbia University Press, 1990), pp. 91–93.

10. In the Bronx, connections developed first as north-south extensions from Manhattan: the Westchester Avenue elevated line was completed in 1904 and connected to the Lenox Avenue subway in 1906; in 1908, the Broadway IRT (Interborough Rapid Transit) line was completed to Van Cortlandt Park. After 1916, several other major lines were also completed, further opening up the borough. These included the White Plains line in 1917, which extended the Westchester Avenue elevated to the northernmost edge. By 1918, the Jerome Avenue IRT lines had opened to Van Cortlandt Park. In 1920, the Lexington Avenue IRT was extended to Pelham Bay Park. In Brooklyn, the connections were more difficult, but by 1908, the IRT had been completed along Eastern Parkway, and by the end of the next decade a number of the BMT (Brooklyn-Manhattan Transit) lines were completed. In Queens,

which urbanized last, the Queensboro IRT subway was completed as far as Jackson Heights by 1917 and was extended to Flushing by 1928. The BMT line through the East Sixtieth Street tunnel was completed to Astoria in 1917 and to Queensboro Plaza in 1920. In all boroughs, the far-reaching IND (Independent Subway) lines were not completed until the 1930s and later. Their planning served indirectly to reinforce the established development tendencies. See Plunz, *Housing in New York*, pp. 128–130.

11. Whitten, "Building Zone Plan," pp. 3–4. This portion of the manuscript is printed verbatim in the Commission on Building Districts and Restrictions' *Final Report*, p. 48.

12. Whitten, "Building Zone Plan," p. 4; Commission on Building Districts and Restrictions, *Final Report*, p. 48.

13. Whitten, "Building Zone Plan," p. 5; Commission on Building Districts and Restrictions, *Final Report*, p. 49.

14. Plunz, *Housing in New York*, pp. 130–131; Daniel Karatzas, *Jackson Heights: A Garden in the City* (New York: Jackson Heights Beautification Group, 1990), chapters 2 to 4.

15. Whitten summarizes the use of all of these data.

16. Ford, *Building Zones*.

17. The City Club of New York, *Protecting the Future of New York City: A Plea for Stricter Regulations in Certain Matters Before the Commission on Building Districts and Regulations* (12 April 1916): 2.

18. Ibid., pp. 7–8.

19. Ibid., pp. 12–14.

20. New York City Board of Estimate and Apportionment, Commission on Building Districts and Restrictions, Committee on the City Plan, *Tentative Report* (10 March 1916). An enumeration of the proposed revisions is given in "Makes Revisions in Area District," *Real Estate Record and Builders' Guide* (22 July 1916). The final revisions are included in the Commission on Building Districts and Restrictions' *Final Report*, pp. 216–226.

21. The article explained the application of this principle to a section of Bedford Stuyvesant, in which there was probably little danger of large-scale or nonresidential building. See "Brooklyn Districts," *New York Times* (27 February 1916): sec. 3, p. 7.

22. Commission on Building Districts and Restrictions, *Final Report*, pp. 100–101.

23. Plunz, *Housing in New York*, p. 123; Karatzas, *Jackson Heights*, p. 34.

24. "Zone Changes in the Bronx," *New York Times* (21 May 1916): sec. 4, p. 4.

25. New York City Planning Commission and Department of City Planning, *Annual Report* (1940), Tables 6 and 7. See also Makielski, *Politics of Zoning*, p. 45.

26. Based on background material provided by Sandy Hornick, New York City Department of City Planning, November 1991.

27. New York State, State Board of Housing, *Annual Report* (1929), Table VII.

28. For more background, see Plunz, *Housing in New York*, pp. 135–137.

29. Plunz, *Housing in New York*, p. 201; Karatzas, *Jackson Heights*, pp. 67–69.

30. The "garden apartment" involved the fundamental premise of reducing building coverage to the point of opening up a possibility of integrating "garden" courtyards within the mass of the housing. The garden apartment altered the design conventions associated with the tenement air shaft beyond recognition. For a fuller discussion, see Plunz, *Housing in New York*, chapter 5, pp. 122–163.

31. For more background, see Plunz, *Housing in New York*, pp. 123–124.

32. "Old Bronx Areas Must Be Rebuilt," *New York Times* (22 February 1925): sec. 2, p. 10.

33. For more background, see Plunz, *Housing in New York,* pp. 200–206.

34. "Tower in the park" planning and design espoused concentrating development in tall skyscrapers that would be placed at wide intervals in unbounded park space. For a fuller discussion, see Plunz, *Housing in New York,* pp. 184–192.

THE 1961 ZONING REVISION AND THE TEMPLATE OF THE IDEAL CITY

ROY STRICKLAND

This paper will discuss the 1961 revision of New York City's zoning resolution in the context of the economic and social conditions in the city after World War II. The 1940s and 1950s were a period of enormous change in the city. These changes stimulated criticism of the city's 1916 zoning resolution—criticism that prompted the rewriting of the zoning ordinance in 1961. The zoning that was to reshape New York City's skyline and neighborhoods, however, was based on ideas about urban development that had been urged by planners and architects since the late 1920s.

In an era when urban America was reformulated on the model of low-density suburbs, and in the face of centrifugal development forces, New York City attempted to hold its position as a preeminent center of business and industry. The city looked to rationalize its development and land use according to the profitable formula of urban renewal and it sought to provide a level of amenity in open space, light, and air that urban reformers had pursued for decades. These objectives were to be achieved by placing the template of an ideal prewar city on the volatile conditions of a real postwar city. There was a disjunction between the ideal city envisioned by planners and the forces that were shaping the city, though—a disjunction that contributed to many of the conditions that we find in the city today.

NEW YORK 1945

A comparison between New York City in 1945 and in 1961 reveals a wide range of changes that stimulated the comprehensive zoning revision.

THE TEMPLATE OF THE IDEAL CITY

As Jan Morris relates in *Manhattan '45*,[1] New Yorkers felt at their best just after World War II. Their city was physically untouched by the war—quite different from London, Berlin, Rome, or even Paris (which was still intact but had suffered the humiliation and deportations of Nazi occupation). New York City was the embodiment of modern technology, perhaps the only fully twentieth-century city among its peers. New Yorkers felt that they were members of a great social organism and were proud of their city. They were eager to please visitors from abroad, often engaging the world-weary traveler with personal recommendations of what to see, where to shop, and how to master the subway system.

Despite its modernity, the New York City of 1945 had remained relatively unchanged for more than a decade. With limited new construction since the Great Depression, the physical outline of New York City just after the war was similar to that of the 1930s. The primary concentration of office buildings was in lower Manhattan around Wall Street and along Broadway. In the vicinity of Grand Central Terminal, there was a secondary cluster of skyscrapers, which benefited from the relatively generous block sizes of the 1811 street grid and the coordinated planning of Terminal City. Similar high rises were found in Brooklyn, along Court Street near Brooklyn Heights. In Queens, Art Deco office buildings, miniatures of those on Wall Street, were clustered around Queens Plaza in Long Island City. Many of these buildings were products of the 1916 zoning resolution: setback skyscrapers that represented New York City and the United States to the rest of the world. All of these office districts, whose construction preceded the war, were located in places where several rapid transit lines converged.[2]

The city's industrial and manufacturing areas spread between these office districts. In Manhattan, these activities could be found along the West Side, beside the Hudson River, in the garment center along Seventh Avenue, in the center of the island below Greenwich Village, and along parts of the East River. Industry and manufacturing also could be found along the Red Hook, Williamsburg, and Greenpoint waterfronts in Brooklyn; in Long Island City, Queens; and spreading north in the Bronx from the Harlem River and along the New York Central Railroad tracks that were below the bluff of the Grand Concourse.

Where there was waterfront in New York City, there was usually industry and manufacturing. As Richard Plunz writes in his essay, "Battery Park City: Between Edge and Fabric,"[3] New York City historically established a high level of density and amenity at the center of the city then turned its back on the waterfront, which was left to less attractive uses well before such land use patterns were made official policy in the 1916 zoning resolution. One reason was that transportation, critical to industry, was historically provided by the port. In 1945, this was still the case; piers and rail yards had a firm grip on the waterfront. The Port of New York was America's busiest, and glamorous ocean liners mixed with barges and tugs in the bay and on the active waterfronts of Manhattan and Brooklyn.[4]

The city's residential neighborhoods, becoming crowded with returning veterans, also were largely in their prewar form. Poor and working-class people lived in tenements on the Lower East Side, the Upper West Side, and the Upper East Side (east of Third Avenue), in central Harlem, East Harlem, Williamsburg, Greenpoint, Red Hook, and the South Bronx, and behind the Long Island City waterfront. These high-density areas were near employment centers, and many of them had been designated areas of unrestricted use in the 1916 zoning resolution. Unlike exclusive residential districts, which were legally isolated from industry and manufacturing, these neighborhoods (with the exception of central Harlem, which had originally been erected as a middle-class residential community) were mixed use.

A second ring of poor and working-class neighborhoods, including Jamaica, Brownsville, and East New York, mixed single-family and multifamily dwellings and were linked by rapid transit to manufacturing, garment, and printing centers in Manhattan, Brooklyn, and Queens. Some public housing projects had been built (for example, the Harlem River Houses, the Red Hook Houses, and the Queensbridge Houses) but they had yet to become ubiquitous, the ambitions of the Federal Housing Act having been interrupted by the war.

For the middle class and the rich, "name" streets, such as Park and Fifth avenues, Central Park West, the Grand Concourse, and Eastern Parkway, resonated with financial and social achievement while neighborhoods such as Flatbush, Washington Heights, Riverdale, Pelham, Jackson Heights, Forest Hills, and Flushing denoted middle-class stability in their combinations of private houses and low-slung apartment buildings. These neighborhoods often occupied the zone between central business and outlying manufacturing districts or were far from such districts, and zoning often protected them from the incursion of nonresidential uses. In some cases, these neighborhoods' exclusivity could be traced to restrictive covenants that were formulated in the nineteenth century and were translated into law by the 1916 zoning resolution.

Race and class figured in the New York City of 1945—as it did in 1916, when zoning was motivated in part to separate elite retail districts from incursions by the garment industry and immigrant workers. Yet racially, at least, New York City was still relatively homogeneous. Primarily a city of European ancestry, it accepted racial segregation as a matter of course and it developed hierarchies among the white majority as income, ethnic, and religious groups gravitated to certain neighborhoods and, when sharing neighborhoods, often gravitated to certain buildings. "Gentleman's agreements" separated middle- and upper-class Christians from middle- and upper-class Jews; African-Americans struggled to gain access to the better housing from which they were automatically excluded (they even were segregated from whites as part of public housing policy). There were glaring social divisions, such as the ones between African-American Harlem, European-American Upper West Side, and Asian-American Chinatown. There also were subtle divisions: the settlement of Jews was accepted in Crown Heights along Eastern Parkway but it was "restricted" on the other side of Prospect Park, along Prospect Park West. There was pride in being a New Yorker, as Jan Morris attests, but there was also social friction beneath the city's outward civility.

NEW YORK 1961

By 1961, very little about New York City seemed permanent, not along Park Avenue, not along the South Bronx route of the Cross Bronx Expressway, and not in its rapidly developing outer edges. The burst of construction that had been awaited since the Great Depression finally occurred during the 1950s, but the industries and people toward whom this energy was directed were different from those that characterized the city before the war. New York City's white-collar work force was expanding and its population included more people of color and more poor people. Federal mortgage and highway subsidies seemed to conspire against the city as they carried middle-class New Yorkers to newly built suburban communities, even as the private sector and local government invested heavily in new commercial buildings and infrastructure in the center of New York City.

Midtown Manhattan began to rival Wall Street as a business center as many of the city's Fortune 500 companies moved uptown from the Wall Street area. On Park Avenue north of Grand Central Terminal, hotels and palatial apartment houses collapsed under the wrecker's ball and were replaced by office buildings. Lower Manhattan saw little new construction until David Rockefeller, the president of the Chase Manhattan Bank, erected a new headquarters there in 1960 as a gesture of confidence in the Wall Street area. The new skyscrapers looked radically different from the old. They were faced with glass and metal rather than stone and brick, adapting International Style design to traditional "wedding cake" zoning envelopes. Occasionally, as at Chase Manhattan Plaza, Lever House, and the Seagram Building, these buildings assumed the pure geometries and open plazas characteristic of International Style architecture.

In the decade following the war, New York City's economic base was richly diversified, with a growing service sector supplementing manufacturing and the garment and printing trades, but there was slippage in blue-collar employment; other states, both in the region and in the Sunbelt, lured local industries by offering lower wages, favorable taxes, and newer facilities, and as the nation's transportation system became more dependent on highways than railroads, New York City's location became less convenient and less advantageous.

Even the Port of New York (still the greatest in the country) was becoming less Manhattan's and Brooklyn's than New Jersey's Elizabeth and Newark: containerized shipping practices shifted activity from rail-serviced piers in Manhattan and Brooklyn to road-serviced piers in New Jersey. Passenger travel was shifting away from New York's piers, too. Although the superliners *France* and *Queen Elizabeth II* had yet to appear in the harbor, the leisured travel that they represented was well in decline. In 1957, transatlantic air travel surpassed ocean travel for the first time.[5]

As the delicate balance among transportation, industry, and support services began to shift, so did the distribution of the city's residential districts. Portions of Manhattan's West Side, South Brooklyn, and the South Bronx became obsolete, which depressed adjoining working-class neighborhoods. Midtown Manhattan lost much of its residential character in the face of the expansion of office districts, and older neighborhoods near manufacturing areas became poorer as blue-collar employment declined.

Other neighborhoods, though, were expanding as the city filled its empty edges with middle-class housing. Canarsie and Mill Basin in Brooklyn, Bayside and Howard Beach in Queens, and sections of Staten Island were covered by rows of one- and two-family houses. This was housing occupied primarily by white New Yorkers as the racial and class lines of the city shifted but remained drawn. Just as subways transported prewar New Yorkers to the Grand Concourse and Jackson Heights, new roads and bridges took postwar New Yorkers to the periphery of the city and beyond. This process was symbolized best in the construction of the Verrazano Bridge, which was completed in 1964 and opened Staten Island to thousands of Brooklynites anxious to escape the changing demographics of their old neighborhoods. Highways and low-cost federal mortgages opened up vast new areas for suburban development, and 1.5 million middle-class New Yorkers left the city altogether.

Meanwhile, poorer people continued to migrate to the city; they were seeking economic opportunity, as the poor always had, but had the misfortune of arriving just as New York City was losing 600,000 manufacturing jobs in the 1950s.[6] Most of the newcomers were African-Americans and Latinos who settled in East Harlem, Brownsville, East New York, Jamaica, Morrisania, and other aging, working-class neighborhoods that had been abandoned by European-Americans moving to the suburbs. City, state, and federal programs sponsored the construction of enormous public housing projects (averaging 7,500 new units per year during the 1950s[7]) for working- and lower-middle-class New Yorkers—many of them African-Americans and Latinos. Urban renewal projects, public housing, and highways eviscerated many of New York City's working-class neighborhoods during these years. Some 500,000 people were displaced by such construction, resulting in the psychic wounds so compellingly described by Robert A. Caro in *The Power Broker*.[8]

In a city with such immense activity compressed into such a small area, changes in one neighborhood precipitated changes in others. For example, the closing of the Third Avenue elevated train in 1955 opened the East Side to development of middle-class, high-rise apartments. However, as Columbia University urban planning professor Elliott Sclar points out, this also cut off the South Bronx from a direct line of transportation to jobs in Manhattan, which helped depress neighborhoods far flung from the Upper East Side.[9] Fragile balances within and between smaller geographic areas also were upset during this time. As Caro details, urban renewal projects in the Upper West Side strained housing and services in adjacent neighborhoods as the poor were squeezed like mercury from Columbus Avenue to the corridor between Broadway and West End Avenue.[10]

ZONING MODIFICATIONS IN THE FACE OF CHANGE

New York City changed enormously between 1945 and 1961, and, as it had for much of its history, it changed with a combination of progressive and conservative impulses, optimism, and pain. Third Avenue became a gleaming residential and corporate corridor as the South Bronx deteriorated. Expressways were built to rush commercial traffic through the city and helped industry to decamp to cheaper locations. Urban renewal projects flattened slums but, as Peter Marcuse writes, they stratified the city socially and further segregated it racially by locating middle-class Title I projects next to central business districts and public housing in an outlying ring.[11]

In introducing the proposed comprehensive revision of the zoning resolution in 1959, James Felt, the chairman of the New York City Planning Commission, criticized the old ordinance for the following reasons[12]:

- It failed to provide a concept or vision that would absorb and direct the city's changes.
- The complexity of the rules, modified by hundreds of amendments, appeared to undermine good planning.
- The maximum building envelopes allowed under the 1916 zoning law would have allowed some fifty-five million people to live in New York City and some one hundred million people to work in the city.
- The zoning resolution's emphasis on building envelope created a development climate in which new construction tended to fill the permissible envelope to the maximum, with little variety in design.

- The zoning map encouraged development in desirable, high-density areas rather than in slum areas and unbuilt sections of the city.
- Little consideration was given to fine-grained planning, for example, addressing the kinds of mixed uses that might be compatible in a district, the intensity of development, and the use and storage of the automobile.
- Open space, light, and air were forsaken in the high-rise city that New York had become. Generally, most of the zoning districts did not stipulate strong-enough controls over building bulk.
- Under the existing rules, housing too often preempted increasingly scarce sites for "employment-giving and taxpaying industry."

In place of the old guidelines, Felt's City Planning Commission proposed a new zoning law that encompassed what were called "fundamental principles of good zoning" and included:

- A population ceiling in the five boroughs of eleven million people, some three million more people than lived in the city at the time but considerably fewer than the fifty-five million that the 1916 law hypothetically permitted;
- Economic incentives for developers who would build "in the public interest";
- Recognition of the "fact and economics of large-scale projects";
- Performance standards that would guide the appropriate distribution of uses, giving "high-performance industry a wider choice of sites";
- Recognition of the automobile and its off-street storage in all districts—except the "most congested downtown areas"; and
- Simplicity for the user (that is, the developer) in formulating building proposals.

Features of the new resolution included:

- A single set of zoning maps;
- Three broad categories of use districts—residential, commercial, and manufacturing—that were subdivided into twenty-five specific districts (fourteen residential, eight commercial, and three manufacturing); and
- Forty-seven districts created by combining regulations regarding use, bulk, parking, and loading.

Residential districts included single-family districts (R1 and R2) and general residence districts (R3 to R9), which were open to all housing types and in increasing density. There were eight types of commercial districts, ranging from local retail and service districts (C1 and C2) to heavy service uses (C8). There were three categories of manufacturing districts, ranging from

M1, which included low-nuisance uses (such as garment work), through M3, which included heavy, noxious industries (such as oil refining). Residential uses were excluded from manufacturing districts.

At a broader level, these zones were mapped in a series of generally concentric rings. Gradual changes in use buffered residential neighborhoods from the most noxious manufacturing areas. The waterfront was consigned heavily to manufacturing uses, as it had been historically. Large-scale planning, especially in residential districts, was encouraged. Formulas determined how buildings would be positioned on lots. A system of floor area ratios was devised so that building sizes would be a function of lot size. If developers wanted to build larger and potentially more profitable buildings, they were required to provide proportional amounts of open space.

IN PURSUIT OF THE IDEAL: TEMPLATE UPON REALITY

A review of Felt's criticisms of the 1916 zoning resolution and the commission's proposed changes reveals a great deal about the city of New York's concept of itself and of its future, at least the concept held within official and development circles. The proposed changes were based on the principles of good planning that had been advocated in New York City since the 1920s and 1930s by entities such as the Regional Plan Association and the City Planning Commission; the changes expressed explicit preferences for the building forms and site planning principles that had been advocated by a European and American architectural avant-garde since the 1920s.

The 1961 zoning revision proposed a postwar version of the prewar ideal city. The zoning changes had their roots in discussions and city planning theories that dated to before World War II; many of these ideas had, in fact, been adopted by a powerful combination of government and business after the war.

The 1961 zoning revision envisioned a city with a strong manufacturing base, an active port, and a robust middle class, with Manhattan as the focus of the region and with developers enjoying the economies of and profits from large-scale construction. In reality, the city had been busy putting pieces of this vision into place for decades (such efforts included the prewar highway systems and postwar urban renewal projects), so the plan seemed plausible—even as the socioeconomic dynamics of the postwar city would challenge both the vision and the plan.

The well-planned, "modern" city envisioned by the 1961 zoning revision had been detailed in the 1929–31 *Regional Plan for New York and Its Environs.* In that plan, highways radiated from Manhattan across the region, population was dispersed throughout the tristate area of New York/New Jersey/Connecticut, and prototype large-scale development projects were set forth. Large parts of that plan were in place before World War II, shepherded by the productive efforts of New York City's master builder, Robert Moses, and funded by depression-era government programs.[13]

After the war, federal mortgage, housing finance, and urban renewal programs provided powerful tools for filling out the region in the manner envisioned by the 1929–31 regional plan. Highways carried New Yorkers to horizontal suburbs at the periphery of the city and beyond; within the city, vertical suburbs were erected in the image of autonomous residential projects, such as Stuyvesant Town. While the 1916 zoning resolution had encouraged the consolidation of building parcels to enable more light and air to reach the streets, the regional plan and the government now encouraged the consolidation of several blocks into "superblocks" that would allow buildings of reduced ground coverage and would provide more open space. These ideas—a 1930s' vision of New York City adapted through the 1950s—were carried into the 1961 zoning revision.

The participants in the 1961 zoning revision included people who had been active in planning and development and putting these ideas to work for several decades. Planning commission chairman Felt's real estate company had consolidated the site for Stuyvesant Town.[14] Architects from the firm of Voorhees, Walker, Smith and Smith, which had designed public housing projects around the city, conducted planning surveys and drafted the ordinance.[15] Lawrence Orton was an early member of the Regional Plan Association and had been a member of the planning commission since its inception,[16] and, of course, there was Robert Moses.

These people thought that New York City's population could grow by half, that the city's new belt of expressways would make expanded industrial sites in areas such as Brooklyn's Sunset Park and Flatlands competitive with industrial parks outside of the city, and that investment would flow into slums if the city encouraged densities that were proved profitable by urban renewal. Although their zoning proposal was comprehensive, it was nevertheless reductivist (in the tradition of good planning that had been handed down from the 1920s and 1930s): urban functions were separated, proximity between workplace and home was discouraged, and development projects were proscribed by architectural and site models that valued open space over New York City's traditional mixture of pedestrian-oriented activities.

The assumption that a template of the ideal city could be imposed on New York and remold it evolved from a postwar convergence of public and private planning goals: Limit density but raise the city's population; preserve autonomous residential districts but enable industry to expand; and eradicate slums but protect investment by assuring that development would occur at a scale that made it impervious to the volatility of adjacent neighborhoods.

The social implications of the zoning change are of special interest: in 1961, New York City was becoming (at the same time) increasingly white-collar, increasingly poor, and increasingly darker complexioned. With the zoning change, working-class districts in which people walked to jobs were discouraged, the scale of development projects precluded any type of affordable housing other than deeply subsidized, and the financing and marketing of large-scale projects encouraged the segregation of poor and middle-class people into separate superblocks. The radical redesign of New York City solidified historic differentiations of race and class even as the iconic imagery of the prewar architectural avant-garde was applied to both Upper East Side apartment towers and Brooklyn public housing.

NEW YORK 1991: THE TEMPLATE AND ITS GAPS

Thirty years later, part of the 1961 zoning revision's template of the ideal city has, in fact, been filled. As both the 1929–31 regional plan and the zoning revision prescribed, Manhattan is the center of the city, a dense core of high-skilled, service-oriented employment. Along Sixth Avenue below Central Park, a new corporate corridor has been developed. In Midtown and downtown, New Yorkers walk among flattopped skyscrapers and across brick and granite plazas that are the rewards of incentive zoning. The International Style's urban aesthetic of pure geometries has replaced the city's formerly characteristic setback skyscrapers.

In some residential neighborhoods, the template has also been filled—not only in Manhattan but also in the outer boroughs. On Upper East Side avenues once lined by tenements, residential versions of glass and steel office towers provide housing for the upper middle class; clusters of similar buildings loom incongruously above outer borough neighborhoods, such as Riverdale, Forest Hills, and Flatbush. The city's fullest realizations of large-scale development, Co-op City and Starrett City, can be seen from cars hurtling by on expressways. The construction and space standards followed in high-rise buildings like these are hardly different from the standards set for subsidized and public housing, and in newer outlying neighborhoods, especially in Staten Island, housing is neatly separated from shopping centers.

In significant ways, though, New York City only partially fills the template set forth in 1961—or does not fill it at all. The waterfront is now bereft of shipping. The Port of New York, which handled 15 percent of the nation's cargo in 1961, handles less than half that today. Many old industrial buildings have become either de facto or de jure housing or stand empty.[17] Of 1.2 million manufacturing jobs in New York City in 1954, 325,000 are left. Old slums, such as Harlem, Brownsville, and East New York, persist in the face of cuts in federal urban programs while formerly middle-class areas, such as the Grand Concourse, Crown Heights, and East Flatbush, struggle to stabilize themselves.

Today, New York City is, as Peter Marcuse has written, a quartered city, in which racial divisions are subdivided by class divisions.[18] Rich and upper-middle-class New Yorkers, predominantly white, live close to the city center and are separated from African-Americans and Latinos of all classes. The middle class is in an often uneasy holding pattern at the city's edges. The neighborhoods in which the poor and so-called underclass live are expanding, as are the new ghettos described by Camillo Vergara: housing projects surrounded by abandoned blocks.[19] Where abandoned neighborhoods are being recaptured, particularly in the Bronx and in Brooklyn, the big, multifamily buildings that were preferred during the 1960s have been replaced by two- and three-story row houses with strictly enforced private front yards and backyards, an ironic return to nineteenth-century housing concepts. It is less expensive to build these units and easier to transfer the responsibility of maintaining open space—a hidden cost of the 1961 template—to owner-occupants.

The disjunction between the 1961 template and the realities of New York City in 1991 provides clear evidence that the centrifugal forces of postwar American urban development have fulfilled Lewis Mumford's prescient observation of 1924:

> The community is on the eve of a ... migration. The occasion is electric power and auto transportation, which, plus the radio and telephone, tend to equalize advantages of a great area and thus rob the centralized city of much of its attraction. On top of this is the fact that industry, housing, transportation, and so forth, must no longer operate automatically: their automatic growth tends to pile up embarrassing conditions, so that no industry, for example, can afford to pay for the urban housing of its unskilled workers.[20]

The visionary pragmatism developed from the 1930s to the 1950s—and encoded in the 1961 zoning revision—did succeed in expanding the city's dense core. Yet, from all appearances, this core is increasingly detached from the economic and social structure of the surrounding city and region. If New York City continues emerging as a global city or center for telecommunications and the exchange of ideas, as Mitchell Moss, Saskia Sassen, and others observe,[21] this imbalanced development is likely to continue.

New York City, as a global city, is likely to look beyond its suburban rings to a handful of peer cities throughout the world for innovation, capital, business, and culture. In the region, the process described by Mumford will continue and so-called "edge cities," such as White Plains, will satisfy the regional needs that the city of New York once did. The combination of local and national industries, which created so much of New York City's urban fabric and social organization in 1945, is not likely to recur, rendering the 1961 template of the ideal city as obsolete today as the 1916 zoning law appeared to be in the postwar era.

NOTES

1. Jan Morris, *Manhattan '45* (New York: Oxford University Press, 1987), pp. 3–13.
2. The Williamsburgh Savings Bank building sits in isolated splendor at Atlantic and Flatbush avenues in Brooklyn, atop a Long Island Railroad terminal and a station serving ten subway lines.
3. Richard Plunz, "Battery Park City: Between Edge and Fabric," in Roy Strickland, ed., *Battery Park City: Between Edge and Fabric* (New York: Columbia University Graduate School of Architecture, Planning, and Preservation, 1991), pp. 5–6.
4. Notable exceptions to this pattern included the Upper West Side, where Frederick Law Olmsted and Robert Moses had planned Riverside Park, and the Gracie Square area, where there was housing for the middle class and the rich.
5. John Maxtone Graham, *The Only Way to Cross* (New York: Collier Books), p. 408.
6. Roger Starr, *The Rise and Fall of New York City* (New York: Basic Books, 1985).
7. This figure is derived from averaging annual housing production as noted in *New York City Housing Authority Annual Reports* for the decade.
8. Robert A. Caro, *The Power Broker* (New York: Alfred A. Knopf, 1974).
9. Discussion with the author, January 1989.
10. Caro, *The Power Broker,* pp. 963–964.
11. Peter Marcuse, "Robert Moses: Contradictions In, Contradictions Out," a paper delivered at the "Robert Moses New York" conference, Columbia University Graduate School of Architecture, Planning, and Preservation, February 1989.
12. "Main Points of New Zoning for a More Orderly, Less Cramped City of the Future," *New York Times* (16 February 1959): 22.
13. Robert A. M. Stern, Gregory Gilmartin, and Thomas Mellins, *New York 1930: Architecture and Urbanism Between the Two World Wars* (New York: Rizzoli, 1987).
14. Caro, *The Power Broker,* p. 805.
15. The firm Voorhees, Walker, Foley and Smith (later known as Voorhees, Walker, Smith and Smith) was architect of the East River Houses, New York City's first "tower in the park" housing project, which was completed in 1941. See Richard A. Plunz, *A History of Housing in New York City: Dwelling Type and Social Change in the American Metropolis* (New York: Columbia University Press, 1990), p. 245.
16. Caro, *The Power Broker,* p. 659.
17. "Imports by Rail Cut in Half Amount of Cargo Arriving at Region's Docks," *New York Times* (12 January 1992).
18. Marcuse, "Robert Moses."
19. Camillo Vergara, "Response to Peter Marcuse," a paper delivered at the "Robert Moses New York" conference, Columbia University Graduate School of Architecture, Planning, and Preservation, February 1989.

20. Letter to Patrick Geddes, December 4, 1924, quoted in Lewis Mumford, *My Works and Days: A Personal Chronicle* (New York: Harcourt Brace Jovanovich, 1978), p. 107.

21. Saskia Sassen, "Space and Economy in the City: New York and Tokyo," and a response by Mitchell Moss, papers delivered at the "Density and the City: Is New York Dense Enough?" conference, Columbia University Graduate School of Architecture, Planning, and Preservation, April 1991.

ZONING FROM 1961 TO 1991: TURNING BACK THE CLOCK— BUT WITH AN UP-TO-THE-MINUTE SOCIAL AGENDA

NORMAN MARCUS

Zoning is a land use regulation, a tool that implements a city plan. Despite the fervor that zoning periodically inspires, zoning neither builds nor destroys a city and is only partly responsible for the way the city looks and functions. The marketplace, politics, and charity all share those responsibilities. This paper will attempt a history of zoning in New York City during the last thirty years, since the 1961 Comprehensive Amendment to the New York City Zoning Resolution became effective.

That amendment, the first comprehensive update since the zoning regulation was originally enacted in 1916, reflected forty-five tumultuous years of technological, social, and physical change; incorporated new standards, methodologies, and techniques; and, yes, proposed a radical vision of the future. The 1916 resolution had been amended continuously, almost from the day it had passed. By 1960, it resembled nothing so much as a torn patchwork quilt and had swollen to eighty-five pages, including appendices and a Table of Amendments, and was ripe, in the minds of many, for change.

If the 1916 resolution resembled a patchwork quilt in 1960, then the 1961 revision today resembles a giant maze. Today, the also much-amended 1961 revision stands at 835 pages (and still counting), exclusive of appendices and a Table of Restrictive Declarations. There was no table of amendments to the 1961 revision; indeed, it was necessary to complete a table of amendments for this paper in order to document the trends it describes and belatedly to fill in its missing history lessons.

What have been the common threads running through the zoning land use fabric of the last thirty years that may help us to negotiate this maze?

Two stand out: increasing respect for the built (and the unbuilt-on) environment and the use of zoning as a device to recapture some of the value of private development and use it to generate social benefits. The history of zoning during these last three decades is best understood by examining these common threads to see how they attacked fundamental principles of the 1961 zoning resolution and produced the current regulatory maze.

THE VISION OF THE 1961 RESOLUTION

One of the fundamental principles of the 1961 revision to the zoning resolution was to provide more open space in residential and commercial districts while allowing for absolute increases in density. Over the years, this value was superseded by a concern for existing conditions, a concern that was reflected in the creation of landmark preservation, special zoning rules to protect loft buildings and natural areas, and new special and generic zoning districts that responded more directly to the city's physical context.

The 1961 revision was promulgated at the height of the city's urban renewal program, which was dedicated to replacing "substandard and unsanitary" areas, often densely packed low-rise tenements, with sound and healthy neighborhoods. The program was characterized by the designation of large areas for renewal; new open space ratios, height factors, and parking requirements ensured that new development would little resemble the old city building blocks, whose seemingly outmoded form was deemed responsible for the city's social ills. The U.S. Supreme Court in *Berman v. Parker*[1] dismissed conservative fears that much standard housing would be lost in the giant nationwide urban renewal clearance underwritten by the federal government by saying:

> It was important to redesign the whole area so as to eliminate the conditions that cause slums—the overcrowding of dwellings, the lack of parks, the lack of adequate streets and alleys, the absence of recreational areas, the lack of light and air, the presence of outmoded street patterns. *It was believed that the piecemeal approach, the removal of individual structures that were offensive, would be only a palliative* [emphasis added]. The entire area needed redesigning so that a balanced, integrated plan could be developed for the region, including not only new homes but also schools, churches, parks, streets and shopping centers. In this way it was hoped that the cycle of decay of the area could be controlled and the birth of future slums prevented.

Large-scale clearance would, under the 1961 zoning principles, be followed by new districts separated according to uses, as prescribed by detailed tables in the resolution. The three general uses would be residential, commercial, and manufacturing. While new manufacturing zones disallowed residential use, residential districts disallowed commercial and manufacturing uses. Prior legal nonconforming uses were permitted to remain but were prohibited from enlarging.[2]

In the 1961 revision, new floor area ratio (FAR) limits replaced the more visual height and setback bulk controls that had been set out in the 1916 ordinance. The FAR—based on, among other factors, the capacity of the city's infrastructure to absorb development in each use classification district—governed the amount of floor area that could be built on a zoning lot. Although height and setback restrictions establishing a sky exposure plane to the street remained, it was the FAR control that dominated (discretionary relief from sky exposure planes was available elsewhere in the ordinance).[3]

The 1961 revision set forth several other regulatory reforms. New open space ratios and plaza incentives eschewed familiar and reassuring street walls in furtherance of a strong policy to open up the city physically. Towers were encouraged by increasing their as-of-right coverage from 25 to 40 percent of the zoning lot; this rule markedly changed the standard building form in higher density districts from high-coverage ziggurats and wedding cake architecture to the new monoliths. Parking requirements too were substantially expanded for all residential developments and most other uses outside core areas—a change that would shred sidewalks with curb cuts and extend a city welcome (albeit short-lived) to the automobile.

CHANGING ATTITUDES TOWARD OPEN SPACE

One of the most dominant values reflected in the 1961 revision was the need for more open space in the city. "Light and air" had been one of the values of the 1916 resolution, which required not only setbacks for tall buildings but also front, side, and rear yards in the outer boroughs and rear yards in some areas of Manhattan. Other than that, the only publicly protected open space was city parks and streets.

In 1958, Mies van der Rohe's burnished copper and glass Seagram Building created a sensation with its simple formal reflecting pools in a plaza fronting on Park Avenue. Across the street, Lever House, finished a few years earlier, had created a similar stir by providing a public arcade and open space complete with garden in a catercorner pedestrian route that linked Park Avenue to East Fifty-third Street.

Neither was as large as it could have been under pre-1961 zoning; their corporate developers preferred instead to create a distinctive headquarters image. Both buildings were well received when they were finished and have been designated as landmarks during the past decade[4]; the public has made much use of the voluntary open space amenity each provided.

Planners were struck by the paucity of such amenities in Midtown and lower Manhattan, but rather than require similar spaces in the proposals that became the 1961 zoning revision, planners hoped to induce them with an "incentive zoning" device. Studies of pre-1961 central business district development revealed the average building FAR approached 17. In the 1961 rezoning, planners set the basic density limit to only 15 FAR but allowed developers to build an extra 20 percent, to a FAR of 18, if they provided a plaza or arcade.[5]

Planners were equally intent on securing more open space outside the city's central business district. The device they used in the 1961 revision, the "open space ratio" (OSR), was founded on an inverse relationship between the allowable floor area and the open space that would be required. The higher the permitted FAR (that is, the higher the density), the lower the required OSR. In practice, the OSRs incorporated in the 1961 revision were set up so that a new building would provide about as much open space in a neighborhood as there would have been before development, if undeveloped land and vacant lots were considered open space.

Before long, the 1961 revision's emphasis on providing more open space began to be reconsidered. While planners in 1961 were projecting future needs based on an extrapolation of past data trends, they could not have foreseen that their assumption about crime would change. While street crime occurred at relatively low rates in the 1930s, 1940s, and 1950s, it rose steadily in the 1960s, 1970s, and 1980s. Public attitudes toward new privately owned, public open spaces (as well as city parks) began to reflect the new danger they represented. *Defensible Space,* an influential book by Oscar Newman,[6] responded to the new public fears and began to influence property owners as well as planners. Illegal grills and fences attempted to shut these open spaces to the public at off-hours. Spikes were introduced on ledges and other areas upon which people might sit or sleep.

Meanwhile, architecture writers criticized many of the new towers and plazas, particularly those on the Avenue of the Americas across from Rockefeller Center, for their lack of street walls and street-level retailing and for the vacuousness of their minimally improved plazas. It seemed that the Seagram Building and Lever House were flukes, successful in part because they served as occasional refreshing oases in an otherwise disciplined street wall along an avenue.

Responding to this criticism, planners and urban designers came up with a new bonus: a project could receive extra density if it included shop-lined and covered public spaces.[7] Planners contended these covered pedestrian spaces were often superior to plazas because they were more defensible, all-weather, and all-season. To provide these spaces, however, it was often necessary to increase tower coverage, which lowered height somewhat but also reduced light and air without necessarily joining the contextual street walls on surrounding buildings. Also, these spaces created lower-rent retail frontage, which, it was argued, drained vitality from the street. After a decade, the incentive bonus for these spaces was removed,[8] and their provision became an unsubsidized function of the private market for interior shopping malls.

In the outer boroughs, complying with the OSR as well as providing common open space in "planned unit developments" (PUDs) became two means of preserving large expanses of natural areas, often with recreational facilities added. Open space within the PUD was shared by owners of property within the PUD and was not open to the public. Like Gramercy "Park" in Manhattan, these spaces, which often resembled public parks, were defensible in design and, though elitist, popular with their limited class of users.

In the outer boroughs, the debate about contextual design versus open space was most vividly projected in a controversy two decades ago over high-rise development in Glen Oaks, a community zoned R3–2 (for low-density multiple dwellings, such as garden apartments and row houses) near

FIGURE 27
The IBM Atrium at Fifty-sixth Street and Madison Avenue is a covered pedestrian space for which the building developer received a density bonus.

FIGURE 28
Village Greens, a "planned urban development" in Staten Island.

the Queens-Nassau county line. Much of the testimony at the New York City Planning Commission public hearing addressed the height of the three proposed apartment houses. Speakers argued that the proposed thirty-two-story structures would destroy the suburban character of the neighborhood, would be visually offensive, and would be environmentally destructive.

The proposal left as open space almost all of an existing private golf course, the last remains of a glacial terminal moraine left over from the Ice Age. The ground floor area of the buildings covered only some 2 percent of the site. Moreover, the open space was further protected by a covenant contained in a restrictive declaration that prevented the owner of the property from ever building outside a certain circumscribed area regardless of what the zoning might call for in the distant future. The permanent dedication of open space under this covenant was nearly one hundred acres.

Had the special permit for this large-scale residential development been denied, the developer would still have had the as-of-right option to build more than 2,500 single-family homes. This outcome would have satisfied the community's desire to retain a low-level profile but it would have totally destroyed the golf course and terminal moraine.

Ecologists who appealed to the city to reject the special permit overlooked the fact that developments of single-family homes place a far greater strain on the environment than do apartment buildings in parklike settings. Had single-family homes been built at Glen Oaks, at least 20 percent of the area would have been devoted to paved streets that, in turn, would have substantially increased the requirement for storm sewers since runoff would have been greater. Single-family homes also would have generated more traffic because owners of homes with private driveways and garages tend to have higher car ownership rates than high-rise apartment dwellers.

The city approved the project[9] but the profile of the three thirty-two-story towers looming over suburbia served to fuel many a procontextuality political meeting over the ensuing decades.

In a real sense, the 1961 zoning revision and the concurrent billion-dollar urban renewal program shared common assumptions and principles: large-lot development and large-scale redevelopment. The new zoning controls worked consistently in large-scale developments that were shaped by common assumptions. On smaller lots, where new development would "infill" into existing neighborhood fabric, the new controls either failed altogether or produced awkward dissonance within an established neighborhood. It was not surprising that efforts to rehabilitate existing structures came to little in this "think big" world because the zoning resolution that went into effect in 1961 reflected a disdain for the existing built form.

Within a few years of the 1961 revision, public sentiment began to respond to a different drumbeat. Open space lost its standing as the city's dominant zoning value. As a candidate for incentive zoning, it began to lag

ZONING FROM 1961 TO 1991

behind competing "amenities" on the city's social agenda, and the value placed on contextualism today began to outweigh the value placed on open space. Neither large-lot development nor large-scale redevelopment would survive the political storms of the next decades.

LANDMARK PRESERVATION

When Pennsylvania Station was demolished in the early 1960s to make way for office development (under the 1961 revised zoning rules), people rallied and coalesced behind the creation in 1965[10] of the Landmarks Preservation Commission (LPC), which was granted power to designate and regulate individual landmarks and development within historic districts.

The Landmarks Preservation Law was designed to preserve examples of the very building types that the 1961 zoning revision did not favor. Within historic districts, the LPC now mandated that new buildings resemble their older neighbors—with less bulk but higher lot coverage, comparatively low street walls, and little open space—rather than the zoning prototype. Brooklyn Heights, for example, designated in 1965 as the first historic district, was

FIGURE 29
Carroll Gardens Historic District, Brooklyn.

characterized by high building coverage, low street walls, and private open space, attributes of early nineteenth-century technology and aesthetics.

Something of a shotgun marriage was arranged between the zoning resolution and the landmarks law when landmarks were permitted to transfer their unused development rights to nearby lots even if they were across the street.[11] Limited height zoning districts were entertained in designated historic districts.[12] In the 1970s, developments on landmark zoning lots were able to secure use and bulk modifications of the zoning resolution to foster preservation and harmonious relationships between developments, including landmarks and their surroundings.

While no one could thereafter accuse the zoning resolution of being landmark-blind, the two codes remain in a state of tension with each other. By early 1992, 2 percent of all buildings in the city were subject to LPC jurisdiction and a new proposal for transition districts *around* historic districts, which would soften the boundary shock between zoning and LPC turf, was being discussed.[13]

LOFTS AND WALL STREET CANYONS

In the early 1960s, SoHo's "Hell's Hundred Acres" were studied in anticipation that they would be designated for urban renewal clearance and replaced with new housing shaped by the 1961 zoning revision. The city rejected this initiative on economic rather than aesthetic grounds, relying on a report by Chester Rapkin, who was soon to become a city planning commissioner.[14] The report revealed that "[SoHo's] dingy exteriors, however, conceal the fact that the establishments operating within them are, for the most part, flourishing business enterprises of considerable economic value to the City of New York."

Thereafter, though, many of the lofts were vacated by their manufacturing tenants, and, despite a zoning classification that permitted only manufacturing and commercial uses, they were illegally occupied for residential purposes. Artists liked these lofts because they had large floors and high ceilings, which provided flexible space for working and living. Consequently, artists were legislatively deemed a species of manufacturing to legalize their occupancy.[15]

Although Rapkin found the SoHo cast-iron facades "dingy," the LPC determined they were sufficiently unique to warrant historic district designation.[16] Altogether, lofts were on their way to becoming chic, and loft living was becoming de rigueur to a certain class of professional New Yorkers.

However, a Department of City Planning survey in 1977 indicated that 90 percent of residential (that is, nonartist) conversions were illegal, posing a serious fire danger since the turn-of-the-century loft typically lacked safety

FIGURE 30
The SoHo district, Manhattan.

features required in residential development.[17] In crafting responsive loft zoning regulations, planners in effect rejected the form of development advocated by the 1961 zoning revision and embraced a building type that was originally designed for factories. Loft buildings frequently covered most of their lots, had high street walls, had minuscule rear yards, if any, and cast shadows that afforded minimal light and air in the surrounding streets and rear loft floors—a built form literally impossible to achieve even under the 1916 zoning resolution. The adaptive residential reuse requirements ensured these buildings would be retained, accompanied by amendments to other laws that made the adaptive reuse of these structures safe.[18]

The City Planning Commission in the late 1960s had similarly enshrined the canyonlike Wall Street environment. The commission authorized applications to the Board of Standards and Appeals for height and setback modifications from the uniform 1961 zoning standards for new development on irregularly shaped lots fronting on narrow, twisting lower Manhattan streets.[19] Irony is heavy here since this was the unhealthy breeding ground for the original 1916 zoning resolution.

NATURAL AREAS AND WETLANDS

By 1961, most of New York City had been covered with buildings. Those areas remaining unbuilt were either in the southern half of Staten Island (and fast fading with the opening of the Verrazano Bridge), steep-slope areas, such as the Staten Island Greenbelt and Riverdale in the Bronx, and assorted swamps, ponds, inlets, and shoreline susceptible to landfill. Since New York City is reputed to have a shoreline extending some 578 miles, it was inevitable that new development proposals would be projected in these areas, particularly because redevelopment was increasingly constrained by the shutdown of the federal urban renewal program, the continuing protective umbrella of rent control and rent stabilization, and the expanding reach of landmark and historic district designations.

Although the federal National Environmental Policy Act (NEPA), passed in 1969, mandated environmental assessment of federal government actions,[20] it was not until 1976 that New York State, with the State Environmental Quality Review Act (SEQRA),[21] extended this protection to all government discretionary zoning actions (such as special permits, rezonings, amendments to the text of the zoning resolution, and variances). By this time, the state had in place programs to protect tidal[22] and freshwater wetlands,[23] so the window for development in natural areas was closing fast.

In fact, the city had anticipated this federal and state sentiment to some extent by initiating its own zoning regulatory approach to many of these areas. In the Special Natural Area District, which was mapped in portions of the Bronx,[24] Queens,[25] and Staten Island,[26] all development would be discretionary; approval of a proposal would depend upon the degree to which it impinged on designated natural features, such as trees, botanic environments, boulders, and watercourses. Surveys of such features were required as part of a development application. As in the case of landmarks or historic districts, bulk and yard requirements could be modified from the uniform 1961 zoning standards in order to preserve the natural environment.

NEPA, SEQRA, natural area districts, and landmark preservation laws provided a legal foundation for closing the pioneering, taming-the-wilderness, and wholesale clearance chapters in the city's development and commencing a new era called contextual zoning. The only problem with this was the existence of the wrongheaded 1961 zoning revision, which gave architects and developers a free hand in choosing towers over low-rise configurations without regard to contextuality.

ZONING FROM 1961 TO 1991

CURBING 1961'S LAISSEZ-FAIRE REGULATIONS

The 1961 zoning revision reduced the city's great variety of residential neighborhoods to fourteen basic zoning districts. Only eleven were mapped in Queens[27]; imagine the great diversity of neighborhoods in that borough—Hollis, Rego Park, Kew Gardens, Malba, Whitestone, Rockaway, Rosedale, Maspeth, Ozone Park, Flushing, Corona, East Elmhurst, Woodside, South Jamaica, Jamaica Estates, Forest Hills Gardens, Glen Oaks, Bayside, Ravenswood, Astoria, Hunter's Point, Dutch Kills, Forest Hills, Bayswater, Breezy Point, Sunnyside Gardens, Fresh Meadows, Broad Channel, Howard Beach, Fort Totten, Douglaston, Pot Cove, College Point, Little Neck, Jackson Heights, and still others—shorn of their unique characteristics and forced to renew themselves with only FAR, OSR, and height factors to light the way.

Most neighborhoods had been shaped by the pre-1961 zoning regulations, which encouraged higher coverage and lower rise buildings than those promoted by the 1961 zoning. These pre-1961 regulations related the height of buildings to the width of the street and limited "towers"—exceptions to the contextual rule—to structures covering only 25 percent of their zoning lot at the elevation of the required setback.

FIGURE 31
A typical 1961-style building in Flushing.

FIGURE 32
Schematic drawings of possible development within C5–3 and C5–5 zones for central business districts. The tower maximizes development potential because it takes advantage of a plaza bonus.

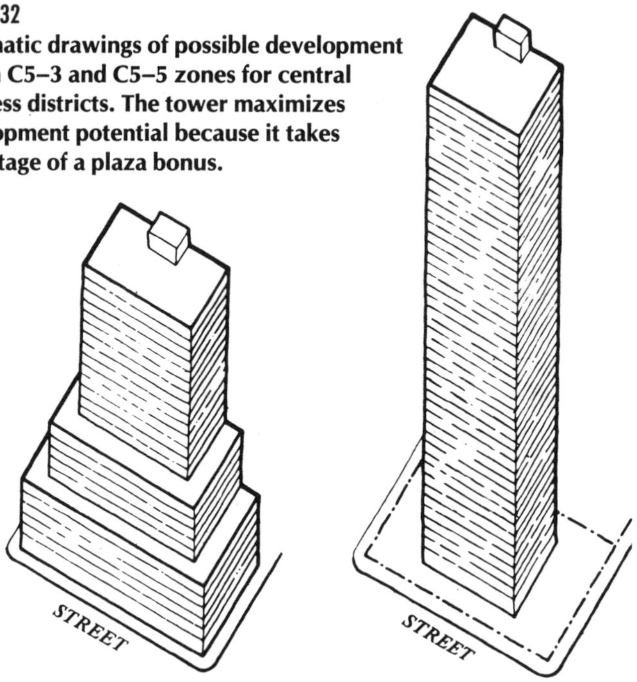

Schematic illustration (25-story building) high coverage

Schematic illustration (45-story building) low coverage

Both schemes possible in C5-3 and C5-5
Highest Bulk Office Buildings, CBD
Basic FAR: 15.00 (18.00 with bonus)
Residential FAR: 10.00 to 12.00
Exempt from parking requirements

Under the 1961 rezoning, each district had a lowest common denominator building that was the most economical to build and the easiest to market but that was frequently at odds with its surroundings in terms of height, scale, or character; that is, the zoning prototype generally did not match the existing built form in the communities in which it could be built.

This happened for a number of reasons. For example, the pre-1961 height and setback rules often dictated floor plans that were too small or intricately shaped to be workable. The 1961 zoning increased the permissible coverage of towers to 40 percent and more (by special permit) of the zoning lot; the fatter tower alternative produced higher, more marketable floors.

At ground level, the OSR required that buildings be surrounded by accessory parking and open space, a practice that ran counter to the tradition of putting up buildings with consistent street walls. Building forms covered less lot area in large-scale developments to satisfy OSR and parking requirements. The plaza bonus completed contextual ruination in high-density areas by creating a strong stimulus for open, public spaces at ground level—rather than buildings with ground-level walls along the sidewalks.

In most of the city—those areas not designated as historic, designated as residential lofts, or within natural areas—the site of the zoning lot was the crucial factor in determining whether development would be low-rise, mid-rise, or high-rise. Since zoning controlled height and bulk primarily through FAR rather than explicit controls on the building envelope, a tower or other bulky building could be built even in a low-FAR district if the zoning lot were large enough. The height factor, which maximized FAR in each residential district according to an upward sliding scale as the densities increased (for example, R5, R6, R7, and so on), was simply too permissive a control to qualify as a contextual tool in the face of the demonstrated market value of higher residential floors.

The commercial districts created by the 1961 rezoning were subject to the same gross bulk generalities as the residential districts. None of these generic districts, in fact, reflected the special characteristics of the city's signature business districts: the theater district, midtown Fifth Avenue, the flower market, Sheepshead Bay, Upper Madison Avenue, City Island, or Hylan Boulevard.

In a commercially zoned central business district, zoning allowed a choice among many uses. However, some of these uses were more profitable than others. The 1961 regulation encouraged the most profitable uses, as well as the most marketable building forms, through its unweighted, egalitarian approach. The distinctive "loss leader" would disappear amidst the higher and ever-increasing land values unless the city could afford to subsidize it.

THE BIRTH OF THE SPECIAL DISTRICT

In 1967, the City Planning Commission proposed an innovative zoning technique that would preserve New York City's position as the nation's theater capital without curtailing construction of the high-rise office buildings that were steadily replacing the old uneconomic, two- and three-story theaters near Times Square.[28] This plan reflected more than just sentiment and nostalgia. There were compelling findings linking New York City's preeminence as a national corporate headquarters to its legitimate theaters, around which so many related activities, such as radio and television, shopping, dining, and tourism, clustered. The catalyst was called incentive zoning.

Rather than inhibit the construction of new office space in the Times Square area, which is well served by the city's mass transit network, the Special Theatre District offered developers an incentive (in the form of a floor

FIGURE 33
The Marriott Marquis Hotel obtained a bonus for providing the Marquis Theatre on site. Three theaters were destroyed to clear the site.

area bonus of up to 44 percent) to construct a legitimate theater as part of a larger project. Through incentive zoning, the city could subsidize the use of desired (in accordance with its comprehensive plan) but uneconomic activities by offering the carrot of additional density. Under this provision, five legitimate theaters were built that otherwise would not have come into being.

The real innovation was that the city did not simply encourage theaters in all areas zoned C6 (for high-bulk commercial uses requiring a central location) or create a new generic theater district (for example, C9). Rather, "the special district" left the basic C6 zone as it was and supplemented its citywide provisions with an overlay of rules that applied only within an idiosyncratic area—the goal being to encourage the use that gave that area its special contextual character.[29] Maintaining the context of the Theatre District meant not only providing incentives for legitimate theaters but also establishing a host of requirements for mandatory retail uses, entertainment-related uses, street walls, pedestrian circulation, and large-scale signs.

The Special Theatre District was not only the first post-1961 zoning amendment that explicitly sought to promote contextualism but also the first attempt to use zoning to recapture the value of private development in order

TABLE 1
Special Districts Designated by the New York City Planning Commission and in Effect on January 1, 1993

24 April 1969	Lincoln Square District [20365A]
9 October 1969	Limited Commercial District [20779]
20 March 1970	United Nations Development District [21014]
4 January 1971	Greenwich Street Development District [21418]
20 July 1972	South Street Seaport District [21975]
28 February 1973	Transit Land Use District [22441]
23 April 1973	Park Improvement District [22240]
13 September 1973	Northside Mixed-Use District [22424]
4 October 1973	Sheepshead Bay District [22171]
20 December 1973	Madison Avenue Preservation District [22350]
28 December 1973	Battery Park City District [22479]
28 December 1973	Manhattan Landing District [22498]
18 July 1974	Planned Community Preservation District [22501]
15 August 1974	Atlantic Avenue District [22670]
24 October 1974	Scenic View District [22750]
21 November 1974	Clinton District [22758]
19 December 1974	Natural Area District 1 [22748A]
9 January 1975	Coney Island Mixed-Use District [22785]
21 May 1975	Natural Area District 2 [22890A]
11 September 1975	Franklin Street Mixed-Use District [23028]
11 September 1975	South Richmond Development District [22972]
18 March 1976	Northside Mixed-Use District [23158]
11 June 1976	Lower Manhattan Mixed-Use District [23198]
20 January 1977	City Island District [23258]
20 January 1977	Ocean Parkway District [23284]
3 February 1977	Little Italy District [N760061ZRM]
1 December 1977	Natural Area District 3 [N770272ZRY]
16 March 1978	Fulton Mall District [N770236ZRK]
26 March 1978	Garment Center District [N870241ZRM(A)]
12 November 1978	Bay Ridge District [N780285ZRK]
20 August 1981	Manhattan Bridge District [N801024ZRM]
3 December 1981	Hunters Point Mixed-Use District [N810538ZRQ]
13 May 1982	Midtown District [N820253ZRM]
28 April 1983	Natural Area District 4 [N821255ZRQ]
10 January 1985	Union Square District [N841006ZRM]
30 June 1987	Hillsides Preservation District [N870002ZRR]
28 September 1989	Grand Concourse District [N890229ZRX]
22 February 1990	Jacob K. Javits Convention Center District [N900053ZRM]

to further the city's social agenda—an issue that is discussed in more depth in a subsequent section of this paper.

In effect, the incentive for providing new legitimate theaters was a refashioning of the plaza bonuses incorporated in the 1961 zoning revision. The same combination of techniques—the special district and density

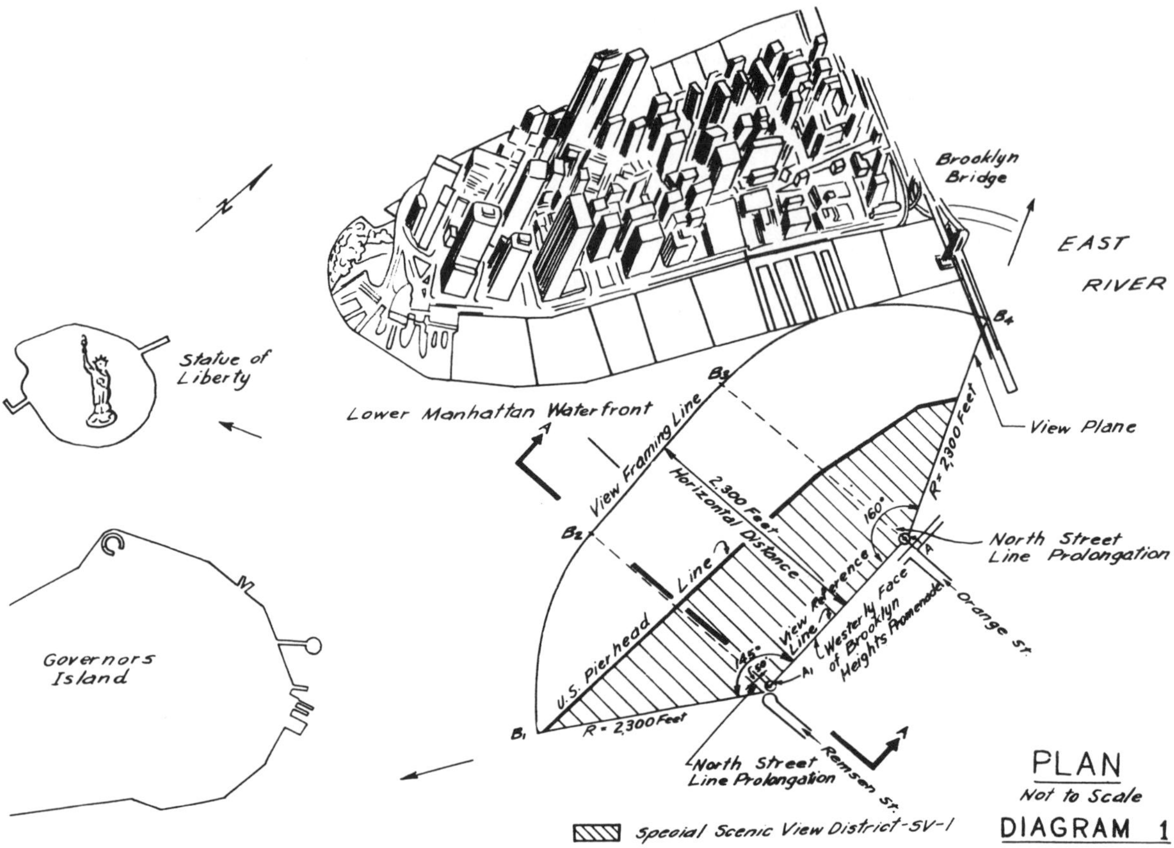

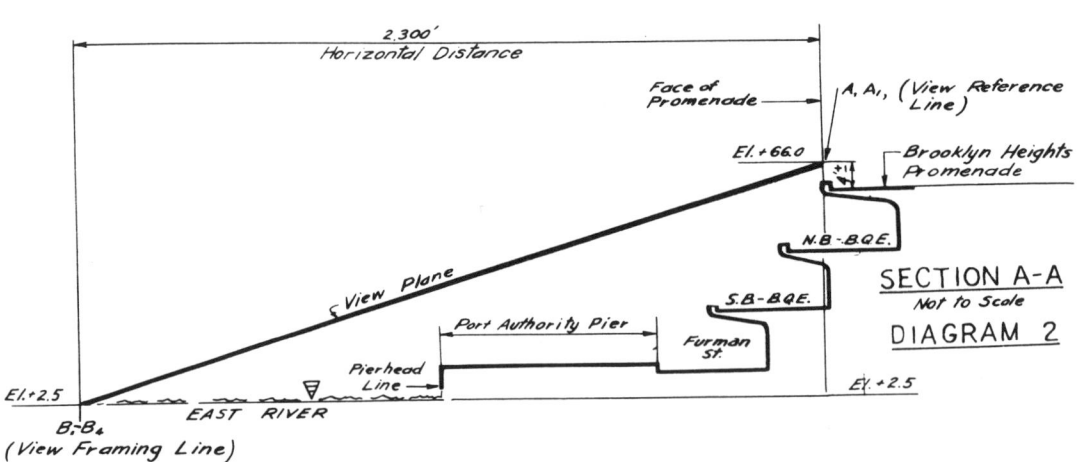

FIGURE 34
Lower Manhattan is the focal point of two scenic view districts, this one mapped from Brooklyn Heights Promenade and another mapped from Victory Boulevard, Staten Island. These diagrams, from the New York City zoning resolution, show how building heights are limited between the Promenade and the East River.

bonuses—were soon used to encourage public rooms and arcades along Broadway near Lincoln Center,[30] extra retail space along Fifth Avenue,[31] and a second-level pedestrian spine along Greenwich Street in lower Manhattan.[32]

During the 1970s and 1980s, more than forty more special districts were designated, but they rarely incorporated floor area incentives. Contextual development was now required, not simply encouraged, through individualized regulations mandating height, setback, street wall, yards, and mixed uses; limitations on uses; requirements for color, materials, signs, recesses, courtyards, development rights transfer, transit easements, open space networks, restrictive covenants, and the provision of infrastructure; prohibitions against plazas and demolition; and countless other conditions about which you always wanted to know but were afraid to ask.

For an area to qualify as a special district, the City Planning Commission required a planning study and some evidence that the district was indeed special. The process of planning with the affected community was usually exhilarating in itself and the experience of citizen involvement a rewarding one, particularly when the involved community used its eyes and ears to enforce the resulting regulations.

The city can be said to have created an even greater number of special districts than those bearing that specific nomenclature. Occasionally, a spe-

FIGURE 35
House being built under special zoning regulations in Borough Park, Brooklyn.

cial provision would be dropped into the uniform regulations to deal with a unique area. For example, one section described a residential area popularly known as Borough Park, in Brooklyn, in which thirty-five-foot height limits would offset a higher FAR, greater lot coverage, and relaxed front yard requirements that allowed the protrusion of balconies.[33] The resulting house type could serve large families and would not require elevators, needs characteristic of a religious community unwilling to use elevators on the Sabbath.

Another example of a special district in all but name is the supposedly generic M1–5A and M1–5B districts mapped only in SoHo and NoHo.[34] Special provisions in these districts allowed joint living-work quarters for artists, a use not permitted in other M1 districts, and restricted ground-floor activity to manufacturing and wholesale use, precluding retail uses otherwise allowed in M1 districts (except by special permit).

For communities concerned about the character of future development, the handwriting was on the wall: a special district could avoid the 1961 zoning "look." It was equally obvious that by the early 1980s no neighborhood ever viewed itself as standard or typical in the sense that the generic districts set forth in the 1961 zoning revision would be appropriate for it.

The proliferation of special districts ultimately eroded the city's capability to enforce zoning—thirty-seven special districts means thirty-seven zoning ordinances in a city whose administrative capacity is geared to one zoning ordinance. The Department of Buildings found it difficult to keep up with so many idiosyncratic provisions in different areas.

It was clear that the city could never map enough special districts to prevent 1961 zoning developments that were out of character with each neighborhood—the task of overlaying the post-1961 zoning resolution would approach the cleaning of the Augean stables and the cacophony of individual special district regulations could approach the commotion at the Tower of Babel.

HOUSING QUALITY AND CONTEXTUAL ZONING DISTRICTS

In the mid-1970s, city planners began to explore other ways of creating regulations that would produce the desired contextual buildings. In 1976, the city created a generic alternative to special districts, available only by discretionary special permit. Called the Housing Quality Program,[35] it recognized the relationship between building design and the quality of life in a dense urban environment. It evaluated the relationship of the design of a proposed building to the surrounding neighborhood, generally seeking to lower the height of new buildings. It also scored the adequacy of on-site recreation space, the safety and security of the building and its occupants,

FIGURE 36
The Bromley was built on the Upper West Side under Housing Quality guidelines, a precursor to generic contextual districts.

and the quality of the building interior. If the evaluation were positive, the city could approve modifications to numerous 1961 zoning regulations, such as those that applied to height, setback, open space, yard, spacing between buildings, parking, window-to-lot-line distance, and zoning lots divided by district boundaries.

After fifteen years of experience with zoning rules that encouraged as-of-right towers in open space, all the city had come up with was a cumbersome application process, subject to the uncertain approval of discretionary waivers, that permitted a contextual building to be built in a neighborhood not fortunate enough to have been designated a special district or a historic district. Ironically, the same building probably could have gone forward as-of-right under the pre-1961 zoning. If Housing Quality buildings were usually superior to "tower in the park" buildings, one might have argued, shouldn't they have traded as-of-right places with the generic rules of the 1961 zoning revision? Another ten years were to elapse, and a million dollars of public funds were to be spent on an environmental impact statement, before this happened.

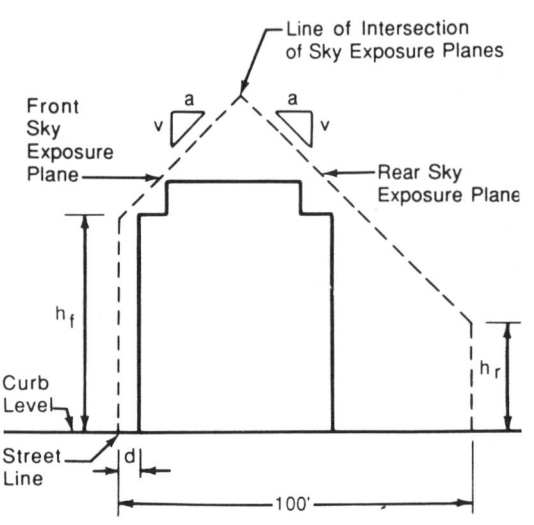
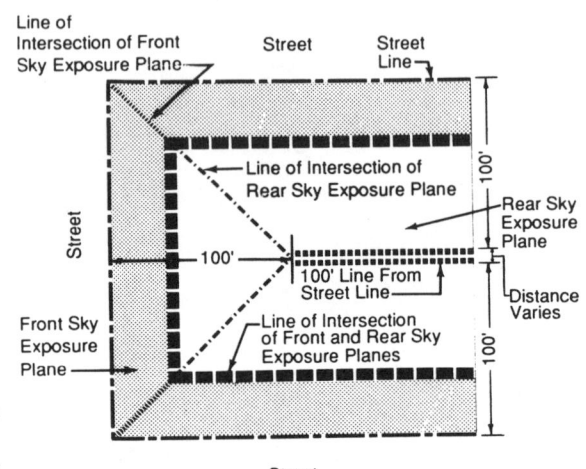

hf is the height at which the *front sky exposure plane* begins at the *street line*

hr is the height at which the *rear sky exposure plane* begins at the 100-foot line

d is the maximum *street wall* setback distance

v is the vertical distance

a is the horizontal distance

FIGURES 37, 38
Sky exposure planes illustrated for R–10 equivalent contextual district.

In the 1980s, proposals were made for a number of generic zoning districts that could be mapped in several neighborhoods.[36] For example, a stretch of Broadway on the Upper West Side had been under study for years for possible designation as a special district; yet its special attributes were echoed not only by its near neighbor, West End Avenue, but also by other Manhattan avenues.

Proponents of generic contextual districts asked, why go through the lengthy and expensive process necessary for establishing a special permit or special district—especially when the effect would primarily be on a few underdeveloped sites in these predominantly built-up environments? A new version of the generic R10 district that encouraged street walls and prohibited plazas and towers was the first (and flawed) contextual approach.[37]

Additional pressures for contextual reform accompanied the growing conviction that as-of-right generic contextual districts would be a better way to accomplish some of the goals of special districts and the Housing Quality program. These pressures resulted, in part, from increased demand during the 1980s for new residential construction, which put more and more neighborhoods at risk of redevelopment.

ZONING FROM 1961 TO 1991

One outcome of this heightened demand was the peculiar phenomenon of the midblock "sliver" building. These towers, erected on lots whose street frontage was less than forty-five feet, mushroomed seemingly overnight in neighborhoods in the Upper East and West sides that had high land values and were made possible through the mechanism of zoning lot mergers. Lots susceptible to sliver construction were typically situated in the medium-density brownstone valleys along the narrower cross streets and between the higher bulk avenues. Since the 1961 zoning regulations encouraged choice along midblocks, options that afforded greater return on investment, particularly from high-rent, high-rise apartments, prevailed over contextual, brownstone-scaled construction there. Prompt "antisliver" amendments[38] were followed by the remapping of these areas with newly created contextual R7B and R8B classifications, which prohibited not only sliver buildings but also other out-of-scale development.[39]

FIGURE 39
Sliver building on East Seventy-eighth Street.

As the 1980s wore on, generic contextual districts were fashioned as equivalents to most of the generic residential districts created in the 1961 revision, and they were mapped wherever existing neighborhood character demanded.[40] Also, the Housing Quality special permit was scrapped in favor of an as-of-right "quality housing" option, which incorporated many features of the Housing Quality formula and further entrenched contextual building design.[41] At the same time, the structure of the post-1961 zoning resolution and the underlying as-of-right choices remain applicable to those areas in which choice and flexibility are still felt to be desirable.

Today, the zoning resolution includes three times as many generic districts as it did when it was revised in 1961, and contextual districts typically require twice as much regulatory text as the districts created in 1961. Moreover, most special districts also remain. Perhaps they have become permanently fused in the collective consciousness of the communities in which they have been mapped; in some cases, they address issues that generic contextual districts, usually spelled out in far less detail, could not.

As a result, the ordinance today is diffuse, unnecessarily complex, and often self-contradictory—a vast, untamed sea of shifting currents and undertows reflecting our changing fashions over a thirty-year period. It is not user-friendly.

VALUE RECAPTURE: THE USE OF ZONING TO PROMOTE THE CITY'S SOCIAL AGENDA

Although the 1916 zoning resolution was conceived as layers of use and bulk prohibitions that varied from place to place, the 1961 revision introduced incentives for developers to include plazas and arcades in market-rate projects and a striking preference, expressed as additional density allowances, for community facilities. New York City's zoning had entered the value recapture era, and it did not stop there. While many of the subsequent changes to the 1961 revision sought to promote the types of buildings put up under the 1916 resolution (as well as those put up before there was any zoning law), others began to advance the city's social agenda. This agenda comprised uses and/or amenities that either the marketplace had ceased to provide on its own or the federal aid-to-cities program had ceased to furnish.

Where this agenda could not be advanced through special districts, special permits, or generic zoning programs (all of which are discussed subsequently), it relied opportunistically on case-by-case private sector applications to change the increasingly outdated 1961 zoning map. The city has not undertaken a comprehensive reexamination of its zoning map since 1961; consequently, many anomalous and seemingly outdated mapping designations remain. For example, large stretches of waterfront, mapped with manufacturing classifications in 1961, are still mapped that way today. Similarly, lower Sixth Avenue is still mapped in a manufacturing category. With the city's precipitous loss in blue-collar jobs since 1961, conforming uses have not emerged to occupy these areas, which are consciously referred to today as "holding zones." A comprehensively updated zoning map would release many of these underutilized parcels from obsolete classification, relinquish the city's site-specific hold over their future, and permit them to be used in accordance with a plan.

Because this comprehensive reevaluation has not yet taken place, individual property owners have resorted to presenting site-specific initiatives for zoning changes. Private owners, responding to market forces, have initiated most of these revisions; public agencies have initiated others, such as the reclassification of the Hunter's Point, Queens, area to allow residential use. The New York City Charter mandates this attention to private requests for zoning changes.[42]

Each approved remapping ensures the city will have intimate control over the resulting development. Moreover, once regulatory discretion has been exercised on a parcel, it becomes inevitable on subsequent changes in that parcel's development. Whether there is a restrictive declaration "running with the land" or a special permit condition on record at the Department of Buildings, once a property is tarred with the special regulatory brush, it must return to the government for permission to change again. In a sense, the property has become "domesticated" or "housebroken."

Discretionary actions that "up-zone" a parcel (for instance, changing from one allowable use or density to another that makes the parcel more valuable) are often seen as an opportunity for the city to recapture some of the new value that is created. Typically, the city sees an opportunity to obtain from the parcel owner some specific community benefit that the private sector and/or the government would not otherwise provide. Often, these benefits are characterized as mitigation for environmental impacts disclosed in connection with the rezoning process. For example, the "value recapture" component of a zoning change approval might take the form of an obligation to provide an open ice-skating rink on the site at nominal charge to the public.[43]

This "opportunity," of course, does not exist when a zoning change is proposed across a large, similarly situated district as part of an areawide plan. Only the proponent of the site triggering the areawide reclassification would have to "give back" something to placate the community. Consequently, piecemeal reclassifications that carried out plans in increments became popular in the late 1970s. They were seen as a method of "having your plan and giving back too," for instance, whenever an owner of a parcel zoned for manufacturing was ready to build a residential project.

The practice of requiring restrictive declarations began in 1966 as a way of mediating conflicts and competing values in the rezoning process. An applicant for a zoning change typically would seek to have the designation of his or her property changed from one generic zone to another, which better suited his development plans. Usually, the pro-choice generic districts established in 1961 permitted a use or design different from that which the applicant was proposing.

The restrictive declaration, therefore, might renounce specific undesirable uses or designs or it might commit to an affirmative obligation, usually in the form of some design feature or amenity on the site. The restrictive declaration would be signed by the property owner and other parties with an interest in the lot and be recorded against the property as a covenant running with the land, binding on future owners. Examples of such negotiated public value recapture abound; there are 134 post-1966 restrictive declarations listed in the zoning resolution.[44]

As a practical matter, the city's ability to obtain a community benefit was limited by the real estate value created by the rezoning, as best as one could determine, since costs and revenues lay in the future. Not surprisingly, the city paid nothing to property owners when "down-zoning," or reducing the value of a given parcel to a level that did not trigger an unconstitutional "taking." Presumably, assessed value would be reduced and along with it property taxes, but by this same test, the city might have been satisfied with the increased assessed value and taxes it would derive from an up-zoning.

All of these up-zoning and down-zoning actions are required to be in accordance with a well-considered plan.[45] Their private significance to the affected property owner is really only an incidental by-product of the larger public interest, the well-considered plan, which is advanced by the zoning amendment. A good plan, of course, should have already considered the impact of the zoning change. In effect, one might argue, a value recapture "give back" to the community is a windfall, the price of a political approval.

EXTRA COMMUNITY FACILITY BULK

The 1961 zoning revision created an incentive for building community facilities, rather than housing, in residential districts by allowing up to twice the floor area for community facilities as they did for housing. Community facilities include libraries, nursing homes, colleges and schools, churches, clubs, first-floor doctors' offices, hospitals, hospital staff housing, and philanthropic or nonprofit institutions without sleeping accommodations.[46]

At no point in the legislative history of the 1961 zoning revision does a need for such a double standard emerge. The consultants who helped prepare the new resolution flagged, in their initial report, the importance of these facilities to local neighborhoods and to the city at large, but they also noted that their proposed ordinance "carefully limits their bulk and requires that parking and other facilities be provided so as to insure their compatibility with the surrounding neighborhood."[47]

I was told afterward by Millard Humstone, who was one of the consultants and later worked in the New York City Department of City Planning—in a conversation when we were both on the department staff in the 1960s—that the community facility FARs were increased late in the adoption process so institutions could better compete with housing for the use of land. The fact that community facilities were largely public or nonprofit and provided needed services justified this unequal treatment in the view of the City Planning Commission.

This is not to say that community facilities are always popular in the neighborhoods in which they are proposed or built. The bulk preference has compounded the tension between community facilities and certain residential communities during the last three decades. A major flare-up occurred in 1974 in Rockaway when the convergence of skewed community facility bulk allowances, the preference of the elderly to live near the ocean, and the availability of federal Lanham Act health-related construction subsidies threatened to inundate the area with nursing homes, health-related facilities, and domiciliary care facilities for adults. To alleviate the problem, the city rescinded the preferential bulk allowances in areas, such as Rockaway, that were already oversaturated with these facilities and required a special permit for the extra community facility bulk, conditioned on "satisfactory site

TABLE 2
Maximum Floor Area Ratio Allowed for Community Facilities in the 1961 Zoning Revision

Zoning District	Community Facility Buildings	Residential Buildings
R1	1.00	0.50
R2	1.00	0.50
R3	1.00	0.50
R4	2.00	0.75
R5	2.00	1.25
R6	4.80	2.00 to 2.43
R7–1	4.80	2.88 to 3.44
R7–2	6.50	2.88 to 3.44
R8	6.50	4.88 to 6.02
R9	10.00	6.54 to 7.52
R10	10.00	10.00

planning and urban design relationships to streets and surrounding developments," among other findings.[48]

Today, the activities that take place in "community facilities" are not always regarded as benign. Drug rehabilitation clinics, homeless shelters, and group homes for troubled children are all considered community facilities. Not surprisingly, the city's inclusion of these uses by right within certain residential and commercial districts generates controversy. A major reassessment of community facility zoning and its relation to contextualism in a citywide framework is badly needed.

PLAZAS AND ARCADES

The 1961 rezoning, as discussed earlier, reserved its maximum density allowance for private projects that provided publicly accessible open space. These maximum densities were comparable to the densities of the largest buildings that had previously been constructed in Manhattan's and Brooklyn's central business districts and in apartment house districts on wide Manhattan avenues. Only from 1961 on would these dense buildings be accompanied by a plaza or arcade—paid for and maintained by the developer and owners—that the public could enjoy.

However, the public became uneasy with these amenities soon after the first few were built; the perception of their value changed, and there were an increasing number of calls requesting that these spaces be upgraded. Architectural critics scored the plazas along the Avenue of the Americas near Rockefeller Center and the resulting loss of street definition. In the late 1960s, activities like drug dealing, crime, and prostitution found a home in the underutilized, undermaintained plazas. Most troubling to the public, perhaps, was the realization that the incentive that encouraged developers to provide the open space, up to 20 percent more floor area than would have been allowed otherwise, was clearly worth much more than the cost to the developer of providing that amenity (often a minimal paving of an open or covered area). When new maximum-bulk buildings appeared with barren minimum-cost plazas, it should not have come as a surprise that the low value recapture was derided as a bad deal for the city.

If a developer were obtaining 20 percent more floor area worth, perhaps, $300 per square foot, his or her plaza should at least provide public seating, landscaping, a water fountain, and a rest room, the public said. Additionally, plazas in commercial districts should be lined with shops or possibly contain a retail kiosk for interest and utility, critics argued, and north-facing or sunless plazas should be discouraged, as should awkward plaza dimensions that raise safety concerns. Owners joined communities in urging that the public space be closed off with gates after dark, a response to fears of street crime.

Many of these concerns became the subject of "value recapture" amendments to the basic plaza text of the zoning resolution in the 1970s.[49] By the 1980s, a more fundamental questioning of the usefulness of plazas to the public led to a reduction in the incentive from 20 percent to a flat 1 FAR in many districts[50] and the outright elimination of the incentive in other districts.[51] It became possible to make discretionary modifications to the plaza requirements in order to create better urban design.[52] In the public's eye, safety concerns, contextual building design, and other value recapture priorities began to counterbalance the advantage that had been seen in obtaining public space on private property via a predictable, as-of-right mechanism.

THEATERS AND OTHER "LOSS LEADERS"

The private market first turned to Times Square as a location for office development in the mid-1960s, but this attention was regarded as a mixed blessing. On the one hand, the western edge of Midtown was the natural direction for the growth of the city's prime office core, but on the other hand, bland office towers set in plazas threatened the nostalgic, raffish character of the theater district.

As described previously, the city responded by creating a special zoning district that sought to maintain the physical character of the area around Times Square and to encourage the construction of new theaters. No freestanding legitimate theater had been built in the Times Square district by the private sector since 1927; the Special Theatre District increased the potential density for office buildings in this area from 15.0 FAR to 21.6 FAR and "recaptured" at least five new legitimate theaters.[53] Clearly, the city had harnessed its zoning resolution to forward its social agenda and to subsidize an otherwise uneconomic use.

Plazas and arcades were amenities that tended to compensate for the additional floor area they triggered, but theaters were a case of rewarding projects with additional floor area for providing an amenity that itself required additional floor area. Whether the additional floor area was economic or uneconomic, there was no compensation in the urban fabric for the additional density. This was equally true of the Special Fifth Avenue District, which provided a floor area bonus for projects that included extra retail space (the effort, in this case, was to recapture Fifth Avenue's vanishing department stores).[54]

These special district value recapture exercises always assumed that the prize gained by the city would be worth more than the "price" the city paid by allowing additional floor area. The first project developed under the Special Theatre District rules, One Astor Place,[55] was finished in 1972; the 21.6 FAR office building remained substantially vacant for years while its "loss leader," the Minskoff Theatre, was continually occupied by hit musicals. New theaters not being a standard construction project, the developer of the Minskoff underestimated the cost of the theater by several millions.

INCLUSIONARY ZONING

In 1970, long before the New Jersey *Mount Laurel* litigation,[56] the City Planning Commission developed a plan for lower Third Avenue that linked a substantial residential up-zoning to the provision of 450 units of lower income housing nearby. This plan was to be implemented through a special zoning district.

The proposal permitted high-density R10 apartment development if the developer built in accordance with design requirements (for example, widened sidewalks and arcades) and shouldered the burden of relocating lower income housing units that would be lost because of the up-zoning. The proposal gave the developer two choices: He or she could utilize 15 percent of the residential floor area for low- or moderate-income tenants or he or she could make a payment to the city representing the pro rata share of the city's cost of acquiring two public housing sites capable of producing 450 dwelling units within the district. Under either technique, the high land value deterrent to class integration would have been removed. Finally, the proposal allowed a developer to resist these blandishments and build under the requirements of the residual, underlying R7 middle-density zone.

The Special Lower Third Avenue District was approved by the City Planning Commission[57] but was defeated by the Board of Estimate. Various reasons have been suggested for its defeat: The adjacent community did not want high-density luxury housing, did not trust the municipal promise of low-rent housing, or feared the "ripple effect" of increasing zoning density on adjacent property, which the adjacent community feared would soar in value so as to put it out of reach of the middle class. I believe the proposal was defeated because the development community, which urged increasing the allowable density, feared a precedent that would make proximate or on-site provision of relocation housing a condition of all rezoning actions that increased residential density.

Despite the defeat of the Special Lower Third Avenue District, four other special districts (Lincoln Square, Clinton, Yorkville, and Manhattan Bridge)[58] incorporated bonus floor area allowances in exchange for the provision of low- or moderate-income housing (the Special Manhattan Bridge District alternatively encouraged provision of a community facility), but none of these recapture schemes worked to produce any lower income units.

It was not until 1987 that the city adopted a generic zoning program to stimulate a private sector provision of lower income housing.[59] This program, applicable only in the highest density residential districts, offers a maximum 20 percent floor area bonus for providing new or preserved lower income housing on-site, within the same community district, or within a half mile of the development that was receiving a density bonus. The legislation provides a formula for relating the amount of bonus floor area to the floor area of the lower income housing provided.

From a public value recapture standpoint, this inclusionary benefit often competed with the plaza or arcade bonus. Where this was the case, a developer predictably chose the less costly alternative (the plaza) to secure the maximum bonus.

At no point in the process of enacting this inclusionary zoning amendment did the city pretend that it would solve the city's serious affordable housing crisis. The program did, however, help perpetuate the myth that all problems are susceptible to a zoning solution by adding a new entrée to the city's zoning menu.

TRANSIT AMENITIES

The social agenda advanced by the city's zoning resolution grew to include the transit system during the 1970s, when the Special Transit Land Use District was mapped along the Manhattan right-of-way of the proposed Second Avenue subway.[60]

Fearing congestion around sidewalk stair entrances to the new subway line, planners mandated that property owners proffer subway stair easements within property lines contiguous to proposed subway station mezzanines. This mechanism would kick in, however, only when lots within the special district sought permits at the Department of Buildings. While not a strict trade-off of a public benefit for the extra value created by additional density, this zoning measure shifted the stair access burden to the private sector, which would benefit from being located near a subway entrance.

Should the Second Avenue subway ever be built, the city holds many easements for station mezzanine access. These will reduce future public costs of building off-sidewalk entrances to the subway and prevent the kind of sidewalk stair congestion so prevalent in certain Manhattan locations.

This idea was recycled into the city's Special Midtown District, which mandated the relocation of sidewalk stairs within the building lines of buildings next to all Midtown subway station entrances.[61] The Midtown rules not

FIGURE 40
Subway entrance and connection built with a transit improvement bonus.

only required owners to relocate and upgrade access stairs but also offered owners a 20 percent density bonus if they made improvements to the adjacent station.[62] A special permit would be required for this bonus, which was subsequently extended to all commercial districts of 10 FAR and above. The subway station bonus, taken together with the devaluation of the plaza and arcade bonus, bumped subway station improvements to the head of the social agenda promoted by the city's zoning.

Each station had a different improvement potential, ranging from new transfer connections and the possibility of new escalators to tiling and fix-up. The New York City Transit Authority would put its wish list in front of the developer, and the public process would refine the resulting transit improvement and determine the extent of the bonus. The parameters of incentive zoning—the cost of the improvement and the value of the additional bonus space—obviously would play a role.

The most controversial proposal for using the transit amenity bonus involved a major upgrading of the station at Fifty-ninth Street and Broadway, which added a 20 percent floor area bonus to a proposal for a tower that would be erected on the site of the New York Coliseum, at one of Central Park's four corners. The project was blocked by opponents who decried the noncontextual design of the proposed tower[63]; their lawsuit successfully challenged the propriety of the city issuing itself, as owner of the site, a transit improvement special permit then selling the site based on the increased value created by the additional density the special permit provided.[64]

BUSINESS RELOCATION ASSISTANCE

Before large areas of manufacturing districts were legally opened to residential loft conversion, concerns were raised about whether there would be increased pressure for businesses to relocate. The city, as part of its loft zoning amendment,[65] required property owners that were converting manufacturing space to residential space to make direct payments to manufacturing tenants who were being displaced and were relocating within the city. If the tenant were not relocating within the city or if the space to be converted were already vacant, then the property owner would be required to make doubled payments to a Business Relocation Assistance Corporation (BRAC). The disparity in payments was consciously intended to foster timely assistance to manufacturing firms so they would be encouraged to relocate in the city.

The extent to which BRAC facilitated direct Robin Hood–like help to displaced tenants has been one of the more effective achievements of the city's zoning value recapture programs. This portion of the program required no government overhead. Payments to BRAC itself have been less successful, primarily because the public officials directing the corporation have had difficulty in spending the millions generated by this zoning device.

Part of the problem of spending BRAC funds was the result of zoning text that was narrowly drawn in order to survive legal challenges based on the theory that the exaction was an improperly levied tax rather than an impact fee. BRAC indeed survived such a legal challenge[66] but found its beneficiaries necessarily limited to initiatives that sought to retain industries by providing relocation assistance. In an attempt to further fine-tune the relocation benefit, BRAC later excluded from eligibility any business that moves to a location south of Ninety-sixth Street in Manhattan, an area apparently thought too valuable for manufacturing relocation despite much M1 mapping. As a result of such self-inflicted disability, BRAC's well-endowed overhead has become the principal beneficiary of this value recapture device.

PROSPECTS FOR VALUE RECAPTURE ZONING

Before leaving this discussion of value recapture, it is necessary to consider the U.S. Supreme Court opinion in *Nollan v. California Coastal Commission*.[67] The California Coastal Commission (CCC), in awarding a building permit to enlarge a beach bungalow into a one-family residence, created a condition: the owner must dedicate a public pedestrian easement along the beach frontage of the lot. The CCC presented a rational-basis case for the requirement; however, the court found that the requirement was insufficiently related to and even condoned the harm created by the expansion of the bungalow (the house would block views of the ocean). Furthermore, the court found, the interest in land that the CCC had hoped to acquire for free was a taking of private property for which a payment of just compensation to the owner was required.

Reading this opinion, one comes away with an impression that a conservative Supreme Court will continue to look closely at the zoning value recapture exercise for evidence of opportunistic leveraging and possible taking of private property by the government. The nexus between the harm prevented and the value recaptured will have to be close and difficult to second-guess. The nature of the value captured by the government regulation had best not resemble the kind of interest normally obtainable in a condemnation proceeding.

Philosophically, at least, the city's zoning value recapture program rides counter to today's conventional wisdom that the private market knows best about these things. Value recapture may be the only game in town, as the saying goes, but its wisdom is worth more than a second thought.

THE LAST TEN YEARS—DISCRETION VERSUS AS-OF-RIGHT

When the city was rezoned in 1961, the zoning map was the result, in part, of the work of teams of planners who went out into the field, measured and classified existing neighborhoods, and often looked beyond the evidence to a longer term planning future. Good planning technique, however, also sought to minimize the extent of nonconformity and noncompliance created by the new mapping. In places where mapping created extensive nonconformity and noncompliance, the result was usually intentional.

As time passes, the relevance of the data-induced policies formed in the 1950s and implemented in the 1961 regulation lessens. The City Planning Commission has reexamined individual areas from time to time, usually at public urging, to test the continuing relevance of 1961 mapping, but the principal, albeit piecemeal, avenue for considering change has been privately initiated requests. Inevitably, this approach devolves into a case-by-case exercise of discretionary planning by the city government.

Increased regulatory obsolescence means that the incidence of exercise of discretion by the government increases, and with it the often irresistible political pressure for value recapture. The result is a distressing, even vicious, cycle.

AS-OF-RIGHT COUNTERCURRENTS

Frequent exercise of discretion on a building-by-building basis is a costly business for city government to be in. It requires architects, lawyers, and planners to match wits and skills with the private applicant's professional team.

In the 1970s, 90 percent of the development in Midtown occurred on the basis of awarding special permits. For example, height and setback waivers for office building towers along the stretch of Madison Avenue from Fifty-third to Fifty-seventh streets produced canyon walls that were reminiscent of the pre-1916 street walls along lower Broadway. The developers of these towers, under prodding by city negotiators, ultimately provided a science museum, a glass-enclosed botanical garden with through-block access to Fifth Avenue, a covered public space, an outdoor plaza with movable furniture, and an art museum.[68]

Whatever the merits of the "give backs," the exercise of discretion, building by building, in one concentrated stretch of Madison Avenue gave away uniform street access to light and air mandated by the 1961 zoning. These negotiated results led the city to overhaul and reform zoning systematically in Midtown and remove the 1961 prescriptive rigidities that motivated special discretionary zoning reviews. Since this revision became effective in 1982,[69] more construction in Midtown has taken place on an as-of-right basis.

Similarly, the transformation of the discretionary Housing Quality special permit into the as-of-right "quality housing" program[70] eliminated many discretionary applications. The complex new as-of-right provisions in the zoning resolution, though, only transfer the heavy burden of evaluating the architecture and planning characteristics of proposals from the Department of City Planning to the Department of Buildings (DOB). Although DOB is considered an agency that makes ministerial determinations without exercising discretion, increasingly complex and novel regulation inevitably invites the agency to exercise discretion in the performance of its duties.

CERTIFICATIONS, AUTHORIZATIONS, AND SPECIAL PERMITS

As special districts and special zoning regulations (particularly for parking) multiplied, a device frequently employed to monitor their administration was the requirement that a development proposal obtain a certification, authorization, or special permit from the City Planning Commission. A certification is legally viewed as a ministerial act, though in practice it often hinged on an exercise of judgment; an authorization involves the exercise of discretion but in relatively minor cases; and a special permit generates a full-scale discretionary inquiry.

In the Special South Richmond Development District, for example, the commission must issue a certification to approve land subdivision, designated open space preservation and improvement, certain yard modifications, additional curb cuts, substitution of other plant materials to satisfy tree requirements, providing a required waterfront esplanade, and other matters.[71] In the Special Midtown District, the builder of an as-of-right urban plaza must obtain a certification from the chairman of the City Planning Commission for any plans to improve and maintain the plaza.[72] Since 1982, proposals for accessory off-street parking facilities in existing buildings and public parking lots of 150 spaces or less in C2, C4, C6, C8, and M districts south of 110th Street have required commission authorization based on findings.[73]

Parking deserves a far more extended discussion than it will receive here, but certain points are germane to the thirty-year overview framework of this paper. Prior to 1961, most off-street parking was provided voluntarily within private garages, private parking lots, and curbside parking, and the number of spaces more or less matched the demand. The 1961 zoning revision substantially expanded the off-street parking requirements for all new development that did not take place in one-fare rapid transit zones. This regulatory objective complemented a city program of building municipal parking garages to intercept commuters before they reach the city's central business districts, making it easier for them to shift to rapid transit or some other mode of transportation. While the parking requirements incorporated in the 1961 revision created a growing reservoir of off-street parking, they also added substantially to the cost and design of all residential development outside the core.

In 1970, though, amendments to the federal Clean Air Act[74] imposed ambient air quality standards on New York City (as well as the rest of the country) and required each state to come up with an implementation plan to achieve these standards. Suddenly, the regulatory objective had shifted. The automobile was no longer automatically regarded as a desirable adjunct to modern living; rather, it was instead becoming a pollution-creating pariah in the eyes of the regulatory bureaucracy.

To address the mandate of the Clean Air Act, environmental impact statements (required for discretionary projects) would have to assess a project's impact on traffic and air quality. Since planners believed in the late 1970s that the availability of parking spaces stimulated automobile usage, they determined that there was a need to review qualitatively all proposals for parking in the core and most proposals for larger parking concentrations elsewhere in the city. Discretionary certification, authorization, and special permit provisions were added for such projects in 1982,[75] and they now coexist awkwardly with the original 1961 parking requirements.[76]

The city generally seeks recourse to discretionary permit reviews in circumstances in which the proposed use or design has the potential for creating controversy. Through this mechanism, the City Planning Commission is able to consider competing-use choices when reviewing proposals for facilities like discotheques, parking facilities, physical culture establishments, and amusement arcades.[77] Similarly, the commission is faced with competing urban design values when it is considering a proposal for transferring development rights from a designated landmark, an action that can result in an overly bulky structure across the street.[78]

However, discretionary approvals also invite political and community participation in the decision-making process on a site-by-site basis. Predictable planning results are better encouraged by minimizing the number and extent of such discretionary variations.

It may be fair to conclude that after decades of experience with the 1961 zoning revision and its subsequent piecemeal revisions, old opportunities for discretionary review have replaced newer ones. Coupled with the ordinance's aging process, they have undoubtedly multiplied the occasions for government intervention in what is euphemistically still called an "as-of-right" system.

THE NEED FOR A COMPREHENSIVE REASSESSMENT

If zoning is a tool that implements a city plan—rather than just a mechanism to avoid the harm created by market-directed development—then one can argue that the 1961 comprehensive amendment to the zoning resolution implemented a plan for the city in 1961. That plan reflected an integrated vision composed of many disparate elements, all grounded in empirical observations and data gathered in the 1950s.

However, the debate over the 1961 comprehensive revision lasted many years, and the key assumptions and policies underlying the 1961 plan were already a decade old when they were adopted. Moreover, those assumptions and policies continued changing during the next thirty years and pieces of the zoning resolution were either jettisoned, amended, or (mostly) added along the way. The zoning resolution and maps we use today are a collage of ad hoc, jerry-built, and, sometimes, thoughtful inspirations grafted onto a long-disowned armature.

We have come to realize that these complicated parts subtract from rather than add up to somewhat less than a whole. The zoning resolution is an integrated ordinance. Tinker with one part and you set another part and its assumptions out of whack. That has been what the city has been doing for thirty years.

At no time since 1961 has an interdisciplinary effort been undertaken to see where New York City stands—to restate a plan or vision for the city's future. Too much has changed since 1961 (really 1951); the common threads that have deformed the 1961 resolution deserve the opportunity to shape the city's plan for the coming decades.

Now that the city charter requires a quadrennial zoning and planning report starting in 1992[79]—a report that includes an analysis of those portions of the zoning resolution that merit reconsideration in the light of planning policy—the time is at hand for a comprehensive reassessment.

In part, the city's past reluctance to initiate comprehensive reassessments of zoning reflects not only timidity but also a concern for its fisc. SEQRA requires a hard look at the environmental impacts of a rezoning[80]—the larger and more generic the area that is being rezoned, the more expansive the look. An applicant for a small site-specific rezoning will agree to undertake the costs of any related Environmental Impact Statement (EIS), but the city has been reluctant to commit its treasury to the unknown cost of an areawide EIS that conservative lawyers say is necessary to repel litigation.

To encourage the desirable step of undertaking a comprehensive reassessment of the city's zoning resolution, the New York State Legislature could spell out the necessary components of the environmental disclosure that would be required. Such a statute would shield the planning initiative from destructive litigation challenges while ensuring responsible environmental review. SEQRA could thus strengthen comprehensive planning instead of inhibiting it.

Just as every rule seems to be proven by its exception, so did the correctness of New York City's 1916 zoning approach always seem confirmed by Houston's lonely and iconoclastic avoidance of zoning for most of this century. In a startling sign of the times, Houston recently announced its intention to pursue the adoption of a zoning ordinance. In New York City, marking the seventy-fifth anniversary of its original zoning ordinance and the thirtieth anniversary of the last comprehensive revision, that news contrasted with increasing local frustration over the zoning resolution's excessive girth, complexity, obsolescence, and, above all, its failure to reflect a current plan for the city's future. All of this suggests that New York City's present system may have come about as far as it can as a credible regulatory mechanism.

A comprehensive reassessment of the past thirty years in light of the city's changed goals and conditions should suggest the need for a simpler regulation that is limited to setting forth basic use and bulk constraints suggested by New York City's present built and unbuilt-on environment. Otherwise, to paraphrase George Santayana, those who will not learn from the past may be condemned to relive it.[81]

ACKNOWLEDGMENTS

This article is dedicated to Julie Spector, Millard Humstone, Pares Bhattacharji, Sandy Hornick, Don Elliott, and John Zuccotti, without whom the past and present zoning would certainly be different.

The author wishes to thank Pares Bhattacharji, Louisa Craddock, and Jaye Fox, for their conceptual and concrete labors on the related zoning resolution legislative history project; Beth Lebowitz, Larry Parnes, and Chester Rapkin, for documenting footnotes; Marilyn Mammano, for directing the Department of City Planning staff effort to make this history a more useful resource; and Sandy Hornick, Eric Kober, Peter Salins, and John Shapiro, for reading earlier drafts and making helpful suggestions.

NOTES

1. 348 U.S. 26 (1954).

2. This system replaced the pyramid of cumulative uses established in the 1916 resolution. In that regime, the pyramid apex was reserved for single-family residential use with increasing cumulative usage as you descended the pyramid levels. The base, or lowest, use classification (called "unrestricted") could contain all uses: residential of whatever nature, business, and manufacturing. Only the heavy industries and noxious uses were confined to unrestricted zones. The targeted zoning of the 1961 resolution forced many changes in land use that might have occurred by right under the 1916 ordinance.

3. The FAR effectively limited the total amount of development that would be allowed in the city and was heralded as the city's first-time population cap. The 1961 resolution allowed enough housing for eleven million people, planners calculated.

4. New York City Landmarks Preservation Commission designations: Lever House LP-1277, 9 November 1982; Seagram Building, lobby interior, Four Seasons restaurant interior, LP-1664, 1665, 1666; 1989.

5. New York City Zoning Resolution, Section 33-14 Floor Area Bonus for Urban Open Space. New York City Zoning Resolution, Section 33-15 Floor Area Bonus for Arcades.

6. Oscar Newman, *Defensible Space* (New York: Macmillan, 1973).
7. New York City Zoning Resolution, Section 74–87 Covered Pedestrian Space, added 16 April 1970, CP 21138.
8. New York Zoning Resolution, Section 81–00 Special Midtown District, added 13 May 1982, N820253AZRM. In 1982, the Covered Pedestrian Space bonus was eliminated from the Special Midtown District. It continues to be available in lower Manhattan.
9. New York City Planning Commission, CP 21651, 11 August 1971.
10. Local Law No. 46 (1965), currently Title 25, Chapter 3, Section 25–301 et seq. New York City Charter and Administrative Code.
11. New York City Zoning Resolution, Section 74–79 Transfer of Development Rights from Landmark Sites, added 22 May 1968, CP 20253. New York City Zoning Resolution, Section 74–79 Transfer of Development Rights from Landmark Sites, amended 4 December 1969, CP 20938.
12. New York City Zoning Resolution, Section 12–10 Definition of Limited Height Districts, added 26 January 1967, CP 19578.
13. Abeles Phillips Preiss and Shapiro, *Zoning and Historic Districts* (New York: Municipal Art Society, 1990).
14. Chester Rapkin, *Report on the South Houston Industrial Area—Economic Significance of Firms, the Physical Quality of Buildings and the Real Estate Market in an Old Loft Section of Lower Manhattan* (New York: City Planning Commission, 1963).
15. New York City Zoning Resolution, Section 12–10 Definition of Joint Living-Work Quarters for Artists, added 28 January 1971, CP 21256A; revised 27 April 1976, CP 23170.
16. *SoHo-Cast Iron Historic District Designation Report* (New York: Landmarks Preservation Commission, 1973).
17. *Residential Re-use of Non-residential Buildings in Manhattan* (New York: Department of City Planning and Mayor's Midtown Action Office, 1977).
18. New York City Zoning Resolution, Section 15–00 et seq. Residential Conversion of Existing Non-Residential Buildings in Certain Community Districts in the Boroughs of Manhattan, Brooklyn, and Queens, added 9 April 1981, N800458ZRM; revised 25 October 1984, N840674ZRY.
See also *Lofts: Balancing the Equities* (New York: Department of City Planning, 1981).
19. New York City Zoning Resolution, Section 73–68 Height and Setback and Yard Modifications, added 14 January 1965, CP 18634.
20. PL 91–190, 42 U.S.C. Section 4321–4347 (1969).
21. Effective September 1, 1976, pursuant to L. 1975 c. 612; New York Environmental Conservation Law, Article 8.
22. New York State Environmental Conservation Law, Article 25.
23. New York State Environmental Conservation Law, Article 24.
24. New York City Zoning Resolution, Section 105–00 et seq. Special Natural Area District, added 19 December 1974, CP 22748A; New York City Zoning Resolution, Section 105–942 Special Natural Area District NA 2—Riverdale, Spuyten Duyvil and Fieldston of The Bronx, added 21 March 1975, CP 22890A.
25. New York City Zoning Resolution, Section 105–944 Special Fort Totten Natural Area District NA 4, added 28 April 1983, N821255ZRQ.
26. New York City Zoning Resolution, Section 105–941 Special Natural Area District NA 1—Emerson Hill, Dongan Hills, Todt Hill, Lighthouse Hill and the central wetlands area of Staten Island, added 19 December 1974, CP 22748A.

ZONING FROM 1961 TO 1991

New York City Zoning Resolution, Section 105–943 Special Natural Area District NA 3—Shore Acres Area of Staten Island, added 1 December 1977, N770272ZRY.

27. The residential districts ranged from R1 through R10; R8 through R10 districts, those that allow the most density, are not mapped in Queens.

28. New York City Zoning Resolution, Section 81–00 Special Theatre District, added 7 December 1962, CP 20000. (Replaced by Special Midtown District, 13 May 1982, N820253AZRM.)

The special district stretched from Fifty-seventh to Fortieth streets and was bounded by Eighth Avenue on the west and the Avenue of the Americas on the east, an area within which most of the city's legitimate theaters presently exist.

29. In 1982, the Special Theatre District became a subdistrict within a larger Special Midtown District. The bonus for a new theater was extended to stimulate renovation of an existing theater. New York City Zoning Resolution, Section 81–70 Special Regulations for Theatre Subdistrict (part of Section 81–00 Special Midtown District), added 13 May 1982, N820253ZRM, N820253ZRMA).

That latter bonus was substantially reduced in 1988 in stunned reaction to the success of the Special Midtown District zoning incentives. As part of that reaction, the bonus for a new theater was also eliminated. (New York City Zoning Resolution, Section 81–74 Special Incentives and Controls in the Theatre Subdistrict, amended 28 April 1988, N880331ZRMA.)

In the late 1980s, the Landmarks Preservation Commission designated many exterior and interior theater landmarks in what could be regarded as a burst of regulatory overkill since their demolition was already barred under the special district zoning. (LP 1305 to LP 1387, Landmarks Preservation Commission, 1982.)

30. New York City Zoning Resolution, Section 82–00 Special Lincoln Square District, added 24 April 1969, CP 20365A.

31. New York City Zoning Resolution, Section 87–00 The Fifth Avenue Special District, added 25 March 1971, CP 21498. (Replaced by Special Midtown District, 13 May 1982, N820253AZRM.)

32. New York City Zoning Resolution, Section 86–00 Special Greenwich Street Development District, added 4 January 1971, CP 21418.

33. New York City Zoning Resolution, Section 23–146 Optional Provisions for Certain R5 and R6 Districts in Brooklyn, added 16 June 1983, N820451ZRK.

34. New York City Zoning Resolution, Section 42–14(D) Special Uses in M1-5A and M1-5B Districts, amended 19 August 1976, CP 23250. SoHo mapping, 27 January 1971, CP 1260 A. NoHo mapping, 31 March 1976, CP 23167.

35. New York City Zoning Resolution, Section 74–95 Housing Quality Developments, added 18 March 1976, CP 23042.

36. Contextual zoning amendment to the New York City Zoning Resolution added 24 May 1984, N840235ZRY.

37. The district lacked a height limit. See the R10 Infill Zoning Amendment to the New York City Zoning Resolution, added 24 September 1981, N810257ZRY.

38. New York City Zoning Resolution, Section 23–692 Additional Regulations for Narrow Buildings or Enlargements, added 3 March 1983, N830112ZRY.

39. Contextual Zoning Amendment to the New York City Zoning Resolution, added 24 May 1984, N840235ZRY.

40. High Density Contextual Zoning Amendment to the New York City Zoning Resolution, added 14 August 1987, N870197AZRY. Low Density Contextual Zoning Amendment to the New York City Zoning Resolution, added 30 June 1989, N890522ZRY.

41. New York City Zoning Resolution, Section 28–00 Quality Housing Program, added 14 August 1987, N870197ZRY.

42. New York City Charter, Section 197-C(3).

43. Remapping of the Coca-Cola site, First Avenue and Thirty-fourth Street, Manhattan, 6 May 1981, C790634ZMM.

44. These are listed in a table in volume three of the New York City Zoning Resolution.

45. New York State General City Law, Section 20(24).

46. "Community Facilities" are listed in the New York City Zoning Resolution, Sections 22–13 and 22–14 Use Groups 3 and 4.

47. Voorhees, Walker, Smith and Smith, *Zoning New York City: A Proposal for a Zoning Resolution for the City of New York* (New York: City Planning Commission, 1958).

48. New York City Zoning Resolution, Section 22–42 Certification of Certain Community Facility Uses; Section 24–111 Maximum Floor Area Ratio for Certain Community Facility Uses; Section 74–901 Certain Community Facility Uses in R1 and R2 Districts and Certain Commercial Districts; and Section 74–902 Certain Community Facility Uses in R3 to R9 Districts and Certain Commercial Districts; added 8 March 1973, CP 22212; amended 10 January 1974, CP 22490A and CP 22566.

49. New York City Planning Commission actions: Establishment of Urban Open Space, 21 May 1975, CP 22784B; Residential Plazas, 27 April 1977, N760066ZRY.

50. New York City Zoning Resolution, Section 81–23 Special Midtown District, Floor Area Bonus for Urban Plaza, 13 May 1982, N820253ZRMA.

51. New York City Zoning Resolution, Section 99–84 Special Madison Avenue Preservation District, added 30 December 1973, CP 22350; Park Improvement District (Park and Fifth Avenues), added 23 April 1973, CP 22240.

52. New York City Zoning Resolution, Section 74–96 Special Urban Design Guidelines—Residential Plaza Modifications, added 21 April 1977, N760066ZRY; Section 12–10 Definitions—Plaza, amended 8 February 1979, N780630ZRM.

53. New York City Zoning Resolution, Section 81–06 Special Theatre District, added 7 December 1967, CP 20000; Special Permit, Minskoff Theatre, granted 17 April 1968, CP 20251; Special Permit, Uris Theatre, granted 17 April 1968, CP 20250; Special Permit, J. P. Stevens, granted 30 October 1968; Special Permit, Marriott Marquis Hotel, granted 8 August 1973, CP 22384, modified 11 July 1979, C790345ZSM.

54. New York City Zoning Resolution, Sections 87–032 and 87–08 Special Fifth Avenue District, added 25 March 1971, CP 21498.

55. New York City Zoning Resolution, Section 81–06 Special Theatre District, added 7 December 1967, CP 20000. Special Permit, Minskoff Theatre, 17 April 1968, CP 20251.

56. *Southern Burlington County NAACP v. Township of Mount Laurel* 67 N.J. 151, 336 A2d 713 (1975) (Mount Laurel I); same title 92 N.J. 158, 456 A2d 390 (1983) (Mount Laurel II); *Hills Development Co. v. Township of Bernards* 103 N.J. 1, 510 A2d 621 (1986) (Mount Laurel III).

57. New York City Planning Commission, Special Third Avenue District, 12 August 1970, CP 21179.

58. New York City Zoning Resolution, Section 82–10 Special Lincoln Square District, added 4 April 1969, CP 20365A; Section 96–21 Special Clinton District, added 21 November 1974, CP 22758; New York City Zoning Resolution, Section 101–06

Special Yorkville–East Eighty-sixth Street District, added 29 May 1974, CP 22529, repealed 30 January 1989; Section 116–12 Special Manhattan Bridge District, added 20 August 1981, N801024ZRM, expired 30 September 1991.

59. New York City Zoning Resolution, Section 23–90 Inclusionary Housing, added 21 May 1987, N850487ZRY.

60. New York City Zoning Resolution, Section 95–00 Special Transit Land Use District, added 28 December 1973, CP 22441.

61. New York City Zoning Resolution, Section 81–47 Off-Street Relocation or Renovation of a Subway Stair (part of Section 81–00 Special Midtown District), added 13 May 1982, N820253ZRM.

62. New York City Zoning Resolution, Section 81–53 Subway Station Improvements (part of Section 81–00 Special Midtown District), added 13 March 1982, N820253ZRMA.

63. Jerold S. Kayden, "Zoning for Dollars: New Rules for an Old Game? Comments on the *Municipal Art Society* and *Nollan* Cases," *Journal of Urban and Contemporary Law* 3 (1991).

64. *Municipal Art Society v. City of New York* 137 Misc. 2nd 832, 522 NYS2d 800 (Sup. Ct. 1987).

65. New York City Zoning Resolution, Section 15–50 Relocation Incentive Program, added 9 April 1981, N800458ZRM.

66. *In the Matter of the Application of Walkbroadway Realty Inc. v. New York City Board of Standards and Appeals* No. 85–3200/85 Slip Op. (N.Y. Sup. Ct., 26 March 1986).

67. 107 U.S. 3141 (1987).

68. New York City Zoning Resolution, Section 74–721 Height and Setback and Yard Regulations, added 9 June 1978, N770669ZRM.

69. New York City Zoning Resolution, Section 81–00 Special Midtown District, added 13 May 1982, N820253ZRMA.

70. New York City Zoning Resolution, Section 28–00 The Quality Housing Program, added 14 August 1987, N870197A.

71. New York City Zoning Resolution, Section 107–00 Special South Richmond Development District, added 11 September 1975, CP 22972.

72. New York City Zoning Resolution, Section 81–231 Standards for Urban Plazas (part of Special Midtown District, Section 81–00), added 13 May 1982, N820253ZRMA.

73. New York City Zoning Resolution, Section 13–451 Accessory Off-Street Parking Spaces, and Section 13–452 Public Parking Lots, added 13 May 1982, N810276ZRM.

74. 42 U.S.C.A. 1857 et seq. (1970).

75. New York City Zoning Resolution, Section 13–40 Special Permits and Authorizations, added 13 May 1982, N810276ZRM.

76. Ironically, further evidence demonstrates that the availability of parking does not necessarily stimulate automobile usage. The number of parking spaces in the central business district decreased substantially after the 1980s' economic boom, but automobile usage seems to have increased nonetheless.

77. New York City Zoning Resolution, Section 73–24 Eating or Drinking Places, amended 18 December 1980, N790716ZRY; New York City Zoning Resolution, Section 74–50 Off-Street Parking Establishments, amended 11 January 1962, CP 17022; New York City Zoning Resolution, Section 73–36 Physical Culture or Health Establishments, added 16 November 1978, N780387ZRY; New York City Zoning

Resolution, Sections 73–35 and 74–47 Amusement Arcades, added 3 April 1979, CP 23128.

78. New York City Zoning Resolution, Section 74–79 Transfer of Development Rights from Landmark Sites, added 22 May 1968, CP 20253.

79. New York City Charter, Section 192 F.

80. *Chinese Staff and Workers Association v. City of New York* 68 N.Y. 2d 359 (1986).

81. George Santayana, *Reason and Sense,* Vol. 1: *The Life of Reason* (New York: Scribner, 1905).

COMMENTARY

This Commentary is edited from a panel discussion that took place after the presentation of the previous four papers at the "Planning and Zoning New York City: Yesterday, Today, and Tomorrow" symposium in New York City on January 30, 1992. Sigurd Grava served as moderator.

SIGURD GRAVA: There are two general observations that I would like to make. The first is that as planners, we have learned, we teach, and we try to practice that zoning is in principle a tool to implement a development plan—to achieve a vision, a policy, or a master plan, if you want. It is a tool that helps shape the urban pattern—the location of activities and land uses—in hopes of making the city function better.

However, the notion that zoning is a tool that can be used to achieve some greater purpose does not seem to have taken root in New York City. For the most part, this is because New York City has never had an overall development plan or master plan. Consequently, there has been no overall picture that we have tried to achieve.

Another point to remember, one that is noted by all the authors, is that the zoning maps that were incorporated within the 1916 and 1961 zoning ordinances have not tried to shape the pattern of growth either. Rather, they accepted the status quo of land use distribution, they looked at the trends, they looked at the existing situation, and then they tried to nail it all down—formalizing already evident general trends in the distribution of zones and zoning districts. The act of consciously shaping the city's development pattern did not take place; one could say then that the zoning ordinances had no vision with respect to the land use pattern. The only exception may be the very recent Special Midtown District, which directed growth from the crowded East Side to the western edge of Midtown.

Is this a situation that can be accepted or is there a major element missing? All the authors note that there have been other planning and development actions that did give, to a large extent, form to the city; the actions to which they refer are principally transportation efforts. One of them is the Commissioners' Plan [of 1811], which is basically a street plan establishing the grid pattern. Another is the construction of the subways and rapid transit lines into the outer boroughs from the late nineteenth century through the 1940s. Another influential transportation network is the highway and parkway system, much of it planned and executed by Robert Moses. Those are the powerful forces that have helped give New York City the form that it has.

The second major theme I want to take up is the question of the grain of development: the bulk of buildings, access to light and air, auxiliary service uses, open space, parking, and all the other elements that affect the quality of life with respect to the physical build-out of the city. These were major concerns in the zoning ordinances, which have had very visible effects, addressing setbacks, plazas, parking locations, and other characteristics of buildings. Much of the discussion in these papers is about what the drafters of the ordinances intended at the time, what they expressed specifically, what was implied, and what actually was accomplished.

Another important point that appears in the papers is that the drafting and approving of the 1916 and 1961 ordinances took a very long time. What consumed years was not only the formal approval process but also the work of collecting thoughts, pulling them together, and reaching some sort of consensus. In New York City, even in the past when things were done more quickly, this has taken decades to accomplish.

That means that by the time the zoning ordinances were implemented, the concepts were already becoming dated. For example, the 1916 ordinance really embodied ideas that were developed in the late nineteenth century or very early in the twentieth century, and the 1961 ordinance is based not so much on the concepts of the 1960s; it really expresses the thoughts that were dominant in the 1940s and the 1950s.

This time lag is probably one of the reasons that each of the zoning ordinances was tinkered with very early on after adoption. Eventually, both ordinances have been subject to a tremendous amount of amendments. This observation allows me to conclude with the sobering thought that if by some miracle we were to decide today to work on a new document immediately, then, possibly, we would have a new zoning ordinance in the year 2006.

FRANCES HALSBAND: I heard and read two dominant themes in the papers presented in this first section, and there is a third theme that I did not hear or read, which I also will mention.

First, several of the authors said that we are talking about "zoning" here. That other word, "planning," which is part of the title of this symposium,

THE HISTORICAL FRAMEWORK

seems to have been left out of the conversation; but reading between the lines, I sensed that the papers said that we do need planning and that planning should take into account *looking at the physical form of the city*. Carol Willis noted "Manhattan's magnificent urban geography"; the work of planners may even include looking at the landscape and looking at urban space and civic space.

There is a continual cry of things being too big. Yet at the same time Carol Willis writes of the love we all have for the tall buildings of New York City. Norman Marcus talked about contextual zoning and special districts as a way of celebrating what I take to be the good design of the places we already have. Richard Plunz observed that the 1916 zoning ordinance enshrined the canyonlike environment of Wall Street. Norman Marcus described how the 1961 zoning revision was subsequently manipulated to accomplish the same thing—yet we were all taught that those narrow, shadowed streets were supposed to be bad.

There were some troubling comments about how we may be losing our open space. Roy Strickland observed that in neighborhoods of two- or three-story town houses, the responsibility of maintaining open space is being transferred to owner-occupants. Norman Marcus argued that the value placed on contextualism today has come to outweigh the value we place on open space. I wonder if there is a trend emerging.

Another theme that I heard is that planning must encompass *more* than just zoning. Maybe it should take into account all systems, all infrastructure, and all perceptual realities of place; this would include both the natural and unnatural landscape, both the built and unbuilt environment. Zoning certainly was not the only force in shaping the city: Richard Plunz noted that there is an intricate balance between building laws, construction costs, and what actually is built. He told us that most of the housing developed in the Bronx and in Queens was shaped more by the building code than by the zoning code. Neither was as influential in channeling development as the emerging mass transit systems. Plunz asked us, "Who planned mass transit?"; it certainly was not the City Planning Commission, which did not exist until years after the 1916 zoning ordinance was passed and much of the transit system had been built.

Norman Marcus talked about preservation law. The implication is that both preservation and environmental planning are being pressed into service in situations in which they are stretched beyond their own limits. Historic preservation and ecology are being used to fill the gaps in our planning law. That is what happens when you have zoning instead of planning.

Finally, as a third comment, what I neither heard nor read was the mention of any other city except, possibly, Houston. I wonder if there is some other city out there from which we could learn.

COMMENTARY

JEROLD KAYDEN: It strikes me that the two most important comments that we heard this morning were that the net effect of zoning was that anyone could build anything anywhere and that the idea that zoning could solve problems is a myth.

I would like to point out four conflicts that I think dominate our ambivalence about zoning and underline the debate we are having about zoning.

First, does zoning confer property rights upon individuals or does it take property rights away from individuals? Certainly, during the past thirty years, the view in New York City has been that zoning, in a sense, confers property rights upon individuals. That is why the city has given more than fifteen million square feet of bonus floor area to real estate developers in order to achieve, at first, a physical objective—such as providing open space in the form of plazas, arcades, and covered pedestrian spaces—and, more recently, a social agenda, such as providing low-income housing. Any discussion about reforming zoning must ask what it is that zoning can really accomplish and whose property rights are at stake.

The second of the four conflicts I see is that while some people feel that zoning gives too much power to developers and lawyers, others feel that it gives too much power to community boards, neighborhood groups, and the Municipal Art Societies of the world. It all depends on to whom you are talking.

Certainly, community groups and others might feel a sense of disenfranchisement and a lack of empowerment because they see what has, until recently, been a very discretionary zoning system in which canny, savvy lawyers and their hired expediters work with the intricacies of special permits, restrictive covenants, and all the tools that were developed after the 1961 revision was adopted. Many people have felt cut out of that process, even though it resulted in more public participation and more public review. Indeed, the City Environmental Quality Review can be viewed as a means of opening up what were the secret corridors of power down at the city planning department.

Of course, developers and their lawyers see too much power going to these other groups. Talk to Mortimer Zuckerman, who was selected to develop the Coliseum site at Columbus Circle, and he will give you a very different opinion than Kent Barwick, president of the Municipal Art Society, would. Even after the Municipal Art Society finally agreed to a negotiated proposal for developing the site, there was yet another group that held it up by filing a lawsuit.

The third conflict is whether zoning should be a Model-T or a Cadillac Seville. The original structure of the 1916 ordinance was along the Model-T line, a clear set of rules, but it quickly became antiquated because everybody wanted to insert their own prerogatives into the ordinance. People also regarded the ordinance as rigid, inflexible, and static and began to ask for positive, aggressive, and flexible tools. Over the years, the city then saw the use—and then the abuse—of variances, the addition of special permits, planned unit developments, and incentive zoning—which was the city's great contribution to zoning and swept across the country like wildfire.

How much responsibility should the city put on zoning? Should it be expected to accomplish, or even advance, our low-income housing agenda? Even if the city wants zoning to accomplish that and decides to give bonuses to developers who build low-income housing across town, as it does now, zoning really ends up accomplishing very little. As Norman Marcus suggested, it is that zoning can further our social agenda, as opposed to our physical planning agenda, or what buildings will look like and how they will be used.

The final conflict is between zoning as zoning versus zoning as planning. In New York City, zoning has really been the unintended plan, but it does not do a good job.

ROBERT A. M. STERN: We have been presented with a picaresque series of talks and a broad agenda, and it is hard for me to come up with some simple responses, but one thing I believe in was confirmed by Norman Marcus's paper: that planning is much too important to be left to the planners. In fact, I do not think planners have any idea about what to do about planning. Lawyers and architects have had the brightest, clearest ideas about planning—although not always the best for the city.

What was the idea behind the 1961 zoning revision? The framers of that ordinance envisioned turning the city into clusters of tall, superscaled buildings isolated from each other and arrayed in a pattern; these buildings would be not so much towers in parks as they would be towers marshaled in a battle against the old city. The vision was fundamentally antiurban.

The 1916 zoning was a set of rules that solidified and structured existing development patterns in the city. The zoning allowed the city to grow in an orderly fashion as new things were happening, ranging from high-rise buildings made possible by the elevator to an increasing intensification of use in the center of a city that had just come together eighteen years before. Even so, the architects who helped shape that ordinance had a very distinct vision of the city. Carol Willis described it. The zoning ordinance of 1916 clearly married a physical vision of the city with observation of existing uses and anticipation of some changes.

Zoning was not the only tool that shaped the city after the 1916 resolution was passed, as Richard Plunz pointed out. Let me describe some of the other important forces. One was restrictive covenants. The developers of most projects on Manhattan's West Side and elsewhere in the city attached restricted covenants that controlled matters such as who could live in a building and how long a building must stand before demolition was possible. This type of planning mechanism still prevails in Houston, which, until recently, had not adopted zoning.

Richard Plunz referred to another control, but I do not think it was emphasized enough in the discussion. Not only the building code but also the Tenement House Law controlled the design of all multiple dwellings, the city's predominant building type. They limited all apartment buildings to twelve stories. Of residential types, only hotels could be taller than twelve stories. Hence, the invention of the apartment hotel, from the point of stable urban living, one of the worst circumnavigations.

A third factor that limited, until relatively recently, the ability for people to build taller apartment buildings was elevator technology. In the early years after elevators were invented, their cost was prohibitive because they had to be manually operated; building owners had to hire elevator operators, which was expensive. Push-button, self-control elevators made possible the six-story apartment house, which is so ubiquitous in New York City. This type was introduced in Jackson Heights.

The implication of all the papers in the first section of this book is that planning is equivalent to zoning. This is wrong; zoning is supposed to be an instrument with which a plan is implemented. These papers do not provide much discussion of planning, and, in fact, there has been little large-scale or small-scale planning done for New York City, and little of what little planning has been done has been sponsored by the planning department or the New York City Planning Commission. The city's 1969 plan was not a plan; it was an inventory, and a rather mediocre one at that.

What led up to the 1916 ordinance was developed by concerned citizens, not professional planners. The Municipal Art Society sponsored a plan in 1907. In the 1920s, there was a major effort at regional planning that paid a lot of attention to the city itself, and in the late 1960s, many plans were offered by extraofficial groups. Since that time, whatever planning has been undertaken in New York City has been reactive, not initiatory, and that reactive planning has been developed by the professional planners and by historic preservationists so that what we have is preservation as a form of planning but not real planning for new growth. No new visions.

If you want to go to the interesting public hearings about planning in New York City, do not go to planning commission hearings, go to Landmarks Preservation Commission hearings. That is where you find out what people really think and worry about, how they struggle to piece together something of the city's past, and what they think is important about the city's built environment. That is where the developers and communities really meet for the action. Landmark designation has, until recently, usurped the planning function of the planning department. Unfortunately, landmark designation is a holding action, not visionary planning.

THE HISTORICAL FRAMEWORK

Norman Marcus, who always inspired me when he was at the planning commission and I was a young troublemaker of a minor kind at the Housing Development Administration, mentioned today that planning is a myth. This observation inspired me to write down my five myths of planning.

Myth number one is that zoning can solve problems. Zoning does not solve problems. Zoning simply records a collective agreement about how we think we have solved problems.

The second myth is that zoning is planning. Zoning is not planning. Zoning is a document that reflects some planning idea or reinforces the status quo, which means somebody else planned it before us.

Then, there is the myth that planners can plan. Nothing New York City's professional planners have ever done has proved that myth to be anything but a myth.

The fourth myth is that planners should plan. I do not believe they should. I think they contribute to planning, as do hundreds of other disciplines, but the feeling planners have that they are the keepers of the flame I do not think is justified or appropriate.

And, of course, the last myth of all, that planners do plan. Well, it has been thirty years since the zoning ordinance was last overhauled, so we know that the claim is not justified. The million dollars that was spent on the environmental study that Norman mentioned was minuscule compared to the cost incurred in this city by planners not doing any planning for thirty years.

GRAVA: I have some questions accumulating here from the audience for Robert Stern, but before we take questions, I would like to ask the authors of the papers if they have any comments.

CAROL WILLIS: One historical point that I would like to reiterate is that the 1916 zoning resolution was a practical, pragmatic document. Its framers were particularly concerned with the constitutionality of writing that legislation, which at the time was innovative and revolutionary. There had been precedents in other cities, but New York City, in combining height and use restrictions, was treading on very tentative ground. We must appreciate the distance that we have come since then and how the whole orientation of our language and rhetoric has changed from those precepts.

RICHARD A. PLUNZ: I would amplify one point, which is that in terms of its development, New York City is obviously in a very different period than it was in 1916. Present difficulties reinforce the importance of planning. The need for planning could seem to be a contradiction in that the city is basically built, but we should not forget that it has also been "unbuilt" in the past decades. At least in 1916, an infrastructure was in place and a marketplace response was predictable and there was a kind of "self-planning" that went on. The complexity of the interrelationship between infrastructure and marketplace today makes it far more difficult to predict what might happen and where while it seems more important than ever for us to know how we might be able to direct the process.

ROY STRICKLAND: I would like to speak to several issues that have been raised by other speakers because I think they open up a possibility for us to see that the 1961 zoning law was actually the natural outgrowth of the city's development.

Throughout New York City's history, there has been an extraordinary struggle around issues of public space and the control of public space. As Carol Willis has described, the 1916 zoning law was in part a reaction to conditions developing on Fifth Avenue, where the Fifth Avenue Association was anxious to exclude immigrant workers from an elite retail district. Before 1916, nineteenth-century restrictive covenants, private parks with gates, like Gramercy Park, and proposals by upper-class enclaves to gate streets demonstrate that control over open space has historically been of concern to the people who had the power to build and develop the city. Nineteenth-century tenement laws, to which Robert A. M. Stern alludes, also were concerned with that control. The legislating of complete apartments that would enable families to live wholly within a building without sharing public facilities was, to a degree, an attempt to make poor and working-class people behave in a middle-class way: discretely, behind closed doors, and off the street.

These examples, combined with many more that are revealed through researching the city's history, indicate that underlying New York City's development was the ongoing concern for controlling urban space, irrespective of the form of the space or its surrounding buildings. In this light, post–World War II urban renewal and the 1961 zoning law, which promoted freestanding buildings surrounded by protected open space, may be seen as deeply rooted in New York City's development history—not antiurban, as Stern argues, but related to nineteenth-century open spaces like Gramercy Park.

NORMAN MARCUS: Although I spent the majority of my professional life in the public sector, for the past seven years I have been in the private sector. Many of the perceptions that I offer in my paper may seem self-serving. On the other hand, my experience gives me a perspective on both sectors that makes a lot of the discussion here quite understandable.

I think we all agreed that New York City was built predominantly by the private sector. The public sector has made some contributions, certainly, Manhattan's grid and the street patterns of the outer boroughs, Central Park, and the basic wedding cake image of the city's older skyscrapers.

Carol Willis said the rules of the 1916 zoning resolution were simple to follow. I can tell you that in the private sector simplicity is appreciated. People know what to do with it; they are intimidated by the size of the government and by its complex procedures. If we hope to reform zoning in the twenty-first century, we must return to a simpler regulation. If we wish to harness the activities of the private sector, the notion of attaching a value recapture, a condition, a restrictive declaration to every private initiative that requires a zoning change will inhibit the extent and number of those changes.

I am not suggesting the zoning should no longer be a tool for achieving the public interest, but I am suggesting that the way it is being done now actually is a turnoff. The notion somehow that a person should pay for his or her zoning changes in the form of a public amenity actually contradicts the very idea of zoning, which is supposed to be in accordance with a plan. If up-zoning is the proper thing, then that is done. If down-zoning is the proper thing, then that is done. No one suggests that in down-zoning property, the government should pay property owners. By the same token, when their property is up-zoned, they shouldn't have to pay for it. The notion of money and zoning combined is one of the more dangerous notions, as was proven in the Municipal Art Society lawsuit involving the Coliseum site, and I will not rehearse the facts of that, but just read that decision. The city has not appealed from that decision.

GRAVA: Most of us would agree that there has not been much planning in this city and certainly not much through the official channels. I hoped somebody would contradict Robert Stern and argue that planners should do planning. I have some questions for you, Bob, from the audience. When was the last time you attended a City Planning Commission or community board meeting? Do you think New York City should have a master plan? And what does planning mean to you?

STERN: Five years ago, or more, to the first question. A master plan—I do not know what a master plan is, so we have to define it. I think the city needs a plan, we have to know where things are going to go and happen, but "master plan" implies that the plan would use the same approaches for every part of the city, which I think is going too far.

And what does planning mean to me? Planning means a strategy for the physical organization of a place, a strategy intended to make a place function effectively and give pleasure to its inhabitants and visitors. It means creating a beautiful environment, which comes under the rubric of city-as-architecture or city-as-work-of-art, and it means many other things, but planning is definitely a physical as well as a strategic operation, and it has a vision. That is, I think, the most serious problem the planning commission faces now: What kind of city is New York City supposed to be?

GRAVA: There are a number of questions from the audience. The first of these is the following: We find ourselves in the last decade of the twentieth century afraid to be visionaries. Why? How can we muster the courage to be visionaries, and can that be a new model for zoning?

COMMENTARY

HALSBAND: It would be very easy. There are many people in this room who care very deeply about establishing a vision for the city. If every one of them were to write down five essential pieces of a vision, we probably would have 80 or 90 percent agreement on what those five pieces of the vision could be. That is how we can start, by reaching out for input.

GRAVA: Since 1961, what have been the most significant clashes between zoning restrictions and real estate market forces?

MARCUS: I am reminded of the conflict over residential development on the Upper East Side in the late 1960s and early 1970s, when the 1961 zoning regulations had prescribed "mountains" of taller, denser buildings along the wider avenues and "valleys" of shorter, less dense buildings on the narrower, midblock streets between avenues. There were a great many sites that had been assembled and actually were "split-lot" sites, part of the site in the "valley" and part on the "mountain." By that time, developers had built very few new units under the 1961 zoning; most that had been built were grandfathered under the grace period during which the old regulation was still allowed to guide development.

The problem of how to regulate these split-lot sites produced a tremendous conflict within the planning commission. Ultimately, the commission turned down a proposal, stimulated by the development community, that would have allowed these split-lot sites to be developed at greater densities than were allowed in the plan. The vote was four to three, and the chair was in the minority. That was about the high point in terms of conflict, and interesting in the way it was resolved within a commission that was viewed very often as simply a monolithic body that did what the mayor wanted.

KAYDEN: The truth is, in New York City there is not that much of a conflict between zoning and real estate developers because the city is very permissively zoned. The zoning ordinance has almost always given real estate developers what they have wanted. It is useful to remember how Voorhees, Walker, Smith and Smith, the consultants who prepared the 1961 zoning revision, determined densities in Manhattan's central business districts. The firm surveyed what the existing floor area ratio [FAR] was for midtown and downtown and found that it was a FAR of approximately 17. So the proposal set a maximum FAR of 15 and added a 20 percent density bonus—up to 18 FAR if developers built a plaza. So the 1961 zoning revision did not take away any great value—not to suggest, of course, that it should have.

The most common conflict between developers and city government in New York City concerns landmark designation. We are all familiar with the Grand Central Terminal, Penn Central case, in which Penn Central, the owner of the terminal, claimed that millions of dollars of value were taken by the landmark designation. The U.S. Supreme Court said so what? Landmark designation is where you have real conflict because there are real dollars at stake.

STERN: You could put it another way and say that there were no conflicts under the 1916 zoning ordinance because the document reflected the kind of city that most people who had thought about New York City's urbanism wanted. Under that ordinance, one could build buildings, very good—and large—buildings, as we all know from Carol Willis's paper. The ordinance did not deal so well with the problems of small-scale development.

KAYDEN: The 1916 zoning ordinance was pushed, in part, by property owners.

STERN: Sure. They wanted to protect their interests, as did the architects who had an aesthetic vision, as did the average homeowner. The 1961 resolution, I am embarrassed to say, was pushed through basically by architects who had an absolute idée fixe about what the city should be like.

KAYDEN: And the Seagram Building was literally the aesthetic model for that.

MARCUS: I will point out that the 1961 idée fixe is still on the ordinance books today.

STERN: The 1961 zoning revision was thirty years out of date the minute it was passed, and it is sixty years out of date today. It was tinkered with within the first year as often as the 1916 ordinance had been tinkered with in the entire forty-five years that it was on the books.

PLUNZ: I do not think the problem, at least until 1961, was between developers and zoning. It was between communities and zoning. The basic issue was the absolute freedom to increase to a level beyond that which the public thought it ought to be—a possibility that zoning not only permitted but also encouraged. There was an enormous vagueness built into the 1916 ordinance, principally in deference to the development community. That vagueness changed considerably in 1961. I do not know why the development community did not figure out the predicament of 1961 sooner, insofar as its interests were concerned.

STERN: The development community opposed the 1961 zoning revision and avoided building under it until the last possible moment. Developers liked building under the previous ordinance better and rushed to construction an enormous amount of projects in the final days before the 1961 revision took effect. The speedy reconstruction of Park Avenue is largely due to that situation and all of the Upper East Side apartment houses that we once hated but now admire as civilized, given what came after the 1961 zoning took effect.

HALSBAND: It has very little to do with density. We kid ourselves if we argue that the problem is with density, that too big is no good.

STERN: No, people love density. The city is supposed to be dense.

HALSBAND: The people on this panel have talked about the magnificence of the Wall Street canyons; look at all the people that live in the loft districts. What do we love about Greenwich Village? The issue is quality, and quality can be dense or not dense. We must avoid the trap of thinking that too big is no good.

GRAVA: I have a follow-up question. Should zoning visions that take decades to enact, or remain in effect for decades, be allowed to enshrine a momentary passion in architecture?

HALSBAND: No.

STERN: No. That is the problem with the 1961 revision.

WILLIS: My answer is not a yes, but my comment as a historian is that I doubt that I'm the only one in the room that sees an irony in the historical presentations of the vision of the city at any particular time. The visions were all well-meaning when they were formulated and had enough support to be made into law, but now they are found to have a horrendous, horrific, debilitating effect.

STERN: People working in the planning department's Urban Design Group and in the Housing Development Administration in the 1960s and early 1970s were struggling to circumvent the 1961 zoning revision and recapture the qualities of urbanism that had prevailed under the previous ordinance. Mayor John Lindsay was elected in 1965 and all through his election campaign zoning already was an issue. That's four years after the ordinance was put in effect! How long must it take before the city comes to the conclusion that it does not work? It was built to replicate the Seagram Building. Do we want whole cities to look like the Seagram Building?

MARCUS: Ironically, the Seagram Building was built under the previous zoning resolution. It became the model for the 1961 revision. The Seagram Building echoes the comment that quality is what counts. How many rip-offs of the Seagram Building can you think of that do not arouse the same love and passion that the Seagram Building does?

PLUNZ: I cannot resist engaging this density question. It strikes me that this is a rather monocultural discussion. Maybe we like density, and maybe I enjoy living in a place that has no light and where some of my cousins would definitely not want to live. But we are a minority. The reality is that an enormous number of people in this city were protecting their houses by fighting for low density during the years between the two ordinances. In another vein, the 1961 revision continued this mind-set. It was not just about an architectural idea. It was rooted in a popular culture that discounted the city. As far as most people were concerned, the less of the city there was, the better. More plazas meant less city. This is a very complicated issue that cannot be addressed completely here, but at the heart of the 1961 revision was an antiurban bias, which pervaded the whole country.

THE HISTORICAL FRAMEWORK

GRAVA: A final question, specifically for Norman Marcus. Would you accept any of the responsibility for the current three thousand–plus amendments to the zoning resolution? More important, other than enabling legislation regarding environmental review, what can we do to correct the current wrongs?

MARCUS: The answer to the first question is yes. As for the second, my paper outlines some steps that could be taken. Piecemeal changes are not the answer because as you change one thing, others will need to be changed. Amending the resolution piecemeal would be like the game of croquet described in *Alice's Adventures in Wonderland:* One played with flamingos' necks as mallets and hedgehogs for balls, so not only the players but also the implements of play were in constant motion. Similarly, the city will not stand still.

Sure, you could change the zoning in Jackson Heights and get rid of prostitutes along Roosevelt Avenue, a problem about which I read in today's newspaper. There will always be those kinds of problems, but the genius in city planning is being able to look at the big picture. That does not mean that what you come up with is going to last forever—it will not—but at least you will have had the opportunity to consider where the city is going, and the city would not have that opportunity if it were to reevaluate the zoning ordinance in a piecemeal fashion. If the city ever were to have a moment to reassess where it is and where it is heading, that moment would be now.

PART II
FUTURE SCENARIOS

THE ZONING OF TODAY IN THE CITY OF TOMORROW

BRIAN KINTISH AND JOHN SHAPIRO

Cities change—in response to world and national events that alter the patterns of migration, to changing family and household structure, to changes in the national and international economy, to the evolution of building, transportation, or workplace technology, to shifting tastes in architecture, and to innumerable other forces. New York City is not the same today as it was in 1916 or in 1961 nor are our ideas of what it should be. Neither the city nor our ideas about it will be the same thirty years from now as they are today.

In the coming decades, New York City's land use and urban form will have to respond to numerous evolving trends. For instance, hundreds of thousands (if not millions) of new immigrants are likely to move to the city; how will they be housed? The city's population will continue to age; how will this affect the demand for community facilities, personal services, and types of housing? More and more people will work at home; how will this shape the workplace and the home of tomorrow? After the current economic slump ends, the city will face renewed demand for large blocks of modern office space; where will new office buildings be constructed, and what bulk and density will be proper? The industrial sector will remain vital to the city's economy even though it faces continued retrenchment and reorganization; will the city accommodate industries' changing space needs, and will viable industrial operations survive the competition from more lucrative land uses?

Inevitably, these trends will cause mismatches between the zoning resolution and the city's land use needs. This will be the case whether the current zoning resolution or a successor is in force; indeed, a new ordinance that is more detailed and prescriptive will invariably produce greater mismatches. If the current zoning resolution remains in place and is amended to adapt to these trends, then it will become more and more of a patchwork of often contradictory amendments—especially as the city moves further and further from the conditions and values of the 1950s that inspired the current resolution. Tensions between newly adopted provisions and the resolution's essential structure will increase.

This paper's underlying assumption is that the New York City zoning resolution will not receive systematic overhaul but that piecemeal changes will be made—much as they have been for the last thirty years. Today, the resolution is a sprawling, adaptable document filled with special exceptions to other exceptions. Its basic thrust is to encourage residential and commercial towers surrounded by light, air, and open space, but it is flexible enough to have accommodated the establishment of generic contextual districts and the Quality Housing option, both of which prevent such towers and promote more traditional urban forms. The 1961 resolution sought to prevent the mixing of land uses, but it has been amended to allow mixed industrial and residential development in several zoning districts and loft areas. If a problem becomes particularly thorny, the resolution holds the possibility of simply treating it as an exception and inventing a new special district or special permit.

There is a price to be paid for such flexibility. Each change makes the resolution more complex and difficult to enforce. At some point, it will grow too cumbersome to accommodate more change without collapsing under its own weight. Thus, in analyzing the resolution's ability to adapt to changing conditions, it is important to evaluate whether a zoning revision would actually be required; if so, whether the problem can be confronted within the context of the existing resolution; and, if so, whether the text revision would seriously convolute the already complex resolution.

Adaptability is only one measure of the resolution's continued utility. In assessing continuing usefulness of the zoning resolution for the foreseeable future, it is important to understand the roles that a zoning ordinance does and should perform. First, zoning should reflect broader planning goals and a vision of what the city is and what it is to become. As conditions change, planners and officials should update those goals and the mechanisms being used to realize them. Second, zoning works by engaging and shaping market forces. If a zoning ordinance is to direct rather than stifle development and if the zoning map is to remain relevant to the actual pattern of land uses, the ordinance must reflect an appreciation of market forces (those elements that determine what types of built space will be in demand and where). In short, zoning is a tool whose usefulness can be judged in relation to how well it addresses the ways in which people live and work, the projects that developers want to build, and the policy objectives that planners and officials are trying to achieve.

Since the zoning resolution functions by dividing the city into various types of districts and regulating land use and building form in those various districts, the most meaningful way to assay how the resolution can accommodate likely future changes is to address each type of district or neighborhood separately: central office districts, satellite office districts, industrial districts, the waterfront, high-density residential neighborhoods, low-density residential neighborhoods, neighborhood retail and services, and low-income neighborhoods. For each type of district or neighborhood, this paper will discuss market trends that will likely affect land use and development and how well the present zoning resolution could accommodate the impact of such changes, assuming the resolution is reformed only in modest ways.

Following those individual neighborhood and land use discussions, this paper will turn to a more general appreciation of the zoning resolution and its continuing viability as a regulatory system. This involves discussions of the zoning resolution's role in the planning process, its role in shaping market forces, and its adaptability to change.

EXISTING OFFICE DISTRICTS

For the next decade or so, by all accounts, there will be a glut of office space. Afterward, New York City will face a renewed demand for office construction. Over the past thirty years, the city's economy has become increasingly white-collar, with declines in manufacturing and dock work and growth in the financial, insurance, and real estate sector and other office work.[1] The trend shows no sign of reversing. Due to the increasing interconnectedness of both the national and the international economies, some forms of white-collar office work will leave the city (particularly routine work that can be performed more economically in places like South Dakota or Ireland), but the city also is likely to become more of a center for international banking and financial services.[2] In other words, the nature of the demand for office space may change but a dominant share of any new economic activity in the city will be performed in offices.

New York City already has the largest and most varied office stock in the country,[3] but much of it is approaching obsolescence. Technological innovation, including firms' increasing reliance on computers and communications technology, has created demand for office buildings with large floor-to-ceiling heights and fiber-optic capabilities. Firms also want operational flexibility, or the freedom to change the ways in which they use and partition the space, which means large blocks of structurally undivided space are in demand.

As a result, older, secondary office space, much of it built before the 1961 ordinance, is likely to go begging.[4] Some parts of the city will likely face proposals for adaptive reuse of secondary office buildings as housing, in response to people's desire to live in closer proximity to their place of work and in response to a trend toward living in mixed-use areas. The city also will face more and more proposals for reskinning older office buildings, a process in which owners strip a building down to its steel frame and then rebuild the building. This enables property owners to modernize buildings that have more floor area than current zoning would allow.[5] If combined with other structural renovations, it also enables property owners to expand buildings containing less floor area than zoning would allow. These trends will collide with increasing public nostalgia for the architecture of the pre–World War II period, resulting in pressure for historic district and landmark designations (for example, a Wall Street or lower Broadway historic district).

The disparity between newer and older office building forms probably will lead to calls for new zoning tools to control the envelope of office buildings. New primary space office buildings tend to be massive in scale. Not only is the contemporary office tower tall but it has a large footprint (the amount of space it covers at ground level) and large floor plates in its upper as well as lower stories. The office towers of the 1920s were tall as well, but they were slender and tapered compared with the new buildings.[6] Whereas the 1916 zoning resolution and 1920s building technology and office economics produced needle-nosed shafts with their trademark setbacks, emphasizing height and the skyscraper's romantic verticality, some of the more massive contemporary office towers have shapes more reminiscent of industrial loft buildings of the 1920s raised to enormous heights.

A public debate has ensued that may temporarily abate with the slower pace of development but will not disappear over the coming decades. The massive office buildings satisfy a desire for large blocks of space, but they also reduce air and light, create wind tunnel effects, and dwarf their historic neighbors. These buildings also have produced potentially threatening increases in density. The subway system has a finite capacity, and environmental considerations militate against increased vehicular commutation into midtown or lower Manhattan. The sidewalks also have a finite capacity; however people get to the central office district, the streets can absorb only so many pedestrians. (One argument in favor of adopting zoning in 1916 was that very large buildings might prove impossible to evacuate because the adjacent streets could not contain the workers.)

The public ire has focused on plaza and other bonus provisions and zoning lot mergers, but the true culprit may be more basic: the reliance on floor area ratio (FAR) as the device that controls a building's bulk. For a building that adopts the zoning resolution's tower regulations, which are available in high-density commercial districts, FAR is the factor that controls the structure's bulk. The tower regulations provide that any portion of the building covering no more than 40 percent of the zoning lot may ignore the otherwise applicable height and setback regulations and penetrate the zoning district's mandated sky exposure planes, rising straight up without setback until it exhausts the allowable floor area.

FAR alone is inadequate as a bulk control, for at least two reasons. First, FAR merely controls a building's maximum floor area. Thus, it is a two-dimensional limitation used as a surrogate to control three-dimensional bulk. A thirty-story building with fifteen-foot floor-to-ceiling heights has the same floor area as a thirty-story building with eight-foot floor-to-ceiling heights, but it is a much larger structure. Second, FAR limits do not prevent a developer from using zoning lot mergers and bonus provisions to amass a substantial allowable floor area and pack it on a portion of the site.

The most obvious and often discussed approach to reducing allowable FAR is to get rid of the bonus provisions.[7] This sentiment is spurred by the many desultory and unattractive "public" plazas that were hardly worth their cost in air and light. Reform in this regard would require not only the jettisoning of a discredited floor area bonus provision but also the relinquishing of one of New York City's most important zoning innovations, incentive zoning, and the resultant loss of a range of public benefits.

Even as plazas have fallen into disfavor, planners and community leaders have become enamored of other bonusable amenities, such as affordable housing and subway station improvements. It would seem that for every bonus provision struck away, another two might be born, like the monster Hydra of Greek mythology. As long as the city relies on the private sector to create public benefits—a trend that is not likely to reverse itself in these fiscally constrained times—bonuses will be a popular tool, and as long as offices are the most lucrative land use, most of the bonus provisions will be attached to zones where offices are likely to be built.

The next most obvious and often discussed approach to stricter bulk regulations, restricting zoning lot mergers, also would be highly problematic. A zoning lot merger is a mechanism for isolating unused development rights from the rest of the property rights bundle and selling them for a negotiated price. The transfer of development rights occurs through a recorded agreement between the owners of adjacent properties rather than through the actual sale of the property. The zoning lot merger is the only form of development rights transfer recognized by the New York City zoning resolution, except for the special permit mechanism that applies only to designated landmarks.

Eliminating the zoning lot merger provision would be a preservationist's nightmare. Without it, the owner of an older, smaller structure would be under more financial pressure to demolish the building and redevelop the property. If developers were required to purchase adjacent properties rather than effect a zoning lot merger on paper, they would be more likely to clear the entire lot, tear down the older structures, and build an even larger tower. There also would be greater pressure to build on undivided sites now occupied by buildings that have large footprints and are used in such a manner that they have resisted development (for example, department stores). A further drawback is that appropriate development sites would be harder to assemble because it is more difficult to convince owners to sell their property than it is to convince them to sell the air rights above their property. Thus, restrictions on zoning lot mergers would have the ironic effect of simultaneously inducing the demolition of older but serviceable buildings and deterring new construction.

A third approach to making bulk regulations more strict would be to design bulk controls independently of floor area limitations. That means concentrating on the building envelope into which any given amount of floor area must fit. One model for doing this was employed in the 1980s "contextual" district regulations, which required a building to fill out more of the lot and limit height by means of flattened sky exposure planes. Although both commercial and residential contextual districts have been created, none of them are applicable to the central office cores. The low-rise, high-coverage contextual model, which produces shorter, bulkier buildings, would be ludicrously noncontextual in these skyscraper districts. Therefore, a new series of high-density commercial contextual zones would be required. A second model for doing this was employed more frequently in the 1970s than it has been in the recent past: creating "special districts" that reflect the particular urban design of office district subareas. Both systems, however elegant from a design point of view, would cause a proliferation of zoning districts. It is uncertain that the present resolution could accommodate itself to such an increase in complexity.

A fourth approach would be to continue to rely on FAR as a control, to continue to allow zoning lot mergers and 20 percent floor area bonuses in exchange for particular amenities, but to reduce allowable FAR. Certainly, no one in 1961 envisioned that the new rules, new technologies, and vast increases in the value of office buildings would combine to make it that much easier to assemble large sites and build gargantuan office towers.

Down-zonings (for example, reducing allowable FARs) are the least likely solution, though, because they would deter new office construction, thus threatening the city's economic well-being and preeminence. Down-zonings or other restrictions would also help push office development into areas outside existing central business districts. Since the central office districts are already heavily developed, demand for large amounts of new office space will require developers to build upward (with ever larger buildings), to build outward (by expanding the central office districts into adjacent neighborhoods), or to build elsewhere (in newly emerging office districts). Bulk restrictions would make the first option less viable, but in any event, economic recovery will entail demand for office construction in new areas, as discussed in the next section.

THE EXPANSION OF OFFICE DISTRICTS

For the time being, the economic pressures that gave rise to the westward and southward expansion of Midtown and to the emergence of satellite office districts in downtown Brooklyn and Long Island City have dissipated. Midtown and lower Manhattan contain approximately sixty million square feet of vacant office space (an amount equal to the total central business district office space inventory of Philadelphia and Dallas combined).[8]

In the long term, however, the expansion of office districts seems likely. First, the Department of City Planning and other observers predict a renewed demand for more office space. Second, the best sites in established office cores have already been picked over, making assemblage of new development sites more torturous. Third, up-zoning in one area is the preferred way to effectuate down-zoning in another; efforts to curtail new office development in the established cores will probably and correctly be balanced with moves to liberalize development rules in other areas. This is precisely what happened in the early 1980s, when the city down-zoned the congested, overdeveloped eastern portion of Midtown and simultaneously up-zoned western Midtown, effectively shifting the focus of development.

There are three forms expansion may take: gradual, site-by-site expansion of existing office districts into contiguous neighborhoods (for example, the transformation of part of the industrial area between Canal Street and the West Village into an area of advertising firms' office buildings now becoming known as Hudson Square); large-scale planned development on an area basis (for instance, Battery Park City); or development of new satellite office districts at locations removed from the Manhattan cores (for example, downtown Brooklyn, Long Island City, and Jamaica).

Gradual expansion into selected contiguous areas represents the most likely scenario. This will occur only where zoning allows it to happen; major office development requires a zoning district that permits commercial uses and that allows sufficient bulk and density. The city's zoning resolution is neither so permissive that such development can occur as-of-right in all contiguous areas nor so differentiated that it deters development in all non-central business district zones.

The current zoning resolution does not deter as-of-right movement of the office core into high-density loft manufacturing districts, except insofar as the city creates special districts, as in the case of the Special Garment Center District, that introduce the very use separations that the body of the resolution eschews. Thus, Saatchi and Saatchi was able to build a 900,000-square-foot office building in a part of Tribeca mapped as a M1–6 manufacturing district because the zoning resolution allows commercial uses in manufacturing districts and because the M1–6 district allows a rather high FAR.

On the other hand, office development bypassed most of Tribeca and detoured north of Canal Street because the lower FAR permitted in the M1–5 zone mapped over Tribeca and SoHo does deter as-of-right office construction in those areas. Since the zoning resolution forbids office development in residential districts, the portions of Clinton, Chelsea, and Murray Hill mapped in R8 (high-density residential) zones are off-limits, absent a developer-initiated map change.

As the Midtown core will probably continue its southward and westward push, and the downtown core will continue its northwestward push, land use conflicts will inevitably occur. Expansion will threaten to displace both industry and residents from Tribeca, Clinton, the garment district, and the East Twenties and Thirties. On the one hand, strangling office development would constrain the city's economic well-being. On the other hand, the city has vested interests in preserving New York City's garment industry, providing housing opportunities within walking distance of the central business district, and preserving the historic and low-scale qualities of much of central Manhattan.

Large-scale planned office development is less likely to be a force in the future. The preferred sites, such as Hunters Point and the Thirty-third Street rail yards, are characterized by extraordinary infrastructure costs for mass transit connections, sewer services, roadway improvements, and so on. The projects of the 1980s, such as the World Financial Center in Battery Park City and Metrotech in downtown Brooklyn, were made possible by enormous up-front public sector investments.

The amount of development in new satellite office districts will depend on the amount of demand generated by the private sector, the availability of suitable sites in Manhattan, and the cost of space (that is, whether Manhattan office space will be expensive enough to induce companies to seek more affordable although less desirable outer borough locations). To the extent that such development proves viable, the zoning issues will be much the same as in central office districts: the proper size and shape of the new buildings and the proper district boundaries. There are important twists, however, especially regarding the boundaries of satellite districts.[9]

In the newer office districts, the central issue is ensuring the size and level of commercial concentration appropriate to an incipient office district that is meant to expand. If the office district's boundaries were drawn too narrowly, either of two unfortunate consequences could occur. The city could inadvertently strangle the new district by not allowing it to achieve the critical mass needed to attract developers and tenants, or developers would propose

FIGURE 41
Skyline of downtown Brooklyn, an expanding satellite office district.

FIGURE 42
Citicorp Building in Long Island City, an emerging satellite office district.

up-zonings of available sites in the general vicinity, seeking to expand the district in an unplanned, piecemeal fashion. Conversely, overly broad or indistinct district boundaries could dissipate the synergistic qualities needed to create a successful office district with needed restaurants, services, stores, and so forth; they would also prompt an inflated real estate market that works to the detriment of nonoffice uses.

A case in point is Long Island City. In the 1980s, the New York City Planning Commission created a three-block, high-density C5–3 district in the midst of a low-density, heavy-industrial M3–1 district. The goal was to accommodate a proposed back office tower for Citibank. There was a vague statement of intent to create a larger office district in the future; a planning study was released recently, but no additional rezonings have followed. At present, the Citicorp tower stands in isolation, devoid of a surrounding office district.

Meanwhile, office conversion projects have occurred or been proposed throughout much of Long Island City, far beyond the areas suggested for office use in the Department of City Planning's Jackson Avenue Corridor Study. The office uses lack the concentration to appear as a coherent office district, but industrial firms are feeling the effects of rampant speculation. A new planning effort by the city planning department should provide guidance, but there is no powerful mechanism in place now by which the city could enforce any plan to focus the office center. Office conversion of industrial buildings is allowed as-of-right, and property owners continue to believe that they can obtain rezonings to build large office buildings.

INDUSTRIAL DISTRICTS

Industry, New York City's most overlooked land use, is more valuable to the city's economy than is generally supposed. Between 1960 and 1980, the number of New Yorkers employed in manufacturing declined by 42 percent, from 870,354 to 507,103, as the city (and the region and nation, to a lesser extent) shed its industrial mass-production sector.[10] Yet New York City remains an industrial center of international importance. Only four of the nation's metropolitan areas have more industrial jobs than New York City alone (without its greater metropolitan area): Los Angeles, Chicago, Detroit, and Philadelphia.[11]

The remaining industry, much of it small-scale and highly specialized, continues to employ hundreds of thousands of New Yorkers. As of July 1991, according to the State Department of Labor, the city had 317,000 manufacturing jobs and another 32,000 trucking and warehouse jobs; together, these categories employed only three hundred fewer workers than the city's banks, security and commodity brokers, and insurance carriers combined.[12] Moreover, these are jobs that do not require high levels of educational achievement. With a 29 percent school dropout rate,[13] with a steady influx of immigrants who often do not speak English, and with an educational system that often fails to educate,[14] New York needs these jobs.

Despite its continuing importance, New York City's industry is quite different today from what it was thirty and seventy-five years ago, when the city's industrial districts were booming. It relies on truck transport, not boat and rail; it now wants to be close to interstate highways, not piers and rail lines. Industry uses equipment and storage techniques that are most efficiently laid out in large, uninterrupted spaces; the demand for multistory space has diminished, and the typical city block and lot pattern is confining. Industrial pollution and safety are more closely monitored so that industry can now be a better neighbor to housing and commercial uses. Industrial operators are no longer simply manufacturers and warehousers of goods; production facilities, showrooms, and offices are typically consolidated in one location. Most important, industry is no longer a high-value use that can expand into residential and commercial districts. The opposite is true; residential and commercial uses are now consistently able to outbid industry in terms of rents and land prices.

Therefore, one challenge is to accommodate the changing space needs of New York City's industries. A second, related challenge is to protect viable industrial operations from displacement by competing, potentially more lucrative land uses. A third challenge (also dealt with in the next section on the waterfront) is to plan for the inevitable continuing shrinkage of industry in New York City.

Of the three basic categories set forth in the 1961 zoning resolution (commercial, manufacturing, and residential), manufacturing zones (or "M" zones) have been scrutinized and altered the least over the past thirty years. A review of the state of industry and how the city regulates it is long overdue, as the city planning department has come to realize.

In terms of both zoning and actual land use, New York City has several different types of industrial districts. The first is the heavy-industrial district, designated M3, "designed to accommodate the essential heavy industrial uses which involve more objectionable influences and hazards."[15] However, there is no longer much demand for uses in this category. Some large factories and oil storage facilities do exist, but the city has lost its shipbuilding industry, its grain depots and processors, the slaughterhouses that once dominated Turtle Bay, all but one of the sugar refineries that once lined the north Brooklyn waterfront, and all of its large breweries.

As the number of heavy-industrial uses has dwindled during the last thirty years, a patchwork pattern of active uses interspersed with abandoned properties has emerged in M3 areas. The active uses tend to be power plants and utility substations, Department of Sanitation garages, an increasing number

FIGURE 43
Waste transfer station on the Hudson River.

of marine transfer stations, petroleum storage facilities, open storage, and uses that could also be accommodated in other industrial districts (docks and container facilities, rail yards, and some clusters of medium- and light-industrial plants).

In fact, M3 districts have become locations not so much for heavy industry as for environmentally noxious uses, particularly those of a public nature: utilities, transfer stations, incinerators, sanitation garages, and the like. Some of these uses are sufficiently noxious to deter other forms of development, including lighter industrial uses.

The second type of industrial area, M2, also does not serve most of the city's current and future industrial needs. It is nebulously called a "medium manufacturing" zone. M2 districts set out performance standards with thresholds between those set out in light- and heavy-industrial areas and exclude the noxious uses reserved for M3 districts, but they allow open storage, unlike light-industrial areas.

The open storage provision makes M2 zones well suited to piers, rail yards, and other transportation and terminal facilities, and that is where most M2 districts are mapped: along large stretches of the waterfront, including swaths drawn between the bulkhead and pierhead lines, and at rail yards and terminals in the Bronx, Queens, and Brooklyn. Some rail facilities remain important, and relatively low performance standards are important to certain operations, but the decline of the shipping industry and rail freight makes much M2 zoning largely irrelevant.

Light-industrial districts, designated M1, can be divided into loft districts (found primarily in Manhattan) and lower density districts. For the most part, modern industrial operations shun multistory space, and the need for truck access makes Manhattan far less convenient than outer borough locations, especially those with highway access. Loft space remains attractive, however, to small firms that require little space and that desire close proximity to jobbers, clients, buyers, and suppliers not always of an industrial nature. The main appeal of loft districts for industrial uses will therefore be for the significant portions of the garment industry that remain in Manhattan, for industrial incubators, for start-up firms, and for printers.

All the same, the amount of available loft space exceeds the demand that these uses can generate; most older loft districts will continue their evolution into mixed-use, quasi-residential, and quasi-commercial districts. The loft regulations in chapter 15 of the zoning resolution and the Special Lower Manhattan Mixed-Use District include useful text intended to provide for an orderly transition from industrial to other uses, allowing a mixture of residential, commercial, industrial, and hybrid work-live uses during the transition period.

To a surprising extent, though, this expected transition stage is emerging as an end in itself. Many people prefer living in these hybrid communities; also, light industry, particularly modern industrial operations with accessory office and showroom operations, is generally more compatible with commercial and even residential activity than with the noxious uses unique to M3 zones. These realizations run counter to the resolution's tripartite division of the urban world into industrial, commercial, and residential sections.

The type of space that appeals most to industrial firms consists of flexible, divisible space in one-story structures. Parking, modern loading facilities, and access to highways should be available. Modern power and communications capabilities, including computer lines, are also desirable. Ceiling heights need be no greater than at most twenty feet; the higher ceilings common in older single-story industrial structures, often reaching forty feet, are wasteful.[16]

In terms of space flexibility, a growing trend is to combine manufacturing, warehouse, office, and showroom functions in one building. Whereas a firm's various functions used to be segmented, with a small office in Midtown, manufacturing operations in Manhattan, and a warehouse in Queens, more and more firms want to consolidate all these operations in one location. Surveys of firms in Long Island City show that whereas ten years ago users of industrial space generally wanted to be able to devote approximately 10 percent of a building's space to accessory office space, now many users want to devote as much as 40 to 50 percent of building space to "accessory" office use.[17]

Thus, there will be a need for considerable rebuilding of the city's industrial stock, for much the same reason that the city has been facing the need for the rebuilding of its office stock: consolidation of operations into larger spaces, flexibility to modify the ways in which those blocks of space are used, and the desire to accommodate ever-changing high-tech capabilities.

If New York City is to remain competitive, it will have to provide the opportunity for such space. The existing zoning resolution allows such space to be built but, for the most part, not in locations at which industrial firms would be shielded from either noxious M3 uses or from competition from more lucrative commercial uses, especially office conversion or development. Also, the street grid and property subdivisions make it difficult to assemble suitable sites.

Moreover, redevelopment efforts have not adversely affected industry. There have been consistent efforts to designate large tracts of vacant and underutilized industrially zoned land (particularly along the waterfront) for higher value residential and commercial development; these efforts have been encouraged by government agencies anxious to maximize real estate values and reclaim the waterfront for presumably more public uses. Land abandoned by other uses, such as in residential neighborhoods in East New York and the South Bronx, is usually earmarked for residential development, in part at the behest of communities wishing to preserve their residential character. A firm effort to maintain or impose industrial zoning, combined with street closings and industrial park management techniques, could meet with surprising success.[18]

A more fundamental zoning issue concerns the ability of industry to compete against commercial uses. Although most of New York City's industry is capable of earning a reasonable return on investment, it cannot compete with the financial return that commercial use can generate. Real estate costs are residential, meaning that the amount a business will pay for property or space in a building depends on its profitability, on projected revenue minus projected other expenses. More profitable enterprises will therefore outbid less profitable enterprises for space. Unless more lucrative uses are excluded from the bidding, industry will be unable to compete.

One function of zoning is to intervene in this free market competition for space, not only to protect public health and safety but also to promote economic diversity and to protect economic and community resources. The low maximum FAR available in most industrial districts is one method of excluding high-rise and mid-rise office development, especially where the existing building stock is not suitable for office conversion, because the conversion costs will make development less lucrative. It is probably desirable, particularly in manufacturing zones in which higher densities are allowed, to go beyond this protection and to exclude various commercial uses.

Making such a zoning modification would not be as simple as one might think. Limiting manufacturing districts to industrial use groups only, and thus excluding all commercial use groups, would be impractical. Such rules would exclude various custom manufacturing, automotive, and semi-industrial uses that are allowed in certain commercial districts and therefore are listed in commercial use groups.[19] Restrictions on retail activities would interfere with the frequently symbiotic arrangement whereby local manufacturers purchase materials from local suppliers, driving up the cost of operations. Elimination of as-of-right support retail would deny workers access to food, banking services, and so forth. Overly restrictive zoning would also prevent the hybrid combinations of industrial, office, showroom, and sales space characteristic of many modern industrial operations.

Clearly, any more purely industrial district would have to permit some combination of uses pulled from various current use groups (such as the catchall collections of "eligible commercial and manufacturing uses" permitted in the Special Garment Center District). This district would also have to distinguish between primary and accessory uses in a way that would allow accessory nonindustrial activities but that would not provide a loophole for office conversion.

The division of industrial zones into the currently permissive districts and new, restrictive industrial districts would constitute a major revision of the existing zoning resolution, entailing an overhaul of the existing use groups. For this reason, such a change would not be probable in the absence of a comprehensive revision of the resolution. Yet the failure to create a more restrictive zone would exacerbate the loss of the city's industrial base.

It should be noted that the weaknesses in the existing resolution do not represent arguments in favor of a zoning ordinance that is fundamentally more or less restrictive. A more restrictive ordinance might limit firms' ability to adapt to changing space needs. A more permissive ordinance might be even less effective at preserving industry (and a mixed economic base in general) than the existing resolution.

THE WATERFRONT

The waterfront now contains some of the city's most inviting development opportunities. Yet, when it comes to waterfront redevelopment, the New York City zoning resolution simply fails.

When the city's zoning resolution was first written in 1916 and when it was rewritten in 1961, the waterfront was designated as an area for industry

FIGURE 44
Marina in Flushing Bay.

and shipping. The crafters of the resolutions logically focused inland, where the subways and new development pressures were located. On the waterfront, all sorts of issues and potential uses were dealt with vaguely or not at all, including floating structures, treatment of underwater land for FAR and for open space, public access, and view corridors. There was no expectation that shipping and industry would decline, that waterfront restaurants and festival marketplaces would become popular, or that recreational boating would become a popular and relatively affordable activity.

The prospect of waterfront redevelopment raises several important questions: What uses will be introduced, what older land uses will be retained, and how will different uses be channeled to appropriate portions of the waterfront? What criteria will guide the size, shape, and design of the buildings that will be constructed? To what extent will public access be mandated and regulated? The existing zoning resolution does not address these questions at all adequately.

Regarding use, it must be remembered that the city's waterfront is, like all land, a finite resource, and only portions of it are really available for development. Parks and public beaches occupy approximately 42 percent of the city's 578 linear miles of waterfront.[20] Large-scale fixed uses, such as Kennedy and LaGuardia airports, will continue to occupy other portions.

Much of the remaining coastline is constrained by narrow lot configurations (such as lots are along the seaward side of major highways), difficult access, inadequate infrastructure, and environmental problems (including wetlands and toxic waste contamination from earlier industrial uses).

The waterfront also remains a special place, and not just because the views add value to residential development projects. Although maritime and other traditional waterfront uses have declined, they have hardly disappeared. New York City remains a major port, and it is likely to remain one for the foreseeable future.[21] In addition to the harbor's role in national and international commerce, intraharbor waterborne transportation (that is, ferry or water taxi service) will probably become increasingly important, particularly as the waterfront is redeveloped and becomes a home or destination to more people. The long-suppressed demand for recreational boating in New York City will also grow in importance if the opportunity exists. All of these are water-dependent uses that cannot exist anywhere but on the waterfront. There are, in fact, relatively few spots with the right combination of depth, currents, access, and upland land area to accommodate water-dependent and maritime uses.

Yet, if the city's waterfront were opened up for development, essentially through the rezoning of areas now mapped with M2 and M3 districts, there would be no guarantee under the existing zoning resolution that adequate space would be provided at appropriate locations for the various water-dependent uses. The existing resolution does not define or otherwise distinguish such uses. The lack of definitions would actually forbid the inclusion of certain uses. For instance, the resolution fails to define "docking facilities" or "marinas" or their various categories. As a result, mooring facilities are treated as though they are the same as major docking facilities or full-service commercial marinas and are therefore disallowed in all but a handful of zones.

In addition to intrinsically water-dependent uses (such as docking facilities for oceangoing vessels, ship loading and unloading facilities, marine transfer stations, boat repair and storage facilities, fueling and other maritime support facilities, ferry and water taxi shops, marinas and yacht clubs, boat sales, and fishing), other uses benefit from the ability to receive waterborne deliveries (for example, cement plants and other heavy-industrial operations). Still other activities, such as restaurants, recreational facilities, and specialized retail establishments, could enhance the public's enjoyment of the waterfront. The existing resolution does not identify or encourage such water-related and waterfront-enhancing uses.

It would be possible to address these various use issues within the context of the existing zoning resolution. The new definitions could certainly be added. Broad definitions of "water-dependent," "water-related," and "waterfront-enhancing" uses could be added, and these uses could be per-

FIGURE 45
South Street Seaport, an entertainment and retail use along the Manhattan waterfront.

mitted in waterfront locations in various existing zoning districts, either as-of-right or by special permit. Alternatively, new zones tailored for the waterfront could be created and mapped in various parts of the city, although this approach would require reorganization of the existing use groups. Either of these approaches would further complicate the resolution, though.

Simply allowing certain uses does not guarantee that they will actually be provided. The city could set aside space for some water-dependent uses by simply retaining the existing M2 and M3 zoning at the appropriate locations, precluding other development options. Much of the rest of the waterfront could be redeveloped with residential and commercial projects. However, the projects would not take advantage of their specialized location to provide opportunities for waterborne transportation and small boat basins; the city would thus lose a number of opportunities to take advantage of a specialized resource.

Whatever type of development occurs, density will also be an issue. Where new infrastructure is needed, where the property owner must clean up toxic contamination before redevelopment can proceed, or where soil conditions or terrain will add considerably to site preparation costs, only high-density development can reduce the unit cost of the needed improvements; but high-density development would generate considerable traffic and would have a substantial impact on the views, property values, affordability, and character of adjacent neighborhoods. Mapping high-density districts would not be easy.

The scale and design of buildings also could be a problem; current regulations allow for the possibility of gargantuan and out-of-scale structures. Under the current zoning resolutions, the allowable size of a building depends on the size of its lot and the density allowed by the zoning district mapped on that lot. This reliance on FAR as a regulator of bulk is particularly problematic along the waterfront, which presents two unusual conditions.

First, waterfront parcels tend to be unusually large. Many have been platted to accommodate land-intensive industrial, storage, or terminal facilities. The waterfront contains vast expanses of land that are not intercepted by streets since the streets running perpendicular to the waterfront tend to end at the roadway running along the inland side of the waterfront property without cutting through to the shoreline itself. Second, waterfront lots do not necessarily end at the shoreline or bulkhead line; in general, underwater land extending as far as the pierhead line is counted for FAR purposes.

Consequently, a single waterfront zoning lot could support an enormous total built-floor area, which a developer could concentrate onto a portion of the property to produce extremely out-of-scale buildings (except in some contextual zones).

On the face of it, this problem could be avoided by mapping more of the waterfront in contextual zoning districts, which use height and setback regulations to control building bulk independently of FAR limitations, but this approach could prove impractical. One of the regulatory devices common to contextual districts is the "front sky exposure plane," which begins at a defined elevation above the "curb level" at the front of the zoning lot. However, along much of the waterfront, the land slopes sharply downhill toward the shore so that the front sky exposure plane might inadequately control the height of buildings constructed nearer the shoreline than the street. Another regulatory device common to contextual districts is the "rear sky exposure plane," which slopes upward and forward from a lower point further back on the lot. This provision, combined with restrictions on how far back from the street a building can be constructed, could effectively bar any development except by variance.

Reconfiguring height and setback regulations so that they were appropriate to the waterfront would be a complicated task. Unless separate waterfront zones were created, the resulting zoning text amendment would provide that different bulk regulations apply within the same zoning district, depending on whether or not the zoning lot were located on the waterfront.

Another major issue that also affects project design is the extent to which the public will have access to the redeveloped waterfront. The prospect of redevelopment provides a good opportunity to integrate esplanades, lookout points, and other amenities into the emerging built environment. Battery Park City has done much to demonstrate the appeal of such access. On the other hand, redevelopment could wall off the waterfront, reestablishing it as off-limits private property and even reducing existing visual access.

The existing zoning resolution does not require public access to the waterfront. Without such a requirement, there is no reason to believe that public access will be incorporated into as-of-right development projects.

FIGURE 46
Public promenade along the Hudson River waterfront at Battery Park City.

The resolution does require "pedestrian ways" or "esplanades" in the South Street Seaport, Manhattan Landing, Battery Park City, and South Richmond waterfront special districts, thus providing a precedent that could potentially be applied to the waterfront in general. The existing resolution could be amended to incorporate a schedule of public access requirements, which might vary by type and density of use. For instance, perpendicular access to the waterfront at some point on the lot might be required in conjunction with industrial or low-density residential development while linear access along the waterfront might be required in conjunction with commercial or high-density residential development. Design standards might also be provided; however, it is hard to imagine any as-of-right design standards that would be able to deal with the immense diversity of the city's waterfront: beaches, wetlands, bulkheads, and all manner of land uses.

Any comprehensive attempt to deal with waterfront zoning would add a further layer of complexity to an already complex ordinance. There would be at least three options for such a revision under the framework established by the existing zoning resolution. First, the city could continue to ignore the special characteristics of the waterfront, resulting in a pattern of development that fails to accommodate the splendid harbor that helps to define the city of New York. Second, it could burden the resolution with a new set of waterfront zones, which would have to provide for all the various permutations of use combinations and densities. Third, it could transform the entire waterfront into what is, in all but name, a special zoning district, in which a zone's usual regulations are modified and supplemented.

The basic alternatives would be to leave zoning in its present unclear and unpredictable state and to rely on discretionary review of private rezoning applications to achieve desired public benefits or to rely on discretionary planning of publicly initiated projects enforced through design guidelines (such as Arverne, Battery Park City, and Hunters Point). The choice appears to be one between more zoning complexity or less as-of-right development.

HIGH-DENSITY RESIDENTIAL NEIGHBORHOODS

The regulations for high-density housing were overhauled in the late 1980s. The new Quality Housing regulations do not satisfy everyone, however. Furthermore, the amendments affected bulk regulations and building layout, not use provisions.

Under Quality Housing regulations, the physical form of new development will be less disruptive of the existing urban fabric than it would be under 1961 regulations. Contextual zoning and the Department of City Planning's proposed "packing-the-bulk" provisions will govern development during the coming decades. There will be fewer towers and more blocky apartment buildings that are reminiscent of apartment construction typical in New York City from the 1920s to the 1950s. There will be fewer interruptions of the street wall and more adherence to the traditional perimeter block.

This does not mean that new construction will be universally popular or that its impact on the urban fabric will not be jarring. New buildings will still tend to be much larger than the ones they replace. If a building boom were to hit a neighborhood and the twenty-story buildings allowed in the highest density contextual zones were to replace lower tenement buildings, residents would find the change startling. Architects will often use contemporary materials and design elements that will not integrate well with the neighborhood's historic appearance. Indeed, as time passes and tastes change, a reaction will set in and organized groups will probably come to object to these new buildings as vigorously as they have objected to 1961 height factor zone buildings. The 1970s and 1980s saw complaints about bleak plazas and excessively tall buildings that towered over their neighbors; the 2000s may see complaints about hulking, massive, "contextual" apartment buildings.

Changing consumer preferences will in time make the details of the Quality Housing provisions antiquated—with its programmatic requirements regarding such design details as street trees, laundry room location, and lobby sight lines. Developers will also complain about the design and review process.

It must be stressed, though, that such conflicts and protests will exist no matter what type of zoning ordinance is in place. A less restrictive ordinance would allow more development, but neighborhoods would change even more radically. A more restrictive ordinance would mean less change, but it could not accommodate changing tastes and technologies. In this regard, so long as it is kept up-to-date in its details, the existing resolution may well strike the best balance.

In residential neighborhoods, more significant changes and controversies are likely to focus on uses rather than bulk and density. The suburban paradigm of spatial separation between workplace and home, with father going off to work and leaving the rest of the family together in a safe residential environment, does not work well in an era of two-wage-earner families and single-parent households.[22] Working parents will increasingly seek work arrangements that allow them to care for their children without significant loss of income or productivity, for example, working at home part-time and in their companies' offices part-time. In addition, more and more workers are becoming self-employed.[23] Finally, small entrepreneurial ventures will probably locate in any available space, including apartments, where half a dozen salespeople might operate via phones or computers or where half a dozen workers might sew clothing or screw together components. The net result will be that increasing numbers of New Yorkers will be working at least part of the time out of their homes—or out of illegally converted units close to home.

This trend will hardly delight everyone. People working in apartments in multiunit buildings will generate more noise, deliveries, trash, and demands for building services; if they see clients at home, the increased traffic could decrease security. One person's convenient working arrangement is another person's threat to peaceful enjoyment of his or her home. Many people want to live in a purely residential environment; they want the strict separation between residential and other uses that is one of the fundamental tenets of traditional zoning.

One psychologist seeing clients or one artist working at home normally will not create much of a nuisance; but if twenty of the residents of a two hundred-unit building work at home, the noise, traffic, trash, and other impacts soon add up. For this reason, although the rise in self-employment will not be unique to high-density neighborhoods, complaints will be concentrated in high-density areas.

Existing zoning is neither permissive enough to satisfy everybody who might want to work at home nor restrictive enough to protect residents who would want to guarantee their peace and quiet. Except for certain loft areas, such as SoHo and Tribeca, the use of apartments for nonresidential purposes is permitted and regulated only according to the definition of "home occupation," which is allowed as an accessory use. The definition contains several restrictions, limiting home occupations to 25 percent of the unit's floor area or five hundred square feet (whichever is less), specifically proscribing a list of occupations (including such less than obvious threats as public relations and interior decorators' offices), specifying that no more than one nonresident employee may work in the unit (and no nonresident employee at all unless the endeavor qualifies as a "profession," which the resolution, of course, does not define), prohibiting the sale of goods not produced on the premises (which helps explain why one must organize a party to sell Tupperware out of someone else's apartment), and warning against "offensive" noise, odors, and other nuisances.

Clearly, these rules forbid completely nonresidential uses, such as a small word-processing firm or sewing shop operating out of an apartment. They also probably outlaw a painter who lives in a one-bedroom apartment and uses the living room for making art, an artist who uses only 25 percent of the apartment for work but has an assistant, a bed-and-breakfast establishment, a consultant who relies on a typist and another assistant who conducts telephone surveys, a publicist who works alone making phone calls and churning out press releases, or a piano teacher or voice coach (provided that anyone considers their students' sound offensive). Yet, a resident can be surrounded by professional neighbors who see a steady stream of clients all day long, and this state of affairs would be perfectly legal under the zoning resolution.

Calls for change will likely come from both sides of the spectrum, and both groups of residents are important to the city's future. It is particularly in the city's interest to enhance the inner city as a place to live and work and as an appealing alternative to the suburban dream.

One solution might be to create a permissive, quasi-residential zone and to map it only in areas near the central business districts, such as the downtown loft neighborhoods in which mixed uses already flourish. This approach would both encourage live-work arrangements and concentrate the phenomenon in certain parts of the city. Since many of the buildings in these areas were designed for industrial activity, they may be better suited to home studio arrangements that involve noise or fumes. Being near business districts, these areas can also best accommodate the need for face-to-face meetings with colleagues or clients. For this reason, these areas are likely to be most popular with, say, self-employed computer programming consultants, architects, or fashion designers who want to live and work in an area convenient to subways, office centers, lunch meeting spots, clients, and so on.

Such a live-work zone would seem contrary to the resolution's basic philosophy of separating uses and to its basic tripartite structure, which divides the city into residential, commercial, and industrial zones. There is precedent, however; exceptions to that structure have been evolving since 1970. These include use group 17D (providing for artists' joint living-work space in the M1–5A and M1–5B zones mapped in the SoHo and NoHo districts), the loft conversion provisions, the Special Lower Manhattan Mixed-Use District (Tribeca), and, to a lesser extent, M1-D and other mixed-use districts. The reform would be to transform these exceptions and transitional rules into generic zoning regulations for a live-work zone.

This solution would not meet the full demand for live-work arrangements. Similar arrangements also will be sought by residents of other neighborhoods who become parents or who decide to go into business for themselves and who do not want to move, whether to the suburbs or to one of a few downtown neighborhoods. These residents probably will want to remain in their apartments and may value the proximity to parks or other amenities. Many home workers will not need employees or face-to-face contacts; they can work alone using personal computers, modems, and fax machines. Others will be doctors, psychologists, home decorators, or others who provide personal rather than business services, for whom a residential neighborhood provides the necessary proximity to clients.

The existing home occupation provisions may be adequate for many of these people's needs; nevertheless, to encourage live-work arrangements, the city may be pressed to liberalize those provisions. More permissive, quasi-residential zoning might also be mapped in other parts of the city, further from the central business districts.

At the same time, the city will be pressed to accommodate people who live in high-density neighborhoods and who value a more purely residential environment. The rise in live-work arrangements, whether or not encouraged by liberalized zoning, will threaten to drive these people out of their apartments.

Caught between two conflicting visions of what a high-density residential neighborhood should be, the city may want to balance increased permissiveness in some areas with greater restrictions in others. (These restrictions would work only if self-enforced by tenants' associations and co-op and condominium boards.) In effect, the city would accommodate both visions by creating two types of residential districts. New residents of the more permissive live-work residential districts would knowingly sacrifice the right to a certain level of peace and quiet for greater freedom to intermingle work and home life. New residents of the more restrictive districts would knowingly sacrifice potential work options for a greater likelihood of undisturbed peace. They could cling to the ideal underlying the suburban paradigm: that the workplace is the workplace and home is home, and the two will remain separate.

Finally, it should be emphasized that social changes, including a trend toward live-work arrangements, will occur with or without zoning changes. To some extent, zoning amendments or their absence can encourage or frustrate the trend or at least New York City's ability to accommodate it. To a greater extent, though, failure to adapt the resolution to changing conditions would merely erode zoning's efficacy as a predictor and regulator of land use.

LOW-DENSITY RESIDENTIAL NEIGHBORHOODS

During the coming decades, the city's low-density residential neighborhoods will experience increasing demand for housing and, consequently, increased housing construction.

One major contributing factor will be a continuing high rate of immigration. Currently, one out of four documented immigrants to the United States settles in New York City.[24] Further influxes are expected, as China prepares to gain sovereignty over Hong Kong and as Eastern Europe faces political turmoil and economic dislocations. Many of the new immigrants will likely settle in low-density Brooklyn or Queens neighborhoods for a variety of reasons, including the shortage of available apartments in higher density neighborhoods, the limited opportunity for affordable new high-rise development, and the fact that earlier immigrants and their children have moved from inner-city areas to lower density neighborhoods. This will represent a departure from past experience; historically, high-density neighborhoods, such as the Lower East Side and Chinatown, were the prime destinations of new immigrants.

Another factor in the increased demand for housing will be the aging of the baby-boom generation. Many baby boomers will be raising their own families in coming years; many will regard proximity of home and workplace as indispensable, but others will regard ample living space and private yards as more important than convenience to work, shops, theaters, and restaurants. Many probably will leave the city for the suburbs; many others will stay in the city but move from their apartment buildings to lower density neighborhoods, adding to the demand for housing in those communities.

Faced with this long-term added demand, developers are likely to call for streamlining contextual zoning rules. The city will be sorely pressed to comply, given its desire to thwart renewed emigration to the suburbs. It may also sense that preventing new construction may have an exclusionary impact on particular immigrant groups.

Conversely, this development pressure and the prospect of unwelcome changes in neighborhood character—increases in neighborhood density, the introduction and proliferation of unfamiliar building types, and changes in the ethnic composition—will produce continued calls for rezonings. Insofar as communities simply request the mapping of zones already on the books, the city will continue to respond to development pressure with mapping actions. However, community and civic groups are also likely to request text revisions to create new zones, including new permutations of contextual zoning.

Under the existing resolution, the bulk regulations will never be so fine-grained that they can force builders to re-create past housing types; the contextual regulations will not and cannot ensure that new buildings will be compatible with the existing homes on every block of every neighborhood in a city with 740,000 residential lots. Some new additions to the repertory of zones are likely over the coming decades, but given the number of residential districts already in the resolution, including the recently enacted lower density contextual zones, the city ultimately will not be able to respond without rendering the resolution unacceptably complex, to the point of deterring new construction.

Two other side effects of continued development pressure, especially in low-density, single-family neighborhoods, will be trends toward illegal additions onto homes and illegal subdivision of homes into multiple units. Increased immigration will produce pressure on immigrant families to provide quarters for relatives who have arrived more recently. The aging of the population will lead to a greater call for separate "granny flats," a common term for a type of small housing unit that is generally ancillary to a larger,

FIGURE 47
House addition along Ocean Parkway in Brooklyn.

single-family unit and that is usually occupied by single adults. Homeowners, particularly those who have extra space in their homes because children have moved out, will want to realize income from rental apartments. If the city does not respond in some way—through increased enforcement or through relaxation of bulk and density restrictions—zoning will be undermined by an increasing pattern of noncompliance, perhaps subsequently legalized through requests for retroactive variances.

In sum, low-density neighborhoods are likely to be more crowded than they are now, and they are more likely to be battlegrounds regarding the extent and nature of new development. The zoning may be more contextual, but the development pressures will be more intense.

RETAIL DISTRICTS

Shopping is a function of the demand for retail goods. As a result, the retail environment in New York City and its neighborhoods is everchanging. The demand for various types of goods and services changes as different communities gain and lose population; as the disposable income, age, and ethnicity of each neighborhood's population changes; and as tastes and styles evolve.

Changes in the nature of retailing also affect the city's shopping districts and residents' shopping patterns. Over the past several decades, large, automobile-oriented, high-volume stores and shopping centers have come to dominate retailing. In the 1950s and 1960s, shopping malls (most of them outside the city) began to lure New Yorkers shopping for furniture, clothing, and other relatively expensive "comparison goods." More recently, large supermarkets and superdrugstores have supplanted smaller groceries, delis, and drugstores. The larger stores can offer greater selection and, because of their high sales volumes, lower prices. The changes also reflect a continuing trend toward two-worker households, so that once-a-week weekend shopping forays have replaced housewives' daily trips to the market.[25]

The configuration of shopping districts in New York City defies these changes, for the most part, and retains an earlier form: that of neighborhood "Main Streets," pedestrian-oriented retail and service strips consisting of blocks of uninterrupted storefronts. Because buildings along these strips occupy the entire street frontage of almost every lot, there is little provision for on-site parking. Because of multiple ownership and shallow retail zoning, there are relatively few large supermarkets or other anchor stores. The zoning enforces this configuration through shallow, linear commercial districts superimposed on residential districts; these overlays preclude large, deep stores or shopping centers set behind parking lots.

Older neighborhood retail centers will largely flourish or fail to the extent that the city suppresses large-scale shopping centers and auto-oriented strip development. This means not mapping deeper commercial zones, particularly in areas such as eastern Queens, and not granting special permits to allow large stores or shopping centers in industrial districts like Gowanus. Since Section 74–922 of the zoning resolution provides for such special permits if the City Planning Commission makes certain findings (spelled out in the section), this section may have to be abolished if the city is to preclude the development of large, auto-oriented stores.

Continued restrictive zoning would provide only imperfect protection to the older retail strips, and at a cost to the city. An unintended result would be a drainage of retail dollars from the city plus a loss of sales tax revenue as residents drive to the suburbs to shop. Many city residents would feel frustrated by the lack of retail choices in their neighborhood and might well be even more unhappy about a noticeable decline in their neighborhood's main shopping street prompted by loss of business to auto-oriented shopping close by.

The elasticity of store quantity and mix and the inelasticity of the location and quantity of space in retail districts have some interesting nuances that will be registered quite differently in different neighborhoods. For instance, in the outer reaches of the city, such as eastern Queens and southern Staten Island, car ownership is particularly high and population densities are relatively low. These areas resemble the adjacent suburbs more than inner-city neighborhoods, and developer interest and consumer support for modern auto-oriented shopping are likely to be high. The traditional shopping centers are likely to suffer declines in size and prosperity. Accommodating this shrinkage will be a planning and zoning challenge, especially since zoning is better at shaping development trends than disinvestment trends.

For quite different reasons, the same may be true in the city's low-income neighborhoods. Due to abandonment and low land values, it is relatively easy to assemble tracts for supermarkets and mini auto strip shopping centers (see, for example, Atlantic Avenue in East New York). For security and image reasons, many residents likewise prefer auto-oriented shopping. Some older retail strips are likely to fail altogether in the face of declining income and increasing competition, as have the once flourishing Claremont Parkway in the South Bronx and Jersey Street in Staten Island.

In other areas, especially the neighborhoods appealing to the city's newest ethnic groups, the older retail streets will probably flourish. New residents to the city are likely to seek out stores selling familiar foods and goods and run by people speaking their own native language. The new

FIGURE 48
Commercial street in Flushing, Queens, a burgeoning immigrant district.

residents also provide an entrepreneurial as well as a customer base. Some retail districts will be transformed from neighborhood shopping streets to regional destinations, as Flushing and Brighton Beach were in the 1980s, with all of the attendant parking and expansion issues.

Shopping districts in high-density, affluent residential neighborhoods face quite a different challenge. The high population densities can support considerable amounts of retail space, of a very varied nature, including many types of specialty stores.[26] The variety and concentration of specialty stores, in turn, give these shopping districts a regional drawing power. They pull in customers from the city's growing residential population, the increasing number of commuters into Manhattan, and the city's increasing tourist population.[27]

In several neighborhoods, particularly the Upper West Side and parts of the East Village, neighborhood-oriented stores have been replaced by boutiques and restaurants. This trend has abated somewhat as a result of the current recession and as once free-spending, newly affluent baby boomers have become fiscally overdrawn parents. In the long term, though, the trend is likely to continue, in part because the city is expected to continue gaining population and jobs, in part because the city's international presence will boost tourist and visitor spending, and in part because the growing presence of national chain stores in the downtowns and the demise of the traditional large department store will increase the popularity of specialty shopping districts.

On the one hand, this trend helps to boost the local economy and to reinforce New York City's position as the premier retail city in America. On the other hand, the competition for retail space diminishes the number of lower rent, personal service establishments (such as shoe repair shops and dry cleaners). Just as industrial firms cannot compete on an equal basis with office developers for space, a shoe repair shop cannot compete with a boutique or chain drugstore, which can sell higher priced goods or do a greater volume of business. The loss of entire categories of stores and services is not in the public interest.

During the next economic upturn, there will probably be renewed calls to protect such endangered retail and service categories. The city could respond by mapping more retail space, thereby allowing demand and supply to reach a new equilibrium. Mapping more retail zones is likely to engender tremendous controversy, however, because it would endanger the residential look and feel of the side streets and avenues where the new retail and service overlay zones would likely be mapped.

Another approach would be to amend the zoning resolution to protect endangered retail and service categories by disallowing higher rent uses. The current zoning resolution does not have a basic convenience retail zone. The C1 commercial overlay functions ostensibly as such a zone, but it is too inclusive to protect basic store and service types. It allows art galleries, antique stores, boutiques, and so on. A more restrictive basic goods and services zone, which might be mapped only along some side streets and other secondary retail corridors, would be limited to a somewhat expanded variation of use group 6A, which is a subset of the permissible C1 uses that consists of more essential convenience stores. The current large-scale residential development regulations allow stores listed in that use subgroup to locate anywhere in the development, whether or not in a commercial zone, as long as they comply with certain size and other restrictions. This would not represent a fundamental change in the zoning resolution.

The results would be unpredictable, though. As time passes, planners may be surprised to learn that desirable types of local stores or services have been inadvertently excluded and that other less desirable establishments have been allowed. The results might even recall the city's attempt (reflected in zoning) to protect neighborhoods against undue noise by limiting the number of musicians that could play in a commercial establishment and the types of instruments they could play. The restrictions effectively discriminated against certain types of bands, such as jazz combos and string quartets. Yet, because the regulations did not restrict amplification, they did not effectively restrict noise. Retail mix may be one component of land use for which fewer restrictions represent the lesser of two evils.

NEIGHBORHOOD SERVICES

It is generally agreed that, aside from waterfront zoning regulations, no aspect of the zoning resolution is in as much need of an overhaul as the community facilities provisions.

In 1961, schools, churches, hospitals, health clinics, libraries, and community centers were viewed as boons to the communities that they served. Most such facilities had minimum floor area needs that exceeded, and often far exceeded, the size of residential buildings allowed in low-density residential districts. It would be unreasonable to build a school that was the size of a two-family house, for instance, and it would be extremely wasteful to restrict the school to such a low floor area ratio that a decent-sized school building would require a vast tract of land. Yet it also would be unreasonable to effectively forbid or deter schools or libraries in low-density residential neighborhoods.

Consequently, to encourage such facilities and to promote efficient land use, the 1961 zoning revision was extremely permissive regarding them. It combined them into a broad category of uses classified as "community facilities" and permitted these facilities in any concentration in any residential district. Moreover, community facilities were allowed up to twice the bulk and density that was allowed for residential uses.

As time passed, the attitude toward community facilities has become decidedly less genial. Part of the problem is that some low-density neighborhoods have attracted an inordinate number of facilities, such as nursing homes, that serve a regional constituency, not just the neighborhood. They generate a level of traffic ill-suited to the area's low density, and, because they are not designed to serve neighborhood residents predominantly, they burden rather than benefit the immediate community.

More importantly, social and demographic changes have altered both the perception and the reality of community facilities. Whereas libraries, day-care centers, and elementary schools are generally regarded as desirable, nursing homes and health clinics are not, and homeless shelters and drug treatment centers elicit extreme aversion. Even school proposals can cause alarm; parents want them in the neighborhood but residents on nearby properties worry about the noise and traffic; high schools and intermediate schools arouse fears of rowdy or even violent behavior. In the age of the "not-in-my-backyard" protest, a reasonable generalization about the response of individuals who will be affected by a facility is, "Whatever community facilities I use are desirable, and whatever community facilities serve other people are objectionable."

The city has adopted "fair share" rules regarding placement of city-owned facilities, but the only way to control the location or size of private facilities is through zoning. If the regulation and distribution of community facilities is to be rationalized, there will be a need to address the definition, categorization, locational requirements, bulk regulations, and parking rules for community facilities. The existing resolution can accommodate such changes, but it would involve a major overhaul of the regulations. Use groups 3 and 4, in which community facilities are now listed, would have to be reworked completely; among other things, they would have to be expanded and subdivided. The changes would have to resonate through the use, bulk, and parking chapters for all types of districts, as well as the special permit sections of the resolution.

LOW-INCOME NEIGHBORHOODS

If the experience of the last thirty years is any indication, New York City's zoning ordinance will have little influence on the pattern of development in lower income neighborhoods.

Any zoning ordinance is a system of regulations that influences land use and urban form by shaping market forces. It sets the parameters regarding what can or cannot be built and what can or cannot be done in existing buildings; its underlying vision of what the city should become is then realized to the extent that new construction or changes in use occur. As a result, its influence is greatest where market forces are strongest, and that is where the loudest zoning debates occur. Zoning has far less relevance or influence where there is little incentive for development.

Development pressures do exist in low-income neighborhoods, but they generally are driven by the government rather than the market. The city's land disposition strategies, decisions about locating facilities and undertaking capital projects, and requests for proposals are the primary means by which it regulates land use and urban form in low-income communities. Politics, expediency, and federal or state guidelines have more influence than zoning over publicly initiated or subsidized projects. In fact, these projects often supersede the city's zoning regulations. Zoning is treated in much the same way as a comprehensive plan and map: It is not ignored but there is no presumption that it must be followed.

Enforcement problems compound the issue; zoning regulations only work if there is an ability and will to enforce them. In neighborhoods where well-organized, well-informed, and well-connected community groups demand enforcement, zoning and other rules tend to be enforced. In more troubled neighborhoods, residents tend to be less influential, they are less likely to be familiar with city regulations, and they often view public officials with mistrust. Consequently, the city is less likely to express concern about illegal additions to homes, subdivision of units, or violations of industrial performance standards in these areas. (Similarly, in such neighborhoods, the city is more likely to ignore abandoned cars or sweatshops and is less likely to determine that an environmental impact statement [EIS] is required for a proposal project.[28])

The net result is that in all of New York City, the greatest departures from traditional built form have occurred in low-income neighborhoods: the towers of Mott Haven, the ranch houses of Charlotte Street, and the superstructures of Far Rockaway. In many low-income neighborhoods, dreary, discredited high-rise public housing projects have become the urban design context, not the exception.

The city can do more than it has in the past to abide by its own rules, enforce regulations, and be more sensitive to the built form and neighborhood character of disadvantaged neighborhoods. Recent actions, such as the fair share rules for the siting of public facilities and the city planning department's increased attentiveness to the impact of its land disposition decisions, indicate that this will indeed be the case. Still, these actions do not alter the fact that as long as the anticipated benefits of new housing and jobs outweigh quality of life considerations and good land use planning, the public sector will be driven more by expediency than by planning principles and zoning rules. Perhaps more importantly, sensitivity to these issues will not create the sort of market forces that can be shaped, appropriately or inappropriately, by zoning.

THE ZONING RESOLUTION'S ROLE IN THE PLANNING PROCESS

No zoning ordinance is any better than the process by which a city's land use planning decisions are made. Although the zoning ordinance implicitly reflects a planning vision, it is not itself a city's master plan. Rather, it is the most important of several tools that planners may use to realize a constantly evolving set of goals and objectives.

The changing tastes, values, and social, economic, and technological conditions require planners and officials to update not only the zoning text and map but also their goals and objectives for the city as a whole and for its specific communities. Such an ongoing comprehensive planning process may involve a formal citywide planning document (long since dismissed as impractical for New York City), separate planning studies for various parts of the city, community district plans, less formal policy statements, or the City Planning Commission's quadrennial reports to the mayor. It is clear, though, that without some form of comprehensive planning, any zoning ordinance will come to seem clumsy and misguided.

Most basically, however comprehensive or haphazard the process may be, planning decisions have to be made, and the zoning text and map must be amended in response to changing conditions. Changes in land use and physical character *will* occur, with or without zoning reforms or mapping amendments. Mapping and text amendments are made regularly in New York City, but more major, complicated reforms are often postponed indefinitely. To the extent that the zoning resolution cannot accommodate changing space needs, many of the land use changes will be illegal and unacknowledged. For instance, this paper includes projections that homes will be subdivided to create new apartments and that residential units will be used for office and industrial purposes, whether or not zoning is relaxed to allow these changes to occur. Stasis merely renders the zoning resolution increasingly irrelevant.

Second, text and map changes should reflect the comprehensive study of particular land uses or parts of the city. Otherwise, in the high-market-pressure areas in which zoning has the greatest potential to influence development, zoning will be a reactive tool, not one that shapes the city, because developers themselves will be framing the issues and initiating remappings. As a result, the city may have difficulty limiting development projects to desirable bulk and density levels; mandating urban design controls, public amenities, or public access; encouraging desirable concentra-

FIGURE 49
Sixth Avenue in Chelsea, zoned for manufacturing uses, is lined with vacant lots.

tions or combinations of uses; and limiting wider speculation and displacement. Unfortunately, in recent years, too many of the city's planning decisions have been reactive and haphazard.

Third, zoning changes should be made in conjunction with the use of other planning tools to advance broader objectives or neighborhood plans. To the extent that planning and zoning are treated synonymously and the zoning resolution is misused as a surrogate master plan, the city largely abdicates its planning role, especially in disadvantaged neighborhoods. Zoning should be coordinated with urban renewal projects, strategic disposition of city-owned land, the siting of public facilities, and capital budget allocations. In past years, the role of the city planning department seemed to contract to that of keeper and shaper of the zoning resolution, the Uniform Land Use Review Procedure (ULURP), and the City Environmental Quality Review (CEQR) process. Recent department initiatives, such as the neighborhood land disposition plans, seem to be restoring the balance.

Finally, planning requires not only concentration on particular neighborhoods but also a certain comprehensive sense of the city as a whole; policy decisions and zoning changes should be made within this broader context. This is the only way in which the city can hope to channel development to particular areas and away from others: to protect historic districts, moderate-income communities, or stable but low-profit-margin industrial concentrations from excessive development pressure and to stimulate development where it has the greatest likelihood to flourish.

Planning is a process by which officials determine where the city and its neighborhoods should be going; the zoning ordinance is the vehicle they use to get there. Divorced from a sound planning process, the zoning ordinance becomes a more or less serviceable vehicle for arriving at the wrong destination. Before we can consider what type of zoning ordinance the city should have, we need to determine what sort of city New York should and can be, since different approaches to zoning are more or less suited to different visions of the city.

THE ZONING RESOLUTION'S ROLE IN SHAPING THE MARKET

No zoning resolution can realize a planning vision in the absence of market forces. Zoning does not so much prescribe what must happen as what shall not be allowed to happen. The market dictates what can happen. Zoning's efficacy as a design tool is derived from the nexus of the range of permitted uses and forms and the set of market preferences. Without an appreciation (and accommodation) of market forces, any zoning ordinance will serve to stifle the economic and social vitality of the city.

First, the ordinance must provide predictability. Developers must be sure of what they can build and, therefore, what they should pay for a property. Uncertainties and delays (which discretionary actions introduce) add to the risk. Markets can change very speedily, as the boom-to-bust pattern of the past five years attests. Developers go bankrupt not because they make or lose a 5 percent margin but because they guess badly about what the market will be like when a project is completed. The more predictable the ordinance is and the more speedily development proposals can be approved, the less risk developers face. This fact underlies the preoccupation with as-of-right zoning.

Second, and somewhat contradictorily, the ordinance must provide flexibility to accommodate change. Market forces are everchanging. Either the guidelines and strictures of the ordinance must be liberal enough to allow a variety of uses and forms or the ordinance itself must be amended easily. Otherwise, the local economy will become more and more inefficient.

Third, the ordinance must recognize developers' inclination to utilize zoning options that benefit particular development objectives and their disinclination to utilize options that they do not perceive to be in their own best interests. As a case in point, a developer is more likely to provide a plaza (ostensibly a public amenity) if it serves the project's particular market niche. The project's market niche will also determine the design of the plaza: whether it will be a small privatized park for residential tenants, a sterile front yard for an office tower, or a truly public place that helps establish a prestigious image. Therefore, zoning provisions designed to prevent readily measurable diseconomies (for example, loss of light and air, pollution, or overcrowding) tend to be more successful than provisions designed to create public amenities whose success hinges on quality of design and execution (such as plazas, facade treatment, promenades, or affordable housing).

Fourth, to the extent that zoning channels development, it is a weak public policy tool in the absence of market pressures. Zoning is a limited planning and design tool in low income neighborhoods and even in stable moderate-income neighborhoods, where development is not likely to occur. Moreover, the effectiveness of zoning as a tool to recapture public value is limited to a small part of the city. If such amenities are mandated (rather than encouraged through incentives), then they add to project costs and deter development in lower value neighborhoods, where the added costs cannot necessarily be absorbed. If such amenities are encouraged through bonuses, then implementation is contingent on developers' desire to exceed the normally allowable density.

In sum, market forces determine what activities and building projects the city and its neighborhoods can support; the zoning ordinance serves to restrict and channel these market forces. Divorced from a sound prediction of emerging market forces, the zoning ordinance becomes more or less ungrounded. Before we can consider what types of zoning ordinance the city should have, we therefore need to determine where the market is headed.

THE ZONING RESOLUTION'S ADAPTABILITY TO CHANGE

Zoning must evolve in response to the multiplicity of social, economic, technological, and demographic changes that will affect market forces, popular tastes, and public policy objectives. If city planners could accurately predict the future, their task would be relatively easy. In reality, of course, no two pundits can agree on what the city's or the region's economy will be like a year from now—let alone on what the city will be like thirty years from now.

The zoning issues discussed throughout this paper are conservatively defined and necessarily quite selective. Most of them arise out of well-evident trends, but values and conditions will almost certainly change in more striking ways that nobody can now foresee. Just as the crafters of the 1916 ordinance could not foresee the full impact of the automobile and air conditioner on the city of the 1950s, and the crafters of the 1961 ordinance could not foresee the rapid evolution and spread of computer technology or the sharp increases in crime and homelessness, we cannot fully identify future economic and social developments or their impact on the city of tomorrow.

For instance, what if environmental considerations or a dramatic increase in the price of gasoline were to curtail reliance on the automobile, vastly increasing the value of mass transit cities and concentrated downtowns and affecting where businesses locate, where people choose to live, and how they shop? What if a small but significant increase in ocean levels were to make the city's waterfront less suitable for settlement? On the other hand, what if New York State and New York City were to improve water quality even further, providing more impetus for waterfront development? How would expanded ferry and water bus services, another East Side terminal, completion of the Second Avenue subway line, mass transit links to the airports, or a subway connection to the Meadowlands affect development pressures? What if the city's school system were to fail altogether and middle-class families were to leave in droves?

Given the unpredictability of future conditions and market trends and the lack of a commonly accepted, well-articulated vision of how the city should evolve, it is hard to assess how well the current zoning resolution will continue to serve the city. The uncertainties highlight one overarching consideration: the ordinance's ability to accommodate change.

The existing zoning resolution reflects obsolescent visions of what the city should be and what it is likely to become, but it has managed to absorb thirty years' worth of modernizing correction. Has it been retrofitted sufficiently to remain serviceable? The various amendments have inevitably introduced an element of self-contradiction, and the corrections have been accomplished by creating exceptions to general rules and by deforming the resolution's essential structure, originally rather straightforward.[29] At what point do the tensions between newly adopted provisions and the resolution's essential structure become too great? Cumulatively, the changes make the resolution more complex and more difficult to understand, interpret, and enforce. At what point does it become too unwieldly to use? When does it become too brittle to accommodate more change without breaking?

One inherent problem is that the resolution is based on a division of the city into residential, commercial, and manufacturing use groupings. These traditional genres do not necessarily continue to reflect social and economic reality. Many people want to combine work and home life in a way that is contrary to fundamental assumptions about the separation of residential and other uses. Small-scale commercial and industrial operations also are appropriate in certain residential neighborhoods, as long as they adhere to strict performance standards.

Yet, there are economic and planning reasons why other uses should be separated, at least in certain neighborhoods. The 1916 resolution protected Midtown merchants by forbidding incursions by industry into commercial areas; changing economic conditions may make it advisable to protect certain healthy or strategically important industrial areas from incursions by office development. Certain types of particularly noxious uses, such as unenclosed solid waste transfer stations, may be incompatible with most types of industry.

Questions of how to define and separate land uses may not always invite general answers; it may be preferable to provide choices regarding, say, different conceptions about how exclusively residential a community should be. As time passes, as social mores and the nature of commercial and industrial operations change, assumptions regarding what uses are compatible with each other will continue to change.

The approach to amending the zoning resolution during the past thirty years has been to leave the use groups, the basic zoning districts, and the three groupings of zones very much as is while creating exceptions. Different use combinations were established for various special districts in which the general rules do not fit well. These special district regulations were tacked onto the primary body of the resolution, virtually as an appendix. Other changes applied to a variety of specialized areas rather than just one area, so they were introduced as new special permit uses. Loft provisions were fit awkwardly into the "General Provisions" article of the resolution, even though they are specialized provisions that are anything but general. As a result of this tinkering, Article I and Volume 2 now provide exceptions to the general use regulations of Articles II, III, and IV, and Article VII provides special permit exceptions to Articles I, II, III, and IV. Nobody can tell where to look, and the document lacks an index.

The most radical solution would be to scrap the concept of strict separation of uses and rely instead on varying performance standards. This approach would totally destroy the very basis of the existing resolution. A more compatible approach, restructuring and expanding the list of zoning districts and reconfiguring the use groups, would still entail significant revision. Even under this approach, each change would affect not only the use regulations but also reverberate through the bulk and parking and loading chapters as well. The existing resolution can accommodate major changes with regard to land use; but if the resolution were to remain (or again become) coherent, comprehensive revision would be required.

Another problem with the zoning resolution is a fundamental confusion about whether it should be a collection of relatively basic zoning districts, which are uncomplicated by nuance and supplemented by additional provisions applicable only in specific special overlay districts, or a collection of diverse and detailed generic zoning districts that make special districts unnecessary. In reality, the resolution has become both, accumulating thirty-seven one-of-a-kind special districts since the late 1960s and adding more than thirty new generic districts (many of them "contextual" zones) within the past five years.

The special districts are neither independent, self-sufficient zones that are mapped instead of basic zones nor overlays that merely add additional requirements to the underlying generic zoning regulations. Rather, they are overlays that in some ways supplement but in other ways modify and seemingly replace the underlying regulations.

The new generic districts include density and bulk restrictions that are better tailored to the existing characteristics of buildings in the neighborhoods in which they are mapped, but the new generic districts include regulations that are not at all basic, bare bones provisions designed to be supplemented where necessary. They can be quite detailed and complicated, including various alternative height and setback requirements, yard and lot coverage requirements, and, in some cases, special programmatic requirements (regarding, for instance, window glazing, laundry facilities, recreational space, and planting areas). These districts are "generic" only in the sense that they can be mapped anywhere in the city.

All in all, it is as if New York City has two or three zoning ordinances superimposed on one another. When considering how to confront issues such as those arising along the waterfront, planners do not know which one to amend. The unwieldiness of the resolution makes change harder to incorporate in a coherent way and often deters thoughts of additional change.

One of the most innovative qualities inherent in the resolution also helps make it difficult to keep up-to-date. The 1961 zoning revision pioneered incentive zoning. The resolution not only tells property owners what they can and cannot do but also what they might be able to do for a specified price. Developers may receive FAR bonuses in return for various amenities; depending on zone and location, these may be public plazas, inclusionary housing payments, or transit improvements. In the past, they included theaters and arcades. Possible future candidates include waterfront public access.

Such incentives quickly become dated, however. In essence, they invite developers to enter into a voluntary transaction, trading an amenity for extra floor area. Voluntary transactions are subject to everchanging market values. Additional floor area becomes more and less valuable with time, depending on real estate market conditions. Perhaps more importantly, the value that society places on a particular amenity changes over time. (Public plazas are worth less to New Yorkers now than they were in the 1960s. Waterfront public access strikes planners as very valuable right now, but it may be much less of a priority in twenty years.) In the marketplace, prices fluctuate to account for changing values, but incentive zoning fixes the price of an amenity by law. Inflexible price systems do not work well when applied to zoning unless they are modified constantly, at the cost of a great amount of time and attention from planners.

A final problem with the current resolution is that it serves to empower some people at the expense of others. Its extraordinary complexity means that only a handful of public officials, civic leaders, consultants, lawyers, architects, and developers fully understand its workings. A successful project application can hinge on a nuance. The resolution's complexity discourages new players from entering the New York City development scene. Furthermore, community groups feel excluded. Community groups feel special districts and discretionary review are the two tools most responsive to their particular concerns, and the trend away from these tools in favor of universally applied, as-of-right rules is likely in the long term to increase community concerns. The misconception that zoning is a master plan for the city exacerbates this problem.

In addition to problems inherent in the zoning resolution itself, legal and financial constraints imposed upon the Department of City Planning also take their toll.

CEQR, conducted under the aegis of the State Environmental Quality Review Act (SEQRA), has made it enormously costly to undertake generic zoning reform. An EIS can easily cost hundreds of thousands or even millions of dollars and can take years to prepare and process. The Arverne EIS alone cost more than $2 million in consultant fees (not counting city staff time); this is equivalent to more than 10 percent of the city planning department's annual budget. The department is chronically underbudgeted; on a per capita basis, it receives only one-fifth the budget that planning departments receive in other major American cities.[30] The agency is strapped to fulfill its charter obligations, leaving precious few funds to pursue major planning and zoning initiatives.

At the simplest level, the prospect of expensive EISs has made it harder to keep the zoning map up-to-date because (in some cases) the Department of City Planning has shied away from map changes that would trigger EISs.

More fundamentally, though, CEQR deters timely or comprehensive zoning reforms. Reforms are not timely because a required EIS takes months or sometimes years to complete and because actions that would trigger an EIS may be postponed to avoid the expense. Reforms are not comprehensive because far-reaching actions, affecting the resolution in more significant ways, are likely to require more expensive EISs. A comprehensive overhaul of the resolution is less likely under these conditions. Adoption of a new, thoroughly revised zoning ordinance, difficult enough in 1961, would face possibly insurmountable obstacles today.

PROSPECTS FOR REFORM

All in all, the zoning resolution has proven surprisingly adaptable, in great part thanks to its very complexity, which allows it to serve many masters and seemingly contradictory goals. Its complexity is now so great, however, that it serves as an argument against any incremental reform that would add to the confusion.

At the very least, therefore, the zoning resolution needs a good, thorough pruning and shaking. Extraneous provisions, zones, and appendages should be removed, anachronisms should be located and discarded, confusions and contradictions should be resolved, and omissions should be noted. Confronting the various contradictions and omissions will not be easy, but to lumber along without a major overhaul may prove impossible.

This overhaul is probably best approached on a comprehensive basis, at the very least land use by land use. This would require a level of commitment, allocation of resources, public outreach, and consensus building far exceeding that employed for the Quality Housing and lower density contextual zoning initiatives of the past decade. It would probably require a state legislative effort to reform SEQRA to allow more sweeping reform and remappings than have been possible in the past decade. It may involve greater use of sunset provisions or expiration dates especially with regard to special districts and bonus provisions that become outdated relatively quickly. It could involve revisions that make communities partners, not commentators, in the zoning process. It can be done, though.

In conclusion, it should be repeated that there are two sets of criteria by which a zoning ordinance is to be judged. First, it should be adaptable to market trends; it should provide a predictable framework within which development can take place and the city can adapt to new economic and social realities. Second, it must be consistent with a shared, clearly articulated vision of the future and our common judgments about what problems are most important to address.

The 1916 zoning resolution was designed for the age of the skyscraper and the construction of the subway system. The 1961 zoning resolution was designed for the age of automobiles and high-rise construction. Compared with the New York City of these eras, tomorrow's city will be more attuned to environmental concerns and limitations, more conscious of its social and ethnic diversity, and more protective of its past. It is time to plan and zone for the New York City of the twenty-first century.

NOTES

1. From 1960 to 1990, services and the "FIRE" (financial, insurance, and real estate) sector grew from a 31 to a 56 percent share of private sector jobs in New York City. Blue-collar work (in manufacturing, construction, transportation, and utilities) declined from 44 to 23 percent of private sector jobs. See *Tomorrow's Jobs Tomorrow's Workers 1991: New York City* (New York: New York State Department of Labor, 1991).

2. Prominent among recent forecasts of this trend has been Hugh O'Neill and Mitchell Moss, *Reinventing New York* (New York: New York University Urban Research Center, 1991).

3. New York's Midtown and downtown office cores are the country's two largest central business districts, as measured by the amount of either primary or total office space. The precise size of the inventory varies according to the criteria used in counting it. The most widely quoted figures are those of Cushman and Wakefield, which counted 163 million square feet of Midtown primary office space and eighty-one million square feet of downtown primary office space as of 1990. Although Cushman and Wakefield's primary space figures are the ones generally cited, the firm does also track the secondary office space inventory; in 1989, the firm's periodical publication, *Manhattantrends,* counted fifty-eight million square feet of secondary space in Midtown and another twenty-six million square feet downtown.

It should be noted that Cushman and Wakefield considers buildings as far south as Canal Street to be in "Midtown." The Edward S. Gordon Company, counting only buildings with at least 150,000 square feet of space and excluding Midtown south, lists 189 million square feet in Midtown and ninety-one million square feet downtown. All of these figures include only private office buildings, not government buildings, such as 26 Federal Plaza and the Municipal Building. The Regional Plan Association simply estimates three hundred million square feet of office space in Manhattan's business districts.

In short, between 240 and 325 million square feet of office space are located in the ten square miles of Manhattan below Sixtieth Street.

4. The distinction between "primary" and "secondary" office space (also known as "grade A" and "grade B" space) is based on several factors. Primary space generally consists of new, modernized, or prestige older buildings with high-quality tenants and at least 200,000 square feet of rentable floor area. Secondary space generally consists of older, less desirable buildings.

5. This is not a new phenomenon. See, for example, "Old Structures Get New Faces," *New York Times* (15 May 1983): 30.

6. For example, the two tallest 1920s towers downtown, 40 Wall Street and 70 Pine Street, have average floor plates of 14,500 and 15,000 square feet, respectively. Compare to buildings put up in the 1980s: The forty-seven-story 7 World Trade Center has floor plates of 47,000 to 49,000 square feet and the thirty-four- to fifty-one-story World Financial Center buildings have average floor plates of 50,000 square feet.

7. The Department of City Planning is in the process of reviewing the bonus provisions.

8. At the end of 1991, the Regional Plan Association estimated that Manhattan below Sixtieth Street had sixty million square feet of vacant office space (*New York Times* [7 November 1991]: sec. B, p. 1). Earlier in the year, the Edward S. Gordon Company counted 56.7 million square feet of available space (*New York Times* [28

July 1991]: sec. 10, p. 1). Downtown Dallas has approximately thirty million square feet of office space, and downtown Philadelphia has thirty-one million square feet (Manufacturers Hanover, *Real Estate Digest* [Summer 1989, Autumn 1990]).

9. Regarding the size and shape of buildings, the point is merely that building envelopes in satellite office districts should not necessarily be the same as in the central office districts because the surrounding urban context is much different and because back office operations have different spatial needs. Under the current zoning resolution, whether or not it is amended to impose stricter envelope controls, the central district and satellite district envelopes are likely to be the same. To distinguish them, and to design the look of each office district separately, would require a zoning ordinance more fine-grained, with an even greater variety of districts, than the existing resolution.

10. U.S. Census Bureau, *Census of Population, Census Tracts: New York, N.Y.–N.J. SMSA* (1960, 1980): Table P-10. It should be noted that the total number of employed New Yorkers declined by 3 percent during this period.

11. Samuel M. Ehrenhalt, "The Competitive Challenges: Signposts for the Future," unpublished paper.

12. *Labor Area Summary: Monthly Statistical Report* (Albany: New York State Department of Labor, September 1991).

13. *Tomorrow's Jobs Tomorrow's Workers 1991.*

14. In 1987, the New York Telephone Company tested sixty thousand applicants for jobs as operators and found that only three thousand had the requisite ability to file names in alphabetical order, read instructions, and do simple arithmetic (*New York Times* [26 June 1988]: p. 25).

15. New York City Zoning Resolution, Section 41–13. Industrial operations in M3 zones may emit more noise, vibration, smoke, dust, and odors than would be permitted in other industrial areas. The zone permits a list of uses forbidden in all other zones: foundries; breweries; glue, asphalt, brick, cement, chemical, fertilizer, glass, and machinery factories; incinerators; tanneries; slaughterhouses; grain processors; oil or sugar refineries; radioactive waste disposal services; repair yards or dry docks for ships more than two hundred feet long; marine transfer stations; power plants; and storage facilities for coal, gas, petroleum, grain, or explosives.

16. Abeles Schwartz Associates, *Regional Industry Market Study* (New York: New York City Public Development Corporation, 1988).

17. Abeles Phillips Preiss and Shapiro (in association with Louis Harris and Associates), *The State of Long Island City Industry* (New York: New York City Public Development Corporation, 1988).

18. This approach has been taken in Port Morris, East New York, and Bathgate.

19. Specifically, use groups 11 and 16.

20. *New York City Waterfront Comprehensive Plan: Summary of Major Goals and Elements* (New York: New York City Department of City Planning, 1991). The percentage may be somewhat misleading, however. If the waterfront were defined as extending inland to the first mapped street, considerable "waterfront" property would be available for development behind public beaches and boardwalks. An example is the three hundred-acre, mostly vacant Arverne Urban Renewal Area.

21. In 1989, the New York–New Jersey port handled $49 billion worth of cargo, according to the American Association of Port Authorities (see Manufacturers Hanover, *Real Estate Digest* [Summer 1990]: 13). It is the second busiest port in the United States, behind Los Angeles. In 1961, though, it was unchallenged as the world's busiest port, and a far larger percentage of the cargo was handled in New York City than New Jersey.

22. Nationally, 52 percent of mothers are working within a year after childbirth, according to the U.S. Census Bureau.

23. The Regional Plan Association has estimated that self-employment in New York City increased by 46 percent between 1977 and 1988 and that nationally it increased by 51 percent from 1978 to 1986, making it the country's second most vigorous growth industry in percentage terms. (See *The New Century 2* [New York: Regional Plan Association]: 4–7.) Self-employment in New York City accounted for 361,500 jobs in 1988, or 8.7 percent of the city's total jobs. It accounted for 15 percent of jobs located outside of Manhattan. The trend will almost certainly continue.

In this regard, it is worth noting the different ways in which the city's employment is measured. The U.S. Census Bureau's *County Business Patterns* measures an area's private jobs, excluding government workers and the self-employed. For New York City in 1988, the figure was 3.1 million. (The U.S. Census Bureau's decennial *Census of Population* counts the number of an area's residents who are in the work force and employed, including those who report being self-employed; this is not a measure of the number of jobs in the city since it does not address commutation into or out of the city.)

The New York State Department of Labor's statistical reports measure an area's total employment in nonagricultural establishments, including government jobs but excluding self-employment. For New York City in 1991, the figure is 3.5 million jobs, including 600,000 government jobs.

The state labor department and U.S. Census Bureau data provide sensitive barometers of economic contraction and expansion, but they underestimate the true amount of employment activity.

The Regional Plan Association uses the U.S. Commerce Department's Bureau of Economic Analysis data, which measure total employment, including self-employment. For New York City in 1986, the figure was 4.1 million, including approximately 360,000 self-employed.

The Port Authority of New York and New Jersey is somewhat inconsistent in this regard. Its publications generally rely on New York State Department of Labor data, but the agency also tracks self-employment, and its total employment figures are inclusive (for example, 4.2 million workers in New York City in 1987).

24. O'Neill and Moss, *Reinventing New York*, p. 41.

25. According to the U.S. Bureau of Labor Statistics, women accounted for 65.5 percent of all employment growth among New York City residents between 1979 and 1987. This statistic is even more striking in light of the fact that this was a period of strong (9 percent) job growth in New York City.

26. New York City has by far the greatest population density of any major American city. In 1980, it contained twenty-three thousand residents per square mile, compared with fifteen thousand per square mile in San Francisco, thirteen thousand per square mile in Chicago and Philadelphia, twelve thousand per square mile in Boston, six thousand per square mile in Los Angeles, and under three thousand residents per square mile in most other Sunbelt cities. See Kenneth Jackson, *Crabgrass Frontier: The Suburbanization of the United States* (New York: Oxford University Press, 1985), Table A-5.

In Manhattan, the density was sixty thousand people per square mile and that had increased to sixty-three thousand people per square mile by 1990. In Manhattan Community Districts 7 and 8, encompassing the Upper West and Upper East sides, the 1990 population densities were 100,000 and 105,000 residents per square mile, respectively (*Community District Needs: Fiscal Year 1991, Manhattan*, and *1990 Census: Population by Race and Hispanic Origin by Selected Ages and Total Hous-*

ing Units—New York City, Boroughs and Community Districts [New York: New York City Department of City Planning, 1991]).

27. Between 1980 and 1990, the city's population, as counted by the Census Bureau, increased by 250,925 residents, or 3.5 percent. The population of New York City's consolidated metropolitan statistical area (CMSA) grew by 547,719 residents, or 3 percent, to a total of 18,087,251. (It should be noted that the Bureau of Labor Statistics, the Regional Plan Association, and the Port Authority use definitions of the "region" that differ from the CMSA.)

Whereas the city's and Manhattan's residential populations grew by 3.5 percent and 4.0 percent, respectively, during the 1980s, the number of jobs in Manhattan increased by an estimated 10.0 percent during the decade (*New York Times* [3 March 1991]: 36). Between 1978 and 1988, Manhattan gained 196,000 private sector jobs, for an 11 percent increase (U.S. Census Bureau, *County Business Patterns* [1978, 1988]).

This indicates that the number of new jobs exceeded the increase in employed New York City residents, meaning the number of commuters into Manhattan increased. This is corroborated by the New York City Department of Transportation, which has been reporting increases in the average daily number of river crossings into Manhattan (Ross Sandler, *An Approach to Reducing Vehicle Congestion in New York City: A Report to Mayor Edward I. Koch* [report issued 10 September 1986]).

Long-term continued population and employment growth is expected. In 1989, the Regional Plan Association projected that between 1987 and 2005, New York City will have gained 423,000 residents, the region will have gained 1,870,000 residents, and Manhattan will have gained 278,000 jobs (Regional Plan Association, *The New Century* [April 1989]).

An estimated twenty-five million tourists visit New York City annually (*New York Times* [5 June 1991]: B2). The number of tourists increased most years throughout the 1980s then declined as the country entered a recession, but foreign tourism continued to rise; the number of international arrivals at LaGuardia, Kennedy, and Newark (New Jersey) airports increased by 5 percent from 1988 to 1990 (ibid.).

28. For example, no EIS was prepared when the city established the Bathgate Industrial Park in what had been a residentially zoned portion of the South Bronx.

29. The zoning resolution consisted of several sections: other brief general provisions, use and bulk provisions applicable to residential districts, use and bulk provisions applicable to commercial districts, use and bulk provisions applicable to manufacturing districts, provisions applicable to existing uses and buildings that became nonconforming or noncomplying under the newly adopted 1961 resolution, and, finally, an administration section that contained variance and special permit provisions as well as a discussion of how the zoning resolution would be enforced and amended.

30. Based on a preliminary analysis prepared by the Department of City Planning, partially updating a 1990–91 survey by the American Planning Association.

ZONING FOR GROWTH AND CHANGE

PETER D. SALINS

This is a challenging opportunity to step back for a moment and take a hard, reflective look at one of New York City's great planning innovations, the local zoning ordinance. We need to step back and reflect because it is increasingly apparent that planners, public officials, and citizens have lost sight of the proper function of zoning. We no longer appreciate what zoning and development regulation in general can and cannot or should and should not try to do.

New York City has adopted a comprehensive zoning resolution only twice in its history, in 1916 and 1961, so 1991 was a special anniversary of both those occasions. Both times the city zoned in response to a discrete set of contemporary concerns and looked to zoning to shape and guide development according to a few simple concepts. Then, in the decades following each zoning event, New York City's citizens and planners increasingly lost their way as they tried to stretch, bend, and massage the zoning resolution to address dozens—perhaps hundreds—of second thoughts, unique situations, and new concerns, concerns that zoning cannot ultimately satisfy. This postresolution tinkering is not proof, as some have alleged, that the resolutions were out-of-date the day they were passed. Rather, it is proof that we expect far too much from our zoning and other development regulations.

Is the 1961 zoning ordinance, encrusted with thirty years and six hundred pages of amendment and interpretative barnacles, broke—as in, "If it ain't broke, don't fix it"? I think it is. It is, that is, if the objective of a good zoning ordinance is to promote the healthy growth and renewal of a municipality's physical stock and the continual redevelopment of its homes and offices, its stores and factories—the vital structural envelope where all its economic, social, and personal activities take place.

As in so many other instances of New York City–style regulation, its zoning ordinance does both too much and too little. On the one hand, the ordinance is a document of staggering complexity. It requires lawyers and expediters to understand and interpret, imposes great burdens on the city's planning and building department staffs, and places costly obstacles of time and expense in the way of all but the most routine residential development. On the other hand, the increments of development that eventually emerge from this regulatory monster are widely despised on all sides; by local communities, by the arbiters of environmentally correct development, and by the architects and planners—despite the resolution's detail, attempts at fine-tuning, layers of discretionary review, and community and watchdog group involvement.

We normally accept the notion that regulation of any sort involves a trade-off, call it trading efficiency for quality. The city of New York's current zoning regime is hugely inefficient—it violates the natural order of the city's land market, distorting its property values and indiscriminately redistributing property rights; and it does all this without making New York City a noticeably better planned, happier, or more beautiful place.

Furthermore, with New York City's economy battered by a recession and facing the prospect of permanent long-term decline, the city should have a strong incentive to promote development. Even if economic exigency were not enough of a motive to streamline its system of development regulation, New York City should want to renew its physical stock, particularly its housing, just to improve its citizens' quality of life.

HOW HAS NEW YORK CITY'S ZONING GONE ASTRAY?

Three impulses have shaped the present zoning ordinance and are responsible for much of its wayward, if unintended, infelicity.

One has been the attempt, especially in the post-1961 modifications of the ordinance, to anticipate every possible contingency of development—a quest for ever more detailed fine-tuning. The 1961 ordinance introduced the idea of alternative zoning options. Then, to accommodate a variety of unique local conditions and unforeseen development depredations, a growing set of special districts was created. Unhappy with the visual consequences of the original development options, complex contextual rules and incentives were added, and, to accommodate the ever-expanding development possibilities, the original zoning districts were subdivided or supplemented. That is how the 1961 zoning document has grown in length from 261 to 835 pages. Certainly in a city of 7.5 million people, more than one hundred square miles of land area, 3.5 million jobs, hundreds of distinctive neighborhoods, and the world's largest central business district, there is a strong temptation to tailor-make development regulation, but in the end, it cannot be done. The temptation should be resisted.

A second impulse, an outgrowth of the first, has been to move New York City development increasingly away from uniform, as-of-right possibilities to a regime of discretionary review. Site-specific regulations are triggered either by offering developers the prospect of economically beneficial development options as an alternative to as-of-right, by special permits and redistricting as standard practice, or, as in the city's thirty-seven special districts, by some quotient of interpretive, ministerial review. In other words, even as the ordinance has grown more complex in its reach for custom-tailoring, it can never quite custom-tailor enough, so it must resort to discretionary devices.

Discretion exercised by the planning process itself might be tolerable, although in a vast city with a relatively small cadre of planning staff, it inevitably leads to clogged review pipelines and careless decisions under the best of circumstances. What has made the growing discretionary zoning elements so intolerable has been their role in triggering two additional levels of review: the ULURP (Unified Land Use Review Procedure) process and the environmental impact statement (under provisions of city and state environmental laws). These two procedures are linked in a costly and time-consuming negative synergism whereby the ULURP clock cannot begin ticking until there is certification that the environmental assessment is complete. Environmental assessments hold up the ULURP process.

Moreover, all elements of the process generate pitfalls along the way. There are challenges to the environmental impact assessment. There are local or interest group challenges during ULURP, and political sensitivity will color the ultimate disposition of any proposal by the planners, the mayor, and the city council. Even if, as defenders of the current process allege, most development does in fact go forward as-of-right, all the larger and more economically vital development projects cannot escape running this gauntlet, and countless other projects never even see the light of day because they cannot afford its financial or physical costs.

The third impulse burdening New York City's zoning system today, again an outgrowth of the other two, is the overwhelming temptation—indeed, mandate—to use the process (or processes) to negotiate (some would call it blackmail) developers to trade approvals for one or another public benefit. Some of these trades are built into the ordinance in a perverse form of the as-of-right concept: extra or "bonus" floor area ratio (FAR) in exchange for plazas or low-income housing or a relaxation of bulk restrictions in exchange for "housing quality" features; but a growing number of negotiations have not been as-of-right, involving swaps of unique zoning concessions for idiosyncratic public benefits recorded in deeds as restrictive declarations.

"Zoning for sale" is a bad idea, however inviting the opportunity and whatever the ostensible short-term aesthetic or functional benefits. It is *unfair* because it is a game that only a handful of well-funded developers, flanked by costly lobbyists, lawyers, and expediters, can play. It is *inefficient* because there is no adequate economic test of the costs or benefits of the trade-offs and because it capitalizes the negotiation potential in arbitrage and speculation, distorting the price of land. Finally, it is *cynical* because it announces that many of the supposedly critical objective parameters of zoning regulation are not so important after all. They can be waived for a price.

BASIC PRINCIPLES

It is clear from all the various critiques of the present regulatory system that further fine-tuning of zoning will not do the job. Therefore, I am prepared to suggest a framework for starting over. Starting over does not merely mean writing a new zoning resolution. It must mean basing that resolution firmly on three simple—perhaps overly simplistic—principles.

First, *trust the market*. We need not fear less regulated market outcomes as much as we often do because the well-understood laws of regional and land economics actually do create quite wholesome, economically beneficial, consumer-responsive, and even attractive and orderly development patterns. The canyons of lower New York City, Manhattan's legendary skyline, the charming brownstone neighborhoods of Brooklyn—as well as such humbler but quite pleasant environments as the tidy working-class neighborhoods of Queens and the middle-class apartment precincts of the Bronx—are natural products of the market only modestly shaped by zoning.

Second, *if we must regulate, keep it simple*. The simpler the regulatory framework, the more predictable are its effects. The more accurately it can be directed to the city's primary development objectives, the less likely it is to distort land values and property rights.

Finally, *once we regulate, leave the system alone*. If the new regulations are sufficiently open-ended and flexible, we can live, this time, with a zoning resolution virtually unamended until it is replaced by a successor a half-century hence.

Going beyond these basic principles, my ideal view of development regulations is predicated on just two operational principles that have resided in the conception of zoning from the outset.

The most fundamental of these principles, addressing its constitutional foundation, justifies zoning as an exercise of the police power to prevent development from imposing *specific harms* (negative externalities, economists call them) rather than as a means to force development to create *specific benefits*. The only reason to interfere in the market is because it operates through trial and error, because market imperatives change, and, above all, because the products of development are so durable.

This may seem to be a mere definitional quibble, but its significance is quite profound. The potential development harms that prompted the introduction of zoning were discrete, easy to identify, obviously deplorable, and thus easy to regulate. The benefits sought by modern zoning, especially New York City's, the nation's most comprehensive and complex, are difficult to define, highly subjective, of questionable value, and thus almost impossible to achieve through regulation.

While planners have long believed that zoning was their God-given and court-sanctioned device for implementing a "comprehensive plan" and pursuing other planning objectives of the moment, zoning was really introduced by lawyers, residential communities, and businessmen, essentially, to prevent just three kinds of harms: excessive density, the juxtaposition of incompatible activities (especially factories near homes), and the most blatant of visual offenses. I propose we go back to the principle that zoning is a harm-preventing, rather than benefit-creating, enterprise and that we concentrate on limiting these three traditional kinds of harms.

Applying this principle means no longer trying to use zoning for promoting ever-changing urban design fashions, securing public amenities, or extracting subsidies for housing or other socially beneficial goods. It also means, for example, that we should not tolerate the involuntary preservation of landmarks, especially at the scale of landmark districts.

Why must this principle be observed? First, and pragmatically speaking, because the law of unintended consequences has caused New Yorkers to regret the outcome that past violations of the principle have produced. The plazas, arcades, and other physical improvements secured by zoning have been visually and functionally disappointing. The housing and other social welfare benefits have proven to be economically infeasible, too, and doomed the projects that depended on them.

The more serious reason for observing this principle, however, is that otherwise development regulation functions as a hidden and insidious tax on development and the land. The benefits sought are not free. They inhibit development and make the occupancy of space more expensive, and unlike a system of open taxation, their incidence and distributive effects are neither readily apparent nor publicly debated.

The second principle, addressing the issue of process, is that zoning should be predictable and certain. This principle—that zoning rules should apply with absolute consistency to all development within identical zoning districts and entirely in terms of precise prescriptive or proscriptive parameters—has governed zoning practice for most of its history. This principle was embodied in the Euclid, Ohio, law that provoked the landmark 1926 Supreme Court test of zoning, *Euclid v. Ambler Reality Co.* (27 U.S. 365 [1926]) and since then in countless model zoning ordinances.

Under such a format, anyone reading the ordinance knows exactly what can and cannot be built on every site in the municipality; in other words, what can be built as-of-right. Such a principle, by eliminating any role for discretionary review, except in the case of appeals, devolves the approval process, essentially, to clerks in the building department who ensure that applicants comply with the rules. Buried deep inside New York City's current zoning behemoth there resides, even today, the vestige of an as-of-right soul crying to be heard. We should return to a regime in which virtually all development, except on city-owned or waterfront property, can take place as-of-right with no discretionary review, returning the approval process to the clerks.

Applying this principle to New York City's development regulation regime means no more special districts, no more site-specific amendments, no more discretionary reviews, and no more site-specific bargaining. It also means no more use of environmental impact assessment as an indirect form of land use regulation. It also means no more ULURP. In fact, the most distressing aspect of the city's discretionary zoning procedures is its role in triggering mandatory environmental impact assessment and ULURP procedures.

Given the long, incremental battle that planners and community planning advocates in New York City and elsewhere have waged over the years to win more discretionary powers, they can be expected to reject this principle bitterly. They will argue, as Brian Kintish and John Shapiro imply in their paper in this book, "The Zoning of Today in the City of Tomorrow," that the growing complexity of New York City requires, if anything, a more complex and discretionary zoning regime; or, in the words of Michael Kwartler in his paper in this book, "Planning and Zoning for a Mature City," they will reject the notion of "one size fits all" zoning.

My response to such arguments is that we cannot custom-tailor development regulation precisely because the city is so large and complex. All we do when we violate this principle is distort the price of land and favor development by those developers rich enough, well-connected enough, or clever enough to play the discretionary game.

These principles are essential to allow zoning to meet two fundamental tests of viable land use regulation.

First, zoning must continually accommodate the market, at least in general terms. While not bending to every market force, the classical zoning ordinance recognized the hierarchy of density that characterizes all metropolitan areas and the need to accommodate every kind of economic and residential activity. In other words, zoning was meant, by and large, to support, not thwart, the realization of most sites' "highest and best use." For many planners and civic planning advocates, as well as many local communities, "highest and best use" are fighting words today. Nevertheless, I suggest, without blindly accepting every development proposal as an embodiment of market wisdom, that we design a zoning ordinance that displays a healthy respect for the natural economic development of the city.

This might seem a gratuitous principle to invoke at a time when the city is accused of bending too much to market forces, but would that it were so. There is no question that when market forces were very powerful, as in Midtown Manhattan during the 1980s, they were able to overcome regulatory obstacles—at a price—but elsewhere in the city, particularly in the outer boroughs, zoning has thwarted the market in a number of significant ways. The zoning map has many outmoded district boundaries and designations. Many districts, especially commercial ones, have unrealistic density ceilings. Many industrial areas are no longer suitable for industry. Many residential areas artificially restrict dwelling types. This is aside from the major market-thwarting effects of landmark districting and environmental impact assessment.

The second test, based on nothing more than common sense, has demanded that zoning be flexible enough to accommodate all the unknown and unknowable increments of future development. Zoning must be flexible because planners and other public officials have not been, and cannot be expected to be, accurate in their assessment of future development trends; nor can they correctly foresee changes in the infrastructure and the general culture.

At the same time, the principles of development regulation set forth earlier preclude tinkering and discretionary procedures and strongly argue against frequent changes in the zoning map or in zoning rules. What to do?

The traditional approach to securing flexibility, increasingly abandoned by New York City, has been to rank zones in a hierarchy of nuisance and density, with single-family homes on large lots at the top and large factories and other noxious uses at the bottom, with the rule that you could always place a higher rank activity in a lower rank zone. This feature, coupled with a tendency by municipalities to overzone for lower rank districts, has ensured that zoning in most cities is flexible enough to accommodate an open-ended quantity and variety of new development.

New York City's present ordinance, by and large, follows this principle, but with several glaring exceptions. The most critical is the prohibition of all residential and much commercial activity in manufacturing zones. This might make some sense until we recognize that many of the city's manufacturing zones dominate areas ripe for residential or proscribed commercial development.

To give the city's future development maximum flexibility, New York

City's zoning ordinance should return fully to the hierarchical format. High-density commercial and residential activity could immediately move into Manhattan's exclusive manufacturing zones, such as the garment district. In the outer boroughs, much vacant manufacturing land could be developed residentially. Such a rule in New York City would also preclude the existing practice of setting lower density ceilings in lower order districts than in higher ones.

The application of the hierarchical rule to New York City's zoning might create some messy short-term juxtapositions of activity or it might threaten some established manufacturing districts, especially those already in a state of terminal decline, but these effects, even if they materialize, are a small price to pay to achieve a zoning framework that can accommodate about any volume or character of future development and rebuilding.

THE BUILDING BLOCKS OF THE PROPOSED ZONING ORDINANCE

A new zoning ordinance to promote growth and change should reflect and embody the principles set forth above. While the new rules should be kept simple, they must prevent the most likely and egregious harms of unregulated development, apply uniformly and consistently as-of-right, accommodate New York City's natural economic and spatial order, and be inherently flexible. In many ways, this proposal will look quite familiar, restoring many elements and concepts from the city's original 1916 zoning ordinance, a far more suitable framework for New York City than its successor.

The basic building blocks of any zoning scheme are the zoning district categories, the development variables that are regulated within each district category, and the parameters of these variables. Clearly, the fewer the districts and the variables, the more accommodating and development-friendly the ordinance. Without enumerating the myriad exceptions and details that encumber the present zoning, it consists of 125 regular district categories, thirty-seven special districts, twenty or so regulatory variables, and dozens of formulas and calculations to determine how the rules apply to specific structures and sites. This is the as-of-right part of the ordinance, before getting into the twilight zone of negotiation and discretion.

What I propose in its place is a system of eighteen district categories, no special districts, about twelve regulatory variables, a few simple calculations, and no exceptions other than administrative (Board of Standards and Appeals) or judicial appeals. My proposal is, at this stage, merely schematic and illustrative. I have not visited, and cannot envision, all the actual and potential configurations that can or do arise in New York City's developed landscape. This zoning scheme attempts to imagine and anticipate a wide variety of the city's present and future residential, commercial, civic, and industrial settings. It attempts to be stringent enough to prevent most development outrages while being flexible and user-friendly enough to accommodate and encourage most needed and desired construction. Undoubtedly, any serious attempt to implement such a scheme will contain somewhat more detail, but even a doubling of my building blocks would still represent a quantum leap toward a simpler and more wholesome zoning future.

RESIDENCE DISTRICTS

Most of New York City's land area, exclusive of roads, other aboveground infrastructure, and open space, would continue to be zoned residential. The objectives of zoning for residential neighborhoods would be to limit their population density and, as unintrusively as possible, to regulate their appearance, primarily to promote construction at a suitable human scale. In the new zoning plan, there would be ten residence districts, running from R1 to R10, with uniform standards and restrictions applying to each district. The present system also runs, ostensibly, from R1 to R10 but, because of numerous interpolations, variations, and subdistricts, actually consists of thirty-one discrete districts, with many superimposed overlay options permitting dozens of unique development configurations.

The proposed schedule of residential districts is based on a hierarchy of density, density being measured by only one standard: lot area per dwelling unit. Within this density hierarchy there would be three kinds of residential districts. R1 through R5 districts would permit only low-rise structures (such as single-family, semiattached, row house, or two- and three-story apartment buildings). R6 through R8 and R10 districts would allow mid- to high-rise apartment towers. R9 would be designed for the kind of high-density town house districts found in Manhattan and brownstone Brooklyn.

Only five regulatory variables would apply in the new residential districts. In addition to density (measured as lot area per dwelling unit), dwelling size and building setbacks would be regulated in R1 through R5 districts, building height would be directly or implicitly restricted in all districts, and off-street parking would be required in R1 through R7 districts.

Height would be restricted in two ways. In low-rise districts (R1 to R5), there would be a fixed height limit, probably twenty-five to thirty-five feet. In all other residential districts, height would be limited implicitly by a permissible building envelope. At the street property line, the constraint would be a vertical plane whose height could not exceed the width of the mapped street. From the top of this plane would spring that venerable New York City zoning device, the sky exposure plane (SEP). In residential districts, the SEP would rise from the top of the street wall at a three to one vertical angle. This rudimentary scheme should adequately regulate the two most serious concerns of most residential neighborhoods: excessive density and anticontextual building heights and setbacks.

In order to create further flexibility and permit new residential development as market conditions and locational characteristics change, developers would be permitted to build, as-of-right, under the parameters of the next less restrictive district category by purchasing surplus density from underdeveloped sites *in the same block*.

For example, assume R3 districts would require 2,400 square feet of lot area per dwelling unit. Suppose a developer owned an 8,500-square-foot parcel in an R3 district, which would otherwise permit three dwellings. Adjacent to this property are two houses, each on a three thousand-square-foot lot. By purchasing six hundred square feet of excess lot area from each of his neighbors (recorded as a permanent restrictive covenant), the developer can "enlarge" his site to 9,700 square feet, allowing him to put up a fourth dwelling.

Note that the parameters of the residence districts would be completely silent as to the type of dwelling unit that could be built. As long as the density, height, and setback limitations were met, this scheme would be indifferent as to whether the homes are single or multifamily, detached or not, houses or apartments. The important variables are density and scale,

TABLE 1
New Residential Districts

District	Density Lot Area per Dwelling Unit	Maximum Height[1] (feet)	Setbacks		
			Street	Side	Rear
R1	7200	25	20	20	30
R2	3600	25	20	15	20
R3	2400	25	10	10	20
R4	1600	35	10	—	30
R5	1200	35	10	—	30
R6	800	65	—	—	60
R7	400	100	—	—	40
R8	225	150	—	—	—
R9	150	65+SEP[2]	—	—	20
R10	75	200+SEP[2]	—	—	—

[1] The height of pitched roofs, gables, and so on, is divided in two when calculating the total vertical height.

[2] The slope of the sky exposure plane is three to one.

not dwelling type. If this was good enough for such New York City area development gems as Forest Hills Gardens, Radburn, and Garden City, not to mention the new towns of Europe and the United States, it should be good enough for the New York City of today.

Incidentally, these rules would also easily permit some popular residential adaptations that usually occur by breaking the law. As long as the lot area were sufficient, or could be enlarged with a neighbor's surplus, underoccupied older homes could be converted to higher densities and an honest house would be made of the notorious "illegal three."

HIGHER DENSITY CORRIDORS IN RESIDENTIAL AREAS

As a quick tour through any residential area in the city reveals, New York City's neighborhoods are laced with commercial activity, and even the lowest density areas have apartment houses nearby. While reflecting market forces, this arrangement has been legitimated by commercial and high-density residential strip zoning along major arterials, as well as spot zoning, variances, and grandfathered nonconforming uses.

The proposed zoning ordinance will continue this general pattern, but in a more systematic and simple way. Following the rule that district boundaries are never to be drawn down the middle of streets, all arterials running through residential areas, including the major thoroughfares of Manhattan, can be classified as "higher density corridors," in which compatible higher density residential structures are permitted. Higher density residential structures must conform to the standards of districts two notches below those of adjacent primary residential districts, and commercial structures or spaces within larger buildings are limited to two stories and must conform to the facade restrictions of the lower density commercial zones.

COMMERCIAL DISTRICTS

The present zoning ordinance lavishes more attention on commercial development than on any other category. There are seventy-eight separate district categories. The regulated variables are few but onerous, involving exquisite gradations of density, as measured by FAR, varied parking requirements, and complicated rules and formulas for establishing structures' bulk. Furthermore, since commercial development is most likely to be caught in the web of discretionary review, it is also most subject to site-specific design and functional tailoring and most apt to be involved in negotiated trades of zoning concessions for public benefits of one kind or another. What generates most of the commercial zoning overkill are three planners' concepts:

the belief that the hundreds of actual and potential commercial activities need to be sorted in schedules of permitted use groups, the preoccupation with fine-grain density variations, and the desire for proactive planning participation in urban design.

Most of the really bitter zoning and land use battles in New York City have been waged over commercial development, especially high-density projects in Manhattan. Few office towers have been built in the last fifteen years without obtaining special permits or zoning amendments and without generating a great deal of haggling and delay as they moved through the approval process. Yet for all the city's intrusiveness and exercise of discretion in the commercial development process, many New Yorkers are sharply critical of the size and design of the most recent crop of skyscrapers.

In sharp distinction to current zoning practice, my zoning proposal would radically simplify commercial zoning, concentrating on a few critical issues. The purpose of commercial zoning would be to regulate the appearance of commercial buildings, to keep them in scale with each other and nearby residential buildings, and to regulate their activities and density of occupancy without unduly thwarting the operation of market forces.

The allowable building envelope would be the primary regulatory tool for two reasons. The appearance and size of commercial structures are their most prominent and publicly sensitive aspects, and for commercial structures "function follows form." That is, most commercial functions can operate only in the right kind of structural envelopes. Thus, by regulating some important characteristics of commercial structures, you can efficiently achieve the two key objectives of harm-preventing commercial zoning: generating visually benign structures and naturally sorting commercial uses in a nuisance-based hierarchy.

I propose the creation of four commercial districts, C1 through C4, graded by the scale and visual prominence of permitted structures, with the following features. The only uses prohibited in any commercial zone, other than by the natural operation of structural constraints, would be amusement parks, marine activities, and manufacturing. There would be six regulatory variables: height restrictions, setback restrictions, lot coverage ratios, facade restrictions, parking requirements, and requirements for visual buffers between commercial properties and residential zones. Within each commercial district, the parameters of the variables would be identical.

The kind of convenience retail stores and professional offices found in most residential areas would be accommodated in C1 districts or by C1 standards in higher density residential corridors. C2 districts would permit somewhat more intensive retail and office clusters. C3 districts would accommodate the major commercial subcenters of the outer boroughs and the less intensive commercial areas of Manhattan. C4 districts would be reserved for Midtown and lower Manhattan. Intensive automobile-related

TABLE 2
New Nonresidential Districts

| District | Maximum Height | Parking Spaces[1] | Street Facade Elements ||| Buffers ||
			Unfenestrated Walls	Sign Restrictions	Auto Access	Visual	Noise
RC	[2]	1	No	Yes	No	Yes	—
C1	35	1	No	Yes	No	Yes	—
C2	SW + SEP A[3]	1	—	—	Side	Yes	—
C3	2SW + SEP B	—	—	—	Side	Yes	—
LX1	20	—	—	—	—	Yes	Yes
LX2	30	—	—	—	—	Yes	—
LX3	—	—	—	—	—	Yes	—

[1] Spaces per one thousand square feet of built space.

[2] See residential district regulations.

[3] SW = street width; SEP A = sky exposure plane with a slope of three to one; and SEP B = sky exposure plane with a slope of four to one.

uses would be effectively barred from all commercial zones but would be welcome elsewhere.

In C1 and C2 districts, the height of the commercial portion of structures would be restricted by fixed building height limitations (fifteen or twenty-five feet). In C3 and C4 districts, height would be constrained somewhat by the street wall/SEP envelope, as in the higher density residential zones, except with different parameters. The street wall would be limited to twice the mapped street width, and the SEP would have a four to one vertical slope. Structures in C1 through C3 districts also would be subject to minimum setback requirements from adjacent residential structures.

Buildings in C1 through C3 districts would be subject to lot coverage ratio ceilings. Unforeseen changes in market or location conditions and the underutilization of some sites in commercial districts would be accommodated by permitting developers to purchase surplus lot coverage from other lots *in the same block.*

Note the disappearance of FAR as a regulatory device. Intrinsically, FAR is an attractive and simple concept for controlling density. Nevertheless, there are two good reasons to scrap it. In most commercial areas, including Manhattan's central business areas, most people are more concerned with the height and shape of structures than they are with their nominal density. Second, FAR has become the basis for much of the negotiating and discretionary activity that has bedeviled the city's zoning process. In my proposed ordinance, the primary tool of density control would no longer be FAR; density constraints would be imposed by the structural envelope, supplemented by lot coverage ratios for low-rise structures in C1 through C3 districts.

Facade restrictions would be designed to regulate scale, with rules aimed especially at making the scale of commercial structures conform to nearby residential buildings. These restrictions, most stringent in C1 and C2 districts, would determine whether facades may or may not be windowless, whether garage doors or loading docks are permitted, and the maximum width of storefronts and commercial bays.

Off-street parking standards would be set for C1 through C3 districts. All properties in C1 through C3 districts also would require visual buffers at the edge of residence districts.

This limited set of building blocks for commercial district zoning should be sufficient to finely modulate the density, scale, and character of commercial areas, meeting contextual objectives for adjoining residential areas while keeping the volume of activity and the appearance of structures within reasonable bounds in the core and the major subcenters.

LESS RESTRICTIVE DISTRICTS

There are a great many activities, essential elements of the metropolitan economic repertoire, that generate significant unwelcome visual, functional, or other impacts. Right now, New York City's zoning relegates them to one of its twelve manufacturing districts and the high-nuisance end of the commercial district hierarchy.

The primary purpose in zoning potentially noxious activities is to keep them away from as many other activities and people as possible and to minimize their negative spillovers. As in the format for commercial districts, I propose that we give up trying to preclassify activities as noxious. Instead, we should segregate them from residential and commercial areas by confining their structures to certain districts and by imposing a few other restrictions related specifically to their most egregious impacts. In my zoning scheme, such activities would be accommodated in one of three less restrictive districts, LX1 through LX3. These districts would be the areas in which all manufacturing uses, as well as other nonresidential activities whose structure requirements do not conform to commercial district standards, could locate.

The regulatory variables in LX districts would address the major negative impacts of activities at the low end of the traditional nuisance hierarchy. These variables would include restrictions on lot coverage, building height, vehicular traffic, and noise and odor impacts and would include requirements for visual buffering from adjacent districts. Restrictions in LX2 districts would be considerably more liberal than those in LX1 districts.

LX1 districts would accommodate many of the kinds of activities now permitted in the less restrictive commercial districts—ones that are truck and automobile related, ones that require space for loading or storage of merchandise and food, and ones whose structures, while homely, are visually less obtrusive. LX2 districts would be designed for activities that require larger structures and generate moderate levels of noise or odor. LX3 districts would be unrestricted zones in which virtually any legal activity would be permitted. New activities in LX3 districts would be the ones most apt to generate problematical environmental impacts and thus would be subject to the restrictions of city and state environmental reviews.

COMMUNITY FACILITIES

Community facilities have traditionally posed problems for most zoning ordinances. Both court decisions and custom have decreed that elementary and secondary schools and houses of worship must be welcome virtually everywhere. Public facilities, such as libraries, museums, police stations, fire stations, public universities, and public hospitals, can generally be located at the pleasure of the relevant public agency, subject primarily to community reaction expressed through the political process. Only nonreligious and private community facilities can be strictly regulated by zoning.

The present New York City zoning ordinance regulates community facilities by making a distinction between those that might be welcome in residential areas and those that are not, with the latter set requiring special permits from either the planning department or the Board of Standards and Appeals.

Since most community facilities pose few problems, apart from the size of their structures, the proposed ordinance would permit all community facilities to locate in any district in which the structural envelope constraints permit. This rule, of course, would relegate most community facilities to commercial or higher density residential districts. Public schools and houses of worship could continue, as is customary, to locate anywhere.

LANDMARK DESIGNATION AND ENVIRONMENTAL IMPACT ASSESSMENTS

Zoning should not be inconsistent with other regulatory rubrics. Therefore, I have suggested that we contemplate two modest changes in New York

City's present regulatory landscape: doing away with mandatory landmark designations of private structures and districts and eliminating the environmental impact assessment of proposed structures.

Landmark designation confers a valuable public benefit by preserving structures and collections of structures of distinctive architectural and historical character, but while such a designation confers a *benefit* on the public, it does not prevent a harm, in that the public is not constitutionally *entitled* to view and use distinctive structures or spaces when their owners wish to tear them down or modify them. We should, by all means, maintain the landmark designation process, just as we maintain the National Register of Historic Places, but the preservation and maintenance of designated sites should be voluntary for their owners unless the owner is a public agency. If the city or nonprofit groups wish to preserve a threatened structure, they should pay for the privilege.

Mandatory landmark designation must be eliminated because, under the present regulatory system, especially as it pertains to the growing number of landmark districts, the landmarks law often prohibits what zoning might permit, thwarting a great deal of desirable development, particularly in New York City's prime development areas. Furthermore, even where landmarking does not actually prohibit development, the landmark designation overlay triggers further discretionary review, forcing projects through a costly, time-consuming, and often unsuccessful obstacle course.

An overlay to zoning even more intolerable than landmark designation is the environmental assessment process. The overdefinition of environmental impacts, and the provision that all discretionary zoning actions trigger environmental impact assessments as a prelude to the ULURP process, more than anything else has made the development regulation process as nasty and costly as it is.

The definition of environmentally sensitive actions and activities has, by now, been broadened far beyond the traditional and legitimate concerns about the degradation of air, water, or earth so that any intrusion on the municipal status quo is labeled an environmental impact. It is precisely these extraenvironmental, status quo–disturbing impacts—traffic, density increments, aesthetics, and shadow casting—that zoning is meant to regulate. To label these things environmental impacts and subject them to the contentious, and highly imprecise, realm of environmental impact assessment robs zoning of a great part of its rationale while doing nothing to actually improve the environment.

True environmental impacts can and should be mitigated at their source. We know how to generate cleaner auto or smokestack emissions and sewerage discharges and how to properly dispose of solid waste. The extraenvironmental urban impacts cannot be mitigated at the source because they are primarily the result of the city's aggregate demographic and economic profile. All we can do about them is to shrink the demographic or economic universe, clearly something no responsible New Yorker would advocate, or shuffle these "impacts" from one part of the city to another.

There are two ways to make the process more benign, both of which I advocate. First, as outlined earlier, design a zoning law that reduces the scope of discretionary review. The other, more radical, proposal is to eliminate environmental impact assessment altogether with respect to the development or modification of *structures*. Legitimate environmental impacts are generated by *activities,* not buildings. The environmental assessment process in New York City should thus be returned to evaluating the specific activities, many of them public, incidentally, that contribute to measurable environmental degradation.

MAKING THE CHANGE

It took twenty years to develop and obtain approval for New York City's 1916 zoning ordinance and ten years before the current (1961) one was adopted. The sheer physical extent of New York City, and the hundreds, even thousands, of interested parties, makes the prospect of drafting a new zoning scheme a daunting, if not hopeless, undertaking. Furthermore, my suggestions for eviscerating landmark and environmental rubrics would not make the task any easier. Nevertheless, there are some procedural ideas that might expedite the design and implementation of a new zoning plan, even if the plan does not turn out to be as ambitious as what I have envisioned.

To begin with, one must separate the notion of crafting the zoning building blocks from the issues of district mapping. I suspect that developing the architecture of the ordinance will be a lot less contentious than deciding the zoning fate of particular areas of the city. Thus, I suggest a thorough and meticulous effort, originating in the New York City Department of City Planning, with both central and borough offices working in consultation with the borough presidents and professional and civic organizations, to establish the basic zoning concepts, rules, and parameters. Once this tool kit of regulatory devices (hopefully a more detailed and thoughtful version of the ideas set forth in this paper) were accepted by all concerned parties and the political process, it would definitely determine the nature of zoning districts and the development variables they could regulate. Naturally, some elements of the scheme would be subject to modification and refinement, as the district mapping efforts reveal regulatory lacunae to be remedied.

The heroic, and much more disputatious, effort will be the mapping itself—the superimposition of district designations on the city's complex and varied physical landscape. This exercise should be, as it was not in 1916 or in 1961, highly decentralized, with the greatest possible degree of citizen participation. This phase should devolve primary responsibility for district mapping to the boroughs, specifically the offices of the borough presidents working responsively with their community boards and cooperatively with the borough offices of the planning department. Not only should community districts have a strong voice in the process, if not an outright veto, but zoning district boundaries must be coterminous with those of community districts. If this occasionally violates my rule that zoning district boundaries should never run down the center of streets, community district lines might be redrawn or my rule superseded.

I foresee two problems with delegating districting decisions to the boroughs and the community boards. One is that much of Manhattan, the central business areas, plus the most prominent and symbolically important parts of the city—the visitors' New York City, if you will—belong to the entire city. Its fate should not be decided by Manhattan residents alone. Thus, to assure that this New York City core, defined as Manhattan below Ninety-sixth Street minus the Lower East Side, is zoned with citywide interests in mind, its district mapping should be turned over to a citywide panel with representatives from all boroughs.

The other problem that will arise is that many local communities in the city reflexively oppose development and will either sabotage the liberal provisions of the zoning tool kit or attempt to vitiate them by mapping too restrictively. To overcome this tendency, borough and community district residents must be given an incentive to welcome new development. What better way than to turn over a large share of the property tax base to the boroughs to pay for the delivery of their basic municipal services? To devolve this incentive further to the grass roots, the boroughs could turn over half of all property tax revenue generated by new development to the community districts to be used solely to supplement or enrich their own service delivery. Thus, we could simulate some of the trade-offs and dynamics that animate zoning decisions in the suburbs: the impulse to curtail development being offset by the desire to expand the local tax base.

CONCLUSION

New York City needs a new zoning ordinance, indeed, an entire new development regulatory framework, to promote its economic growth and enhance its citizens' quality of life. Neither of these can occur without the continuous renewal of the city's physical stock, and the physical stock cannot be sufficiently added to or rebuilt under the sclerotic rules and capricious procedures of today's combined zoning, ULURP, and landmark and environmental regulations.

ZONING FOR GROWTH AND CHANGE

The ideas set forth in this paper on how to revise New York City's zoning while trimming back the conflicting regulatory overlays of landmark designation and environmental impact assessment are at the same time highly conventional and impetuously radical. They are conventional in the literal meaning of the word because they would anchor development regulation in the time-tested conventions of traditional zoning, as implemented in U.S. cities and suburbs, even in New York City at one time, since early in this century. These conventions are far from ideal in their arbitrary distinctions and their distortions of free market development trends, but intelligently deployed, they would protect the public, especially residential neighborhoods, from the most unacceptable development impacts while permitting the market to decide the location and shape of physical development.

The ideas are radical, on the other hand, because they would move New York City's development regulation regime far from where it has drifted, one restrictive step at a time, in the last thirty years. They also are radical in that they dare to envision regulating all development in this vast city with an extreme economy of means. Landmark preservation would have to be purchased. Environmental impact assessment would apply only to activities, not structures. As for zoning itself, it proposes only eighteen zoning districts, a dozen or so regulatory variables, and the deployment of only a few concepts and devices, some lifted from New York City's primeval zoning repertoire. These are the main features:

- Residential density would be regulated by only one variable: lot area per dwelling unit. Contextuality within residential areas and in relation to nearby commercial districts would be regulated primarily by height restrictions. In higher density residential and commercial areas, both density and contextuality would be promoted by resorting to New York City's venerable but novel street wall cum sky exposure plane envelope.
- Local commercial clusters would be kept in scale with surrounding residential areas by means of a limited palate of height, facade, and visual buffer restrictions.
- Use groups would be sorted naturally by regulating and segregating their structures, freeing planners from making countless arbitrary, invidious, and often illogical distinctions.
- To ensure maximum flexibility to accommodate future development, zoning would return to a hierarchical ranking of districts, where the activities or structures of each district would always be permitted in districts lower in the rank order.
- To expedite the pace of development, the entire system would be as-of-right.
- To ensure that the new regulatory system would fit the enormously varied

physical landscape of New York City, its design and implementation would be devolved to the people who will have to live with its consequences.

As I pondered these districts and these rules, I tried, by and large, to follow my principles and my instincts. When I was finished, I was struck by how close my scheme comes to the original 1916 zoning resolution. As some of the other papers in this book reveal, much of the New York City we know and love today was built under the rules of the 1916 ordinance. Furthermore, many of today's postmodern architectural and contextual developments are grounded in the spirit of 1916. Maybe New York City got more out of land use regulation than it suspected the first time around.

PLANNING AND ZONING FOR A MATURE CITY

MICHAEL KWARTLER

Adding together the component partial utilities, the rational herdsman concludes that the only sensible course for him to pursue is to add another animal to his herd. And another.... But this is the conclusion reached by each and every rational herdsman sharing a commons. Therein lies the tragedy. Each man is locked into a system that compels him to increase his herd without limit—in a world that is limited. Ruin is the destination toward which all men rush, each pursuing his own best interest in a society that believes in the freedom of the commons. Freedom in a commons brings ruin to all.

Garrett Hardin
"The Tragedy of the Commons"[1]

It is almost forty years since New York City began reconsidering its first few decades of experience under zoning—an effort that resulted in the comprehensive revision of the city's zoning resolution in 1961. Today, that revised zoning resolution has yielded to the same forces of entropy that ultimately undid the 1916 regulations. Unlike in 1961, when every borough except Manhattan was not yet built out and was still favored with enormous stretches of vacant land, even some farmland, planners now must work with a city that is basically built out. Moreover, the city's residents and planners alike are recognizing the ability of New York City's power of "place," its rich history and urban landscapes, to inform and shape our individual and collective identities as New Yorkers.

Most important, one could say the sense New Yorkers have of their city is changing. The notion that New York City is a developing city was widely held in 1961, but today, city residents are far more likely to think of New York City as a "mature" city. As a result, there has been an increasing tension between conserving and managing the city's "commons," or its extraordinary inventory of neighborhoods and districts, and respecting the city's equally characteristic zeitgeist of dynamic change and often overpowering renewal. As the scale of change has grown and its pace has accelerated in recent decades, the countervailing forces pressing for stability have arisen in an almost Manichaean duality. They are, in effect, "of a piece," two sides of the same coin.

This paper accepts the notion that New York City is a mature city and rejects the notion that the city can be planned and designed through a set of all-purpose rules, such as those promulgated in 1916 and 1961, or sweeping a priori theories. Rather, it argues, the most appropriate approach to planning, designing, and regulating urban space in New York City is fine-grained: each of the city's districts and neighborhoods must be understood both on its own terms and in terms of the contributions it makes to the whole. New York City must, as a city, collectively manage and replenish its commons—its vital neighborhoods and districts—and counter the tendency of the market to maximize the benefit of individuals at the expense of the commons.

NEW YORK CITY: THE MATURE CITY AND ITS CRISIS OF CONFIDENCE

The use of the term "mature" to characterize the way New Yorkers think of their city is intended to be evocative and provocative. "Mature" is meant to subsume the biological, mechanistic, and econometric metaphors that are used to describe large cities into a broader concept that is suggestive of the complexities, ambiguities, and contradictions characteristic of a state of maturity. In a certain sense, maturity is a state of mind that is cyclical; it is reasonable to assume that New Yorkers' perceptions of their city will change as New York City continues to experience the cycles that are unique to great cities.

A mature city is not a physically aging city in which decay has been renamed patina and in which places are treated as museums rather than settings for ongoing life. Rather, it is a vital, fully functioning entity whose citizens have developed an appreciation of limits in a positive way. A mature city is full of places that have distinctive physical attributes and rich associations for neighborhood and city residents, places that signify the durability of the physical and social conventions characteristic of the city and its neighborhoods. The residents of the city recognize the meaning and value conveyed by the physical and nonphysical traces of these past accomplishments.

Nor is a mature city a neutral spatial environment in which the basic utilitarian economics of cost-benefit analysis play themselves out. Rather, it is a great, evolving, humanistic enterprise that Kevin Lynch succinctly called "a vast mnemonic system for the retention of group history and ideals."[2] As a vast memory machine, the mature city is both a physical place and an attitude about place.

The stability of places adds resonance, stability, and well-being to the everyday lives of individuals and groups who regularly inhabit those places, but this resonance does not depend solely on the formal aesthetic content of those places. It also is influenced by the distinctiveness of the physical features and appearance of places, by the activities and functions that occur in them, and by the symbols and meanings that places embody (especially as understood and reinvested with added meaning by the inhabitants of that place).

In almost any city, zoning regulations and urban design plans are usually the playing fields on which the cultural, political, and economic values held by groups and individuals are measured against each other. In a mature city, discussions regarding the structure of the planning process, the content of zoning and design regulations, and efforts to develop or conserve neighborhoods attempt to focus a broad and meaningful question: How can the forces of change be balanced with the environmental stability that supports our cultural identity?

The perceptions people have about a place are difficult to evaluate. While we may know how a place is perceived by a group of people in the aggregate, we do not know what that place means to any particular person in that group. For example, most people might agree that the Empire State Building is a landmark, but what meaning does the building hold for them? That it is beautiful? That it is visible from anywhere in the city? That it is a symbol of unbridled materialism? No matter how difficult they may be to understand, people's perceptions are real, in many ways more real than facts, and planning must deal with both.

A mature city is in many respects a state of mind. Its inhabitants' perceptions of their city reflect the city's mid-life crisis. The world seems more complicated than it was before: childlike notions of omnipotence and control are counterbalanced by experience, which results in self-doubt and, to some degree, a wavering confidence. New York City's inhabitants have thought of their city as a developing city for the better part of the last forty years; now they are coming to grips with its maturation.

This maturation has brought on a crisis of confidence that is characterized by the role people see mature cities, such as New York City, playing in their regions and in the nation. The image of New York City and other mature cities as the centerpiece of their region (with the hinterland playing a supporting role) is in flux. While New York City is still central, its historical importance to the people elsewhere in the region appears to be waning; increasingly higher percentages of nonresidents are loosening their working, cultural, and recreational ties with the city.

Tellingly, the perceptions that new immigrants to the United States have of New York City have changed. As Samuel M. Ehrenhalt, the regional commissioner of the Federal Bureau of Labor Statistics in New York, told *The New York Times* in 1991, recent immigrants, who tend to be young, innovative, and entrepreneurial and who tend to move to where the best opportunities are, are bypassing New York City for surrounding urban centers.[3] "Twenty-five years ago, there was no alternative," one such entrepreneur agreed in the same article. "If you were an immigrant from India, you went to Queens. Now you move to Jersey City or Middlesex County, where everything is available."

A poll taken by *The New York Times* in 1991 underscores the sense that New Yorkers have lost confidence in themselves, their neighborhoods, and their city.[4] An accompanying article noted that the poll measured the highest level of pessimism about the city's future since 1973, when the poll takers first began asking about people's confidence in the future. In the recent poll, only 19 percent of the respondents (versus 38 percent in 1973, also a recession year) said that New York City would be a better place to live in ten or twelve years from now; 58 percent (versus 32 percent in 1973) said it would be worse.

As an example, the article cited respondents' attitudes toward the quality of the city's drinking water: "In a striking illustration of a frame of mind, even the water tastes better to suburban residents than to city dwellers—even when it's the same water." Most disturbing were the comments of one city resident who said that the city's problems were "insurmountable ... the place is a mess, you see it everywhere. And I don't see the will or the way to really clean it up.... It's a shame [to have to leave] because I really love New York. I just feel that a lot of things here are getting out of control."

The pessimism and perceived loss of control that *The New York Times* poll reported, and what they imply about our inability to sustain an ambient environment that is nurturing and stable, are a function of many forces, only one of which is land use planning policy. These attitudes result, in part, from problems that are national in origin. There is a growing sense that mature cities have been pushed to the margins throughout the United States. The nation's last two presidents, Ronald W. Reagan and George H. Bush, have had little evident sympathy for cities, and they were elected without winning the support of virtually any of the country's older cities. Although many urban problems, such as personal safety and the quality of the public schools, cannot be solved solely through planning and regulation that address the physical environment, they very much contribute to New Yorkers' sense of their city and their confidence and attachment to it.

It also is likely that the geographic atomization and fragmentation of the city have contributed to this sense of instability. Overlapping political and service delivery jurisdictions (such as community districts, city council districts, health districts, parks, police, and school districts) are organized, at best, in an effort to optimize or maximize the efficiency of each system. Consequently, they rarely bear a relationship to the real boundaries of neighborhoods, disconnecting them from spaces people understand and undermining accountability, responsiveness, and control. This fragmentation contributes to the city's crisis of identity by atomizing social and political relationships that could support a sense of place.

It appears that the processes of fragmentation and change, both good and bad, have challenged New Yorkers' sense of stability and made them feel that change is out of control. One could surmise that the government's responses to the city's immediate needs have not convinced the majority of those interviewed that those responses will make the city a more satisfying place to be. The most significant result of the poll may be that it indicates the willingness of New Yorkers to dissolve their long-held ties between themselves and the places with which they have identified as individuals and as members of their community: a substantial number of those who have the option to leave the city told the poll takers that they are actively considering doing so. This is due, in part, to people's fear that places they hold dear will no longer be distinct and complete.

CHALLENGES FOR PUBLIC POLICY AND THE PLANNING PROCESS

In a mature city the size of New York City, a varied pace and scale of change is not unusual—in fact, it is characteristic—but the crisis of confidence in the ability of city government and the development community to provide a stable, ambient environment for New Yorkers suggests the need for an entity closer to community residents to assume a stronger role in determining the city's destiny.

Some type of localized empowerment to plan—one that provides a local context for a broad-based planning and regulatory system—would begin to demonstrate the city's commitment to the well-being of its diverse neighborhoods and districts. At the same time, it is critical that responses to immediate local problems be perceived as contributing, ultimately, to the well-being of the entire city. Policies that reinforce a place's identity, residents' sense of real control, and accountability by city officials are critical to restoring confidence.

The development pressures of the 1980s, which many people perceived as a threat to the integrity and stability of places with which they were familiar, have cooled considerably. The oversupply of high-end housing and commercial office space in Manhattan will take years to occupy; as a result, the focus of development probably will shift to the attractive and increasingly vibrant neighborhoods in northern Manhattan and the boroughs, where the scale of development will also tend to be smaller. It is likely there will be a tendency to homogenize these traditional neighborhoods and districts with inappropriate, generalized zoning regulations and through efforts to promote suburban-style privatized developments. Together, these forces will threaten the unique identities of the city's mature communities—the proverbial bedrock communities of the city.

These communities need protection; their stability as viable places must be reinforced. These resources can be conserved through public policies that involve citizens as equal partners in the decision-making process and policies that recognize that there are other places where more dramatic change is appropriate.

The trend toward the decentralization of the workplace is well under way in the region's suburban counties, which are no longer solely "bedroom communities." As this trend manifests itself in the city, one can expect pressures for similarly decentralized workplaces to infiltrate residential neighborhoods. The question of what types of work should be allowed in stable neighborhoods is one that the residents themselves must help answer.

Similarly, the potential of the city's economic development zones (EDZs) to become true mixed-use neighborhoods that provide local jobs is a prospect that should be encouraged; public policy ought to be directed toward evolving innovative mixed-use neighborhoods and districts that would bring the much-needed jobs to these areas in transition. The blurring of the boundaries between the workplace and home, whether in EDZs or residential neighborhoods, seriously challenges the zoning resolution's explicit separation of uses.

New York City's waterfront has a strong potential to transform and unify the city's image. It is one of the few places in which the physical relationships between the different parts of the city (neighborhoods, districts, and boroughs) can be experienced. The waterways themselves have the potential to integrate the disparate parts of this city into a unified network that is both functional and heightens our experience of the connections between the various parts of the city.

While much of the waterfront is in public ownership, it is also underserved by the city's infrastructure. This raises serious questions about what can be developed along the waterfront and its upland areas and what resources must be allocated to sustain new development. The fact that the waterfront is simultaneously a citywide and a local resource requires a participatory planning approach that ensures attention is paid to the historic connections between the waterfront and the upland. Also, because the waterfront is one of the city's most observable and vital natural features, environmental concerns must be an integral part of planning for its future.

It would seem that there is not an alternative to planning given the condition of the city and the trends that are shaping it. The question, therefore, is how to plan for a city with New York City's complexity, potential, and problems while adhering to a process that establishes an atmosphere of certainty and predictability for city residents and the environments that sustain the city's life.

Unfortunately, traditional physical plans and policy plans fail to define the future form of the city in any predictable way (whether they include detailed maps and drawings or are composed solely of broad policy statements loosely related to amorphous, organic shapes on a map). These plans generally offer end-state visions and have little capacity to respond to unforeseen issues that present themselves as times goes by. Many are too specific and rigid, with little interplay between the plans and the changing world around them. Others are too vague to be compelling, providing citizens with no sense of what their experience would be like in the city the plan anticipates.

The result of these traditional approaches, in many ways, is the incremental planning that is New York City's current practice. The city's zoning resolution (which is the city's master plan by default) has been adapted over and over again as opportunities and crises have arisen. This piecemeal approach, nudged along by both the city government and the private sector, is fundamentally flawed—not because it is unresponsive to changing conditions (which it is) but because it does not include mechanisms for putting what are essentially localized situations into a broader context.

Currently, the city relies on environmental impact statements (EISs) to evaluate development proposals within a broader context and time frame, but EISs have proven to be inadequate, notwithstanding the considerable effort they require. One problem is that EISs are required only for discretionary projects, generally, proposals that require a modification of the existing zoning or involve the disposition of city-owned land. Since most development in the city takes place as-of-right, EISs affect a very small percentage of change. (An EIS must be prepared for proposals to change zoning, which sets the rules for as-of-right development.) Another problem with EISs is that they typically include information and analyses that have been prepared after the development proposal has been finalized. Consequently, the EIS generally is undertaken too late in the planning process to inform the project design in any fundamental way.

Ultimately, the EIS process falls short of the mark because its approach is incremental, oriented toward individual projects, rather than systemic.

While an individual project may contribute only slightly to a particular environmental problem, the cumulative effects of many similar projects would clearly worsen the situation. To the extent that the EIS-based project requires environmental harms to be mitigated, it does so only on a localized basis. Moreover, most projects are not required to bear the responsibility for their share of the problem unless they happen to be the straw that breaks the camel's back.

The EIS approach, by focusing on the system's breaking point, cannot deal effectively with environmental concerns that require a collective and concerted response. These concerns, familiar to New Yorkers, include: the way that groups of buildings affect wind currents at ground level, cast shadows on parks, and impede or facilitate the free circulation of air; air quality; the relationship between land uses, density, and traffic; and water supply, water quality, and the capacity of water pollution control plants.

Similarly, the incremental approach of the EIS process is inadequate to the task of enhancing the unique aspects of the city's neighborhoods and districts. The land use, urban design, archaeological, and historical sections of the EIS, which require documentation of local conditions, often provide insight into the context that surrounds a project, but they do not add up to coherent public policy. For example, conflicts that often emerge between the qualities that define a place's physical properties and environmental issues, such as districts with uniform, canyonlike, high street walls that tend to inhibit the free circulation of air and degrade air quality, are districtwide rather than project-specific issues.

Finally, the engineering-based optimization and maximizing strategies characteristic of EISs pose problems when applied to the planning of mature cities. The problem lies not only in the absoluteness of their abstraction but also in the notion that there is a unitary, optimal answer to planning questions. In a mature city, such as New York, this assumption is absurd; the planning equation is filled with ever-shifting situations and events that are beyond the city's control, suggesting that at any given time, there are multiple right answers.

Ironically, EISs, which were conceived as tools to support responsible land use planning, actually thwart the areawide zoning that could implement areawide planning. The city is reluctant to undertake such areawide plans because the necessary environmental studies would be complex and costly. Moreover, such studies would be undertaken at a stage in the planning process at which they inform the public about the impacts of a plan but do not necessarily assist in the formulation of a plan. A strategy that reestablishes the EIS as an integral part of planning would offer a viable alternative to what is currently, at best, an approach to localized problem solving and realizing opportunities presented by the market.

PLACE-BASED PLANNING AND ZONING

Place, as many commentators and jurists have noted, is essential to an individual's and a community's sense of identity and well-being. The physical environment is both the setting and locus for the complete range of human activities and associations, both good and bad, and is the vessel that encapsulates the individual and collective experiences of its constituents. The diversity of places in which people work, reside, and play should be the basic units that serve as the context for incremental planning decisions, which would be examined in terms of how they contribute to the overall well-being of each place. These places are immediately experienced by the people who live and work in them; they are understandable to people and capable of being designed, conserved, and managed.

New York City, as a mature city, should reject traditional methods of planning and zoning as being inappropriate to its future. An alternative "place-based" approach to land use planning and regulation would place a greater emphasis on a public planning process that makes citizens and city government, not the market, the dominant force in determining the form and spatial distribution of land uses. This approach would rely on strategic planning to set the context for programmatic land use planning. The strategic plan would anticipate, spot opportunities, project important trends, and evaluate their impact and potential at the citywide level. Programmatic land use planning would comprise the specific and localized response to these issues at the neighborhood and district level.

This fine-grained approach to planning and zoning at the local scale would be premised on three interrelated propositions for envisioning a better designed city: New York City is a mature city with neighborhoods and districts that are valued physical resources to be carefully conserved; government, through the public planning process, ought to manage the rate, scale, and location of development while managing the city's physical and environmental diversity; and, in so doing, government is conferring the "good" of reinforcing the sense of place characteristic of New York City's diverse neighborhoods and districts as well as preventing the "harm" typically associated with environmental degradation.

In a place-based planning approach, the emphasis would shift from maximizing the efficiency of the individual systems to grounding these systems in real and identifiable places. What are now placeless and discrete systems would be reorganized into a unified system whose subunits are coterminous with the geographic boundaries of neighborhoods and whose performance would be evaluated on the basis of how well the entire system satisfies the everyday needs of the residents. The coterminality of the system with recognizable neighborhoods and districts would combine with other layers of meaning and associations to increase the resonance and richness of these neighborhoods for their residents. Reawakening users' and residents' sense of place in this way can increase the sense of control they have over places where they live and work.

The place-based system of planning and regulation is based on the notion of "satisficing"[5] rather than optimizing or maximizing. This approach asks the question: "Are you satisfied or content with the outcome?" not "Is this the optimal outcome?" "Satisficing" requires that discrete policies and responses designed to deal with short- and mid-range problems be located in a broader frame of reference and a time frame of five to ten years. It asks, "What kind of a block, neighborhood, borough, and city do these policies add up to and is that outcome okay?"

Before pursuing the specifics of a fine-grained, place-based planning approach, it is critical to establish the context in which this planning will occur. The structure that is envisioned begins with the conception of New York City as an entity composed of distinctive and recognizable places that, in combination with and in relation to each other, reinforce each other's sense of place and the sense of the city's environmental and demographic diversity. Just as fragmented service delivery systems should be reorganized into a system that adds resonance to people's perception and experience of places, the multiplicity of places that constitute New York City also should be conceived as a system, not merely a collection of atomized and fragmented parts. The image of New York City that would emerge would be one of a complex city composed of extraordinary physical and demographic diversity and energy—heterogeneous on the broadest scale yet characterized by homogeneity of place on a local scale.

Strategic planning—which means identifying trends and opportunities and projecting their implications for both broad-based and localized initiatives—provides the context in which decisions about place-based planning and land use regulations should be made and in which those decisions can be evaluated in terms of how they contribute to our collective, individual, short-term, and long-term well-being. Similarly, the primary characteristic of a fine-grained approach to land use planning is to ensure that decisions are made at the appropriate scale—beginning with the basic unit, the place or neighborhood, and increasing in scale to include aggregations of neighborhoods, the borough, and the city as a whole.

For example, assume strategic planners identify changing work patterns that imply if the city is to remain competitive, it should pursue land use policies that accommodate decentralized workplaces in the city's neighborhoods and districts. The strategic plan would translate this policy into an agenda for action: It would describe in broad strokes the contribution each neighborhood would be required to make toward meeting the citywide objective. The strategic plan might suggest localized thresholds and criteria for locating workplaces in neighborhoods, such as the proportion or amount of floor area dedicated to work space, access to transportation and other support facilities, and a profile of prospective workers.

The context for determining how each neighborhood would contribute to the whole would be established by place-based preservation, conservation, and development plans that would be formulated by the residents in each place. Continuing the example, the local plan would establish the appropriate locations and sizes of these new workplaces based on an understanding of both citywide and local needs. Each community could experiment with models and approaches that make sense in its own context. Moreover, each community would monitor the implementation of its plan, gaining experience that would be useful in the continual reevaluation of strategic and local plans.

The structure, components, and analytical techniques of place-based preservation, conservation, and development plans would be based on a common model developed by the city's planners in consultation with the community and borough planning boards. These plans would characterize existing conditions, propose areas that are to be conserved and areas in which new development is appropriate, and analyze proposed and alternative courses of action. Each place-based plan would contain components set forth in the citywide model, but the community would calibrate its plan to the specifics of the neighborhood and district being planned.

Under this process, the place-based plan and its EIS would be a single document. The EIS, rather than focusing on specific development sites or being generically unspecific, would correspond to real and perceivable places that are defined by the community. Environmental analyses—which would be undertaken at the same time that place-based preservation, conservation, and development plans are being formulated—would provide the systemic analyses suggested by broader-based strategic planning and inform the fine-tuning of zoning regulations at the neighborhood and district levels. The analyses would be used to inform and adjust the place-based plan, in contrast to the current type of EIS, which is solely a public disclosure document. Undertaking the environmental and planning analyses at the same time would eliminate the current problem of the EIS being an impediment to areawide plans and legislative actions.

The place-based planning effort would enlist local citizens in documenting and assessing existing conditions. The participation of residents is critical on two levels. The first is that residents can obtain a self-conscious understanding of a place only through a structured analysis that gives them knowledge as to how that place is structured. The second is that it allows residents to explore their unconscious experience of a place. The combination of the two methods—one analytical, the other experiential—allows the residents of each neighborhood and district to determine what characterizes their place and to recommend action consistent with their understanding and experience of their neighborhood.

This information would establish the base from which a community could apply the citywide criteria contained in the model preservation, conservation, and development plans to identify areas that are "stable," "in transition," or "to be transformed." A stable area might be a traditional, older neighborhood whose physical form is intact, such as Washington Heights. An area in transition would be a place in which the physical environment is basically intact but the balance of land uses is changing, such as SoHo, NoHo, Tribeca, and the city's EDZs. An area to be transformed might be the waterfront, where manufacturing and industrial uses are declining and where there is a void as to what this land "ought to be" transformed into.

The citywide planning model would include not only quantitative planning and urban design analytical methods but also qualitative, cognitive mapping techniques that evaluate the coherence of places being studied in terms of how clear or stable its image is to residents. Based on that qualitative analysis, places would be generally characterized as having a stable image (people's images are similar); variable images (competing images), which would indicate areas in transition; and unstable images (neither strong nor competing images emerge), which would indicate areas to be transformed. The place-based plan's characterization and mapping of areas as stable, in transition, and to be transformed would provide the context in which the responses to the trends and policies formulated at the strategic level would be shaped in the form of preservation, conservation, and development policies and zoning regulations.

Conserving stable places is an obvious policy in a city in which so much seems to be in flux or "out of control." Conservation policies are critical to reestablishing people's confidence in and commitment to their city and neighborhoods, but such policies cannot be formulated on the basis of a priori judgments and abstract reasoning; they require place-based research that is based on thorough empirical analyses of a place, including the perceptions of the residents.

Areas that are perceived to be stable could be conserved by adopting policies and legislation that would conserve resources and manage the overall rate of change by accommodating evolutionary change. Areas in transition would be encouraged to change while maintaining a continuity with its history. Transforming areas, where continuity with the past is tenuous, would be places in which change would be actively and decisively pursued.

DESIGNING THE ZONING REGULATIONS

New York City's efforts to circumvent the grinding uniformity of a "one size fits all" zoning resolution through special zoning mechanisms and historic districts are well documented. In recent years, the city has created as-of-right contextual zoning districts that are intended to produce buildings whose form complements that of the city's traditional residential neighborhood building stock and scale and has mapped these districts selectively to replace the ubiquitous tower regulations. However, rather than acknowledging the variations of traditional urban design attributes that help define the differences between neighborhoods, the contextual regulations have stressed the traditional urban design commonalities, such as the traditional perimeter block form of city building. In that regard, the contextual regulations are similar to the 1961 "tower in a park" regulations—they attempt to legislate a building type on a citywide basis, regardless of local building traditions and neighborhood form.

"One size fits all" contextual zoning, although clearly superior to its as-of-right predecessors, tends to be a contradiction in terms because of the obvious number of exceptions to the rule. The number of contextual zoning districts has multiplied in an attempt to respond to the diversity of the city's neighborhoods—a logical approach to zoning a mature city. Rather than biting the bullet and recognizing that "contextual" means specific to a particular place, not "kind of" specific or "kind of" contextual, planners are trying to address what they consider to be two opposing goals: improving the sensitivity of new development to particular places by increasing the amount of specific language and keeping the regulations as short, simple, and understandable as possible so they can be administered easily, as-of-right.

Attempting to write such zoning so it works on an as-of-right basis is an approach unique to New York City and not generally adopted by other large, mature American cities. These other cities are neither as large nor as diverse as New York City, and they have tended to administer areas of special character on a discretionary basis that goes beyond establishing urban design guidelines to include the equivalent of our own Landmarks Preservation Commission, which reviews the architectural design of alterations to landmarks and buildings in historic districts. This use of discretion on such a broad scale has been acknowledged as neither desirable nor practical for New York City.

Instead, we should consider replacing the current set of land use regulations with a new, unified set of predominantly as-of-right rules governing activity, form, and density. These rules would be established only after an analysis of current trends and their implications for the city as a whole (a strategic plan) and for its constituent neighborhoods and districts (a place-based plan) was conducted. The rules would draw on the common urban design characteristics of a mature city yet be responsive to and reinforce the diversity of the city's neighborhoods and districts; and they would require that citizens be directly involved and actively participate in the planning and design of their neighborhood and in the implementation of land use regulations.

Place-based zoning regulations would be grounded in the recognition that New York City is a mature city. Stable areas, in which it would be important to conserve valuable and shared resources that make apparent the history of the city and people or to support the maintenance of community character, would require one set of zoning responses. Areas in transition or to be transformed would require different responses, depending on their local and citywide circumstances. No matter what the specific place-based response, the proposed regulations would share a common conceptual base that would inform their structure and content:

1. *The city's four hundred-year history, its evolving form, and its people are a highly valued asset to be conserved.* The diversity and quality of the city's built environment are extraordinary. The regulations should be responsive to and reflect this cultural wealth by building on the common threads upon which the city has developed. They include the openness of the block and street system, the conventions of public and private space that clearly differentiate urban (public) and suburban (privatized) values, and the intensive and varied use of urban land and space.
2. *Promote the concept of the city as a heterogeneous assemblage of typically homogeneous and imageable places.* This recognizes the appropriateness of regulations that are based on the commonalities observable in the city as a whole (such as an emphasis on defining public space) while ensuring that the differences that help people distinguish one place from another are equally apparent. The value here is not an aesthetic preference, although such preferences have their place, but, rather, the individual and group well-being gained from living in an environment whose visual character is clearly understandable.
3. *The standard embodied in the regulation should be to reinforce the sense of a place.* As a rule, legislative standards should derive from the place and be empirically based, unless a consensus deems the empirically derived regulation unacceptable. Under this regime, standards typically associated with zoning (such as use, density, daylighting, sunlighting, front yards, side yards, rear yards, exterior courts, street wall heights, and setbacks) should be place-based or tuned to the characteristics of each place. They are, in combination, often very specific in places that are built up (for example, the distance between row houses in Greenwich Village and on the Upper East Side is characteristically not the current standard of thirty feet). The place-based approach is not at all radical for a

mature city, in which most standards are not immutable but either habituated or acculturated and specific to each place. (For instance, the daylighting standard for Midtown is based on a historical legislated expectation of daylight that is different from the history of and expectations for daylight in lower Manhattan.)

4. *The level of the public interest, as expressed in the coarseness of the grain of the regulations and in the levels of control, will vary in accordance with the place-based plan and be contingent to the place.* The designation or characterization of areas as stable, in transition, and to be transformed will suggest the appropriate degree of response. For example, in a stable area, fine-grained regulations would be appropriate while those formulated for an area in transition, where change is desired and encouraged, might be less specific.
5. *New development and adaptive reuse should be responsive to environmental concerns.* Issues like the quality of air, water, and microclimate and the amount of sun and daylighting are significant. This is particularly true in to be transformed and transition areas, where change is occurring on a broader scale and these issues can be dealt with systemically rather than anecdotically.
6. *Citizens should participate in the development of the plans and regulations.* The application of this principle is meant not only to empower but also to enlighten people. By helping to document and assess their neighborhood, people can obtain an appreciation of it and of the complexity and subtlety of its construction. Additionally, by participating in the local planning and legislation process, citizens hopefully will obtain a stronger sense of control in a rapidly changing world.
7. *The regulations should be as-of-right to the degree that it is practical.* They should be based on a common kit of parts that represents the urban design conventions and values (activity, form, and density) characteristic of New York City's neighborhoods and districts and would be self-adjusting to each place.

THE KIT-OF-PARTS ZONING REGULATION

The charge that zoning regulations should be tuned to the specifics of each particular place while simultaneously recognizing the common characteristics of the city's built environment suggests two alternative approaches to design and planning regulation. The first and most obvious approach would be to treat all areas of the city as unique and designate them as special zoning districts. Each area, neighborhood, or district (depending on how fine-grained one wanted the regulations to be) would have its own set of zoning regulations that would be specific to the place and as-of-right. This approach has its drawbacks: the total number of special zoning districts would probably be several hundred and special districts have been difficult to administer.

The second alternative would be a "kit-of-parts" approach to urban design regulation, such as that proposed here. Unlike typological regulations that legislate building types, kit-of-parts zoning is based on the full range of attributes (including activities, building forms, and densities) that are characteristic of the city as a whole. These citywide attributes would be combined with local attributes and modified by place-based standards in order to give definition and identity to each neighborhood and district. Somewhat akin to a deck of cards or a box of Lego building blocks, the kit of parts would be a coherent system that would allow an almost limitless number of combinations and permutations, making it adaptable to virtually all conditions.

The generalized kit-of-parts zoning would be designed to be self-adjusting for each development (depending on its location, site size, and configuration), which would be regulated by layering elements from the kit of parts. Moreover, the kit-of-parts zoning regulations would be tuned to the preservation, conservation, and development policies articulated in the place-based plan and would be calibrated to the degree of certainty and control required to implement those policies. Additionally, they would address the issue of commonalities and differences by maintaining the common threads that are woven into each of the city's places.

The attributes that comprise the components of kit-of-parts zoning are commonly called urban design conventions. For example, the kit of parts would include the conventions that define and shape public space, such as street walls, the location of buildings relative to the street, the length of buildings relative to the side lot lines, building height, the visual permeability of facades, recesses and projections, and ground floor uses. These conventions, and the manner in which they are assembled, help shape our experience in a place.

City planning department staff would compile the urban design conventions using the department's existing information and other sources of public information, such as the Department of Finance photo records of all the city's buildings and streets. This information could be augmented by field research, for instance, documenting existing conditions and asking residents to make cognitive maps.

The kit of parts might contain conventions that describe the sense of a place and conventions that describe the particulars of a place—as well as other types of commonly used and idiosyncratic conventions. The kit of parts would be generalized in the sense that the conventions would be included without the physical dimensions that would make them specific to a particular place.

PLANNING AND ZONING FOR A MATURE CITY

Some general categories of conventions that describe the sense of place would be:

- Street and block conventions, which describe the visual properties of a street, such as the abrupt disjuncture of fine-grained, low-rise midblocks and coarser grained, high-rise avenues in Manhattan or the combination of semidetached houses fronting the same street as apartment buildings typical of Jackson Heights, Queens.
- Building type, lot width, or "grain" conventions (such as freestanding, semidetached, or perimeter-block buildings).
- Use conventions that describe the degree to which uses and activities are separated or mixed and describe their spatial distribution within buildings and larger areas.

Some conventions that describe the particulars of a place would be:

- Conventions that describe the area between the public space of the street and the entrances of buildings, such as yards, courts, driveways, steps/stoops, gates, and landscaping.
- Conventions that define and shape public space, such as the location, height, and length of street walls.
- Facade conventions that articulate the public space of the street, such as courts, recesses, signs, storefronts, entries, and stoops.
- Streetscape conventions, such as street trees, paving, and landscaping.
- Privacy conventions, such as exterior courts, alleys, yards, and distances between windows.
- Conventions that accommodate the automobile, such as curb cuts, parking, and the screening of auto storage or parking.

The matching and/or assigning of the kit of parts to areas in a neighborhood or district is the process by which communities would come to understand the urban design attributes that contribute to the sense of place of their neighborhood. Specifically, it is the process through which the community allocates, in combination and permutation, the conventions contained within the kit of parts to areas and subareas delineated in the place-based plan. The characterization of these places as stable, in transition, and to be transformed would provide the context for both the allocation of the parts and degree of control one could envision. Most important, the generalized urban design conventions selected from the kit of parts would be given dimensions by drawing on the documentation in the place-based plan, adjusting the conventions to local conditions. For example, the depth of a front yard in a row house district would vary from as little as one foot on the

Upper East Side or Greenwich Village to more than twenty feet in Carroll Gardens.

Computer technology would be used to organize the conventions into both the generalized and place-specific kit-of-parts zoning regulations, allowing the user to generate a complete listing of all the zoning regulations pertaining to the site being studied. The computer also would perform the sorting and cross-referencing necessary to accommodate the high degree of sophistication that this proposal requires. Obversely, the work of checking for compliance with the zoning could be assisted by the computer.

HOW IT WOULD WORK

The place-based plans and kit-of-parts zoning regulations would be conceived as an integrated whole. The plans would set the context, type, and degree of regulation necessary to achieve the policy objectives. The manner in which the kit-of-parts zoning is applied to each place (each neighborhood, district, community board, and so on) would depend on whether the place is characterized as either stable, in transition, or to be transformed and whether places are designated as the locus of preservation, conservation, or development implementation strategies and policies.

A place-based plan would be fine-grained in the sense that each place in the city would be documented and would be assessed in terms of its potential to address the short- and long-term issues and trends to which the city must respond and of its contribution to agreed-upon local and citywide needs. The unique combination of zoning regulations for each area, no matter how it is characterized, would be selected from the same citywide kit of parts. Stable preservation and conservation areas would generally require a tight fit between the new and existing structures, reinforcing the existing sense of place. In transition and to be transformed areas, where the sense of place is far less articulated, would be assigned a coarser set of regulations that encourage innovative architectural and urban design and promote the evolution of new building and district types. These new designs would be based, in part, on new urban design conventions that derive from environmental concerns—as well as the urban design conventions that in general are common to the city's neighborhoods and districts and are characteristic of New York City's position as a mature and historic city.

The following examples illustrate how the place-based plan and kit-of-parts zoning regulations could be applied to development sites in stable, in transition, and to be transformed areas.

Sites located in neighborhoods characterized as "stable." These sites would tend to be located in areas that are designated in the place-based plan as appropriate for preservation or conservation policies. Generally, preservation areas would be places with environments that tend to be highly specific and imageable and whose development history has resulted in a unique environment. Conservation areas would tend to be those in which the building and urban design conventions are less idiosyncratic than those in preservation areas and where it is a unique combination of conventions that informs the sense of place. Jackson Heights could be considered a preservation area while Flatbush and Brighton Beach, both in Brooklyn, could be designated conservation areas.

For sites within preservation areas, such as Jackson Heights, the kit-of-parts zoning computer would display both the common and idiosyncratic conventions typical of Jackson Heights. This would include the array of placed-based standards for exterior courts; front, side, and rear yards; recesses; and privacy between windows. The dimensions attached to the place-based standards would be based on those that are typical of Jackson Heights and derive from the documentation done by area residents with the participation of public planners.

Depending on the location of a project site, its size, and the proposed use, the applicable conventions from the already reduced and localized kit of parts would be further reduced so that they are specific to the site. If the site were a small infill lot, for instance, the applicable conventions would refer to the conventional dimensions of adjacent structures on that side of the street while a larger site, for example, one fronting on an entire block, intended for residential use would tap into the array of areawide conventions that pertain to blockfront apartment buildings. Similarly, use conventions would be governed by location. In Jackson Heights, for example, religious, institutional, and educational facilities are almost always located on a wide street in an otherwise solidly residential area. The preservation designation would require that new institutions be limited to similar locations on wide residential streets.

In stable/conservation and stable/preservation areas, building form conventions would supersede FARs as density controls. If one were building on a block of two-family semidetached homes, one could build a similar structure regardless of the underlying R6 FAR. The logic behind this provision is based on the fact that there will be few new development sites, other than infill sites, in stable areas. Because densities and thresholds have a built-in elasticity that could accommodate small incremental changes, and because these potential additions would have been accounted for in the place-based plan, the plan would allow building form to supersede FAR. Essentially, developments in stable/conservation and stable/preservation areas should respond to the architect Mies van der Rohe's dictum to his protégé, architect Philip Johnson: "It is better to be good than to be original." However, in to be transformed and in transition areas, FAR or other density controls might pertain.

Sites located in neighborhoods characterized as "in transition." These neighborhoods generally will have subareas designated for conservation, development, and, on occasion, preservation (SoHo, for example, would have been characterized as transition/preservation during the 1970s and 1980s). For instance, consider a development site in an area designated for development in an EDZ—an economic development zone—where the balance of workplaces, service, retail, and residential uses is in flux. In an EDZ, the convention that tends to define the place most is that which describes mixed land uses rather than separated uses. Similarly, urban design conventions would be more coarse than in a stable area. The looser, but distinctly New York City, envelope should allow for the experimentation and innovation that ultimately result in the evolution of new urban district and building types.

Given the potential scale of development where environmental concerns could be dealt with systematically, they too would be one set of determinants of the kit of parts for a site.

The allowable development density and the mix of uses would be based on thresholds and capacities established in the place-based plan and EIS. For example, in an EDZ, the threshold for the amount of allowable workplace activity might be the number of jobs generated as a function of the floor area being used as a workplace. Other criteria also would pertain, such as minimizing activities that require a low number of workers per square foot of work space (consequently adding little to building cohesive and experientially meaningful mixed-use districts).

At the point the threshold(s) is (or are) achieved, the plan and applicable kit-of-parts zoning would expire, mandating a reevaluation of the future of the area in transition. At that point, it might be reasonable to adjust the plan and zoning regulations or to recharacterize the area in a more fundamental way.

Sites located in areas characterized as "to be transformed." Areas to be transformed, such as the waterfront or districts like Melrose in the Bronx, generally would be designated as development areas. The place-based plan for areas to be transformed, similar to plans for areas in transition, would establish densities and uses on the basis of capacities and thresholds, as well as the ability to leverage public and private investment. Most importantly, urban design conventions common to the city (particularly the definition of public space and its accessibility) would be reinterpreted in an environmental context.

The scale of the waterfront and its potential for transformation would allow environmental concerns to be expressed as conventions in the kit of parts and to be dealt with systematically. For example, building heights along the waterfront could be adjusted to allow for solar access to streets, parks, and esplanades. The coverage of permeable surfaces could be controlled to prevent the ponding of storm water. Building mass could be arranged to reduce pedestrian-level winds and provide microclimates hospitable to humans and foliage. Given the long time frame involved between the making and the implementation of a plan, mandatory reassessment points could be established and triggered when thresholds in the plan have been achieved or capacities reached.

CONCLUSION

If the dominant characteristic of the mature city is the appreciation of limits, then the first limit that should be recognized is that the unity of New York City can be neither contrived nor forced. The unity of a mature city is organic, resulting from the tension that underlies the interdependence and interrelatedness of the city's diverse places, which, while clearly different—if not contradictory—simultaneously share commonalities that are specific to New York City.

By making the kit-of-parts zoning contingent on community-sponsored, place-based plans, which would encapsulate both the differences and commonalities within the community, and by making a place's boundaries clear, experiential, and coterminous with political and service area boundaries, it becomes possible to put immediate responses to perceived problems into a broader context, and it makes it possible for us to answer Clifford Weaver's and Richard Babcock's "satisficing question": "[W]here will the city be in five or ten years, and how acceptable will that be?"[6]

NOTES

1. Garrett Hardin, "The Tragedy of the Commons," *Science* 162 (13 December 1968): 1245.
2. Kevin Lynch, *The Image of the City* (Cambridge: MIT Press, 1967), p. 126.
3. *New York Times* (7 December 1991): 1.
4. *New York Times* (1 December 1991): 1.
5. Clifford Weaver and Richard Babcock, *City Zoning: The Once and Future Frontier* (Chicago: Planners Press, 1979), p. 264.
6. Ibid.

PLANNING THE EQUITABLE CITY

R. SUSAN MOTLEY

Some planners argue[d] that in order to be useful, the master plan had to be constantly revised and updated, but others began to suggest that planning was not a method of describing the ideal city but a process of decision-making and that master planning was only one tool among many to be employed in this process.

David Sills[1]

New York City's 1961 zoning revision was not intended to address specifically issues of social, economic, or planning equity, nor did it set forth an overarching land use plan or a coherent set of planning policies. In the absence of such a plan, it does not make sense to put forth even the most thoughtful and sensitive recommendations about how the zoning resolution might further issues of equity. Doing so would be putting the cart before the horse. Zoning needs a context; equity needs some agreed upon standard of fairness.

This paper will look at some characteristics and outcomes of New York City's planning policies and the zoning resolution since 1961 from the perspective of equity: Were the results of the application of the resolution perceived as fair? Fair to whom? For what purpose? It also will suggest ways to construct a planning process that would more nearly meet the tests of fairness—a process that recognizes the interests of different individuals and groups and seeks a means by which those interests can be recognized in support of commonly held overarching goals. My argument is that an equitable city can emerge only through a process for making decisions and solving problems that is equitable itself.

The question for me is: In what ways can the planning process, the evolving plan, the zoning resolution, and the other public policies that exercise control over the ownership and use of land and the distribution of capital investment be crafted to encourage and support a healthy, vibrant, economically stable city that meets the needs of each of its unique neighborhoods and builds upon the strengths of its people and institutions? The answers will inevitably point to ways in which we can make New York City an equitable city.

WHERE WE ARE NOW

The New York City metropolitan region is the most intensely settled urban area in the United States; some say it is the model of what a world-class city-region can be. New York City itself is a city with more than 7.5 million residents, five boroughs that anywhere else would be cities unto themselves, and hundreds of unique neighborhoods. It is a city in which no race or ethnic group is in the majority; trends in immigration and in the demographics of the city's native population point toward an increasingly nonwhite city. These remarkable data describe New York City in 1991 as in the midst of "dramatic dynamics of change," with the relatively rich and the absolutely poor left to cope with an increasingly unmanageable city.[2]

What does it mean to plan equitably in such a fluid context—particularly when the traditional engine of land use, the economics of investment and return, simply does not consider equitable outcomes to be a major concern? The disparities seem staggering. For example, businesses, using economic rationales, make locational decisions that almost always ensure jobs will not be located near labor pools that need employment. In every employment sector—services, trades, and manufacturing—New York City has lost jobs in the last five years. Commercial real estate developers, who built about twenty million square feet of space in Manhattan during the last five years, are now living with the effects of that overbuilding: Manhattan alone has more than fifty-five million square feet of vacant office space today. Take another example: Even in the most dynamic residential real estate market, more housing is built directly for "move up" homeowners than for households doubled up in public housing; far less capital is directed toward improving substandard apartments. In Manhattan's hottest real estate markets, more studios and pied-à-terre units are built than apartments that would enable families to live in the city.

Planning is the process of envisioning what the city can be at its best, and zoning is one of the many tools or tactics that can be used to realize that vision. Fundamentally, planning is a process of defining problems and making decisions about how to solve them. Creating and acting upon a vision of "what the city can be" requires that we come to some common agreements about very basic assumptions and values so that the requisite commitment toward effective problem solving can be carried out. Equity is, after all, about fairness, values, and the exercise of power.

Perhaps as a result of the dramatic changes the city has experienced, there are few shared assumptions or common agreements about values or priorities for New York City in general, let alone shared assumptions that relate to land use planning. Moreover, the shared assumptions and common agreements that the city needs are not likely to be reached through discussions among a few technically qualified and well-intentioned lawyers, planners, or designers. Even though consensus among local politicians would be an amazing feat, that, too, would be too narrow a group to consider adequately the chasm of values and assumptions in this city. Economists and financiers, neighborhood leaders and business owners, developers, academics, government agencies, and the average Josephine and Jose have critical contributions to make.

Planning demands a process that reconciles those visions and acknowledges the differences in values that shape our views and confirm our passions. Planning in this era of dramatic change and volatile issues is more likely to result in an equitable city if the process by which those plans are designed and developed is considered by participants and affected parties alike as fair. The planning process must build consensus, it must respect and incorporate the wide range of interests that exist in the city, particularly those of people and organizations that are directly affected by the resulting plans and their consequences.

This process must have clear and mutually enforceable ground rules, but at the same time, it must be flexible and allow for creative and innovative problem solving. While the issues at hand may involve matters of land use or the allocation of public resources, we must remember that any political process has a higher purpose: to reinforce public confidence in the government and improve relationships among the various segments of our society. Accomplishing that, in the long run, can be much more important to New York City than determining the optimal outcome of a particular planning issue and rallying support for it. Discussions about land use planning—which directs the distribution of capital and jobs and which affects the quality of our everyday environments—are one of the most appropriate forums for considerations about equity.

In short, I am suggesting that an equitable city can emerge only through a process that is equitable itself. The planning process must challenge assumptions, question values, critically examine the official data, and play out the likely consequences of various strategies, including their effects on those who might benefit and those who might be burdened. The process must be based on consensus building and creative problem solving.

PLANNING, ZONING, AND EQUITY SINCE 1961

New York City has always been in the forefront of land use planning and zoning. The 1916 zoning resolution was the first of its kind to be enacted in this country, and it is generally accepted among planners that the 1961 revision was a model of innovation. The 1961 revision was proposed by architects and planners who intended it to be responsive to the most modern construction technologies, quality of life standards, and planning methodologies. It was influenced by civic-minded and business interests and ultimately was shaped by the various political entities that would exercise control over its implementation.

The revision fulfilled what had been considered its obligation to set forth a "well-considered plan" in several ways. It mandated the mapping and zoning of all land into three commonly defined use categories (residential, commercial, and manufacturing), established a clear and compelling connection between physical development and the environment and its capacities, and relied primarily on the marketplace and its economic engine to dictate development. The zoning revision, which was greatly influenced by architectural and planning thinking that was then current, encouraged the design of buildings commonly described as "tower in the park."

Despite the clear (albeit singular) vision, the 1961 revision was amended early and often. These revisions occurred, in part, because the resolution relied on the use of discretionary actions rather than as-of-right change, because the planning process and zoning resolution lacked a systematic assessment mechanism, and because people began to turn against the "tower in the park" concept. These amendments influenced the application of the resolution, as well as the planning process, in ways that could not have been predicted upon its enactment. As Norman Marcus so aptly states in his paper in this book, "Zoning from 1961 to 1991: Turning Back the Clock—But with an Up-to-the-Minute Social Agenda," "If the 1916 resolution resembled a patchwork quilt in 1960, then the 1961 revision today resembles a giant maze."

In the mid-1970s, the New York City Charter was revised to include the Uniform Land Use Review Procedure (ULURP), a standard process for evaluating and deciding upon certain discretionary planning proposals.[3] ULURP is intended to provide a mechanism by which the communities most directly affected by any land use or zoning change have an opportunity to review and recommend whether they think the change should be adopted. ULURP, however, is a *review* process, not a *planning* process; it is a systematic and time-limited mechanism that allows community boards and the general public to react to plans and projects submitted primarily by developers (but often by the city itself) and ultimately approved or rejected by elected officials.

What follows is a look at the track record of the 1961 revision (and its subsequent amendments) to see if there are obvious patterns and lessons that lead us to believe that reliance on any of the major thrusts (design, environmental impact standards, or an incentive/market-driven approach) consistently results in equity as an outcome. By equitable, I mean planning and zoning results that recognize different interests and dynamics of change and that seek a means for those interests to be met in support of a commonly held overarching goal; outcomes that have been perceived as fair and both efficient and stable over the long run and have contributed to the health and vitality of the city as a whole.[4]

DESIGN

The tower-in-the-park design template, favored by the 1961 zoning revision, was intended to be the standard by which high-density developments should be built. The hope was that these tall, slender buildings would allow more sunlight to reach the street and provide more open space. New regulations were crafted to encourage taller and more slender (as well as denser) buildings than had been permitted under the 1916 resolution—these rules limited the maximum density of buildings by instituting a floor area ratio, liberalized the maximum coverage of towers, and established a minimum amount of open space that each new project should provide.

This type of building appeared to be an excellent investment—the 1961 rules seemed to allow greater density than the previous rules did, and the broad-based slab towers favored by the revision could be built more efficiently than wedding cake towers.[5] The inclusion of incentives (bonus floor area in exchange for the provision of amenities, such as open space and arcades) was an additional carrot that the city extended to encourage the design of slab towers. These rules appealed not only to private-sector financiers but also to the public and nonprofit sectors, the government, and philanthropy: the private sector set itself to redeveloping high-value areas of the city with mostly commercial buildings, and the public and nonprofit sectors developed urban renewal (that is to say, poor) areas with residential buildings.[6]

The benefits of this design template were challenged early on. Tower-in-the-park residential buildings, spaced widely apart and distanced from the street, almost always created discontinuity in the urban fabric of low-income neighborhoods and virtually isolated families within the buildings. The tower-in-the-park design bias was at first a minor issue in upper-income neighborhoods, but as new housing began to be developed there, concerns emerged—not only because of the interruptions in street walls but also because of the increased densities and the loss of older, familiar building forms and sometimes historic buildings. Residents fought tenaciously to block this new type of residential development. Historic preservation became a benchmark issue, and these neighborhoods battled to receive protection from the Landmarks Preservation Commission.

This design and development approach also came under attack at a national level, and by the mid-1970s, most public financing was denied for this type of development; the availability of public funds for all low- and moderate-income housing development was being cut. By then, it was too late for many communities, such as Coney Island and Far Rockaway, in which whole neighborhoods had been cleared of "slums and blight" and block upon block of high-rise tower-in-the-park public housing developments had been built.

As Marcus again points out in his paper in this book, the zoning rules put in place in 1961 were amended soon afterward to provide protection for the existing character of the city. By the early 1980s, the rules that permitted tower-in-the-park design schemes had been all but reversed, especially in high-value residential neighborhoods. The preservation movement and the hue and cry of neighborhood uniqueness led inevitably to a more contextual set of regulations that produced buildings that fit visually within the neighborhood and did not disrupt street continuity. Special districts aimed at encouraging and supporting unique neighborhood characteristics were enacted.

Early on, each of these "contextual rezonings" occurred on a neighborhood-by-neighborhood basis and, for the most part, were only deemed significant, and therefore worthy of focus, in those neighborhoods that had or appeared to have high market value. Within these historically stable middle- and upper-income neighborhoods, this position culminated in the general acceptance of a contextual approach to building design and the institutionalization of a combination of incentive and remediation strategies frequently peculiar to each development project.

While contextual zoning appears to be desired and appropriate in high-value residential neighborhoods, poor neighborhoods have experimented with other designs, which often are expressive of a desire to live in housing that looks like typical middle-class housing and at the lower densities typical of middle-class districts. For example, on Charlotte Street in the South Bronx, neither tower-in-the-park nor contextual solutions were deemed acceptable or appropriate to the nonprofit developers or the neighborhood. Instead, to the dismay of many observers, these developers insisted on zoning changes that would accommodate single-family, owner-occupied houses. In Brooklyn, hundreds of "Nehemiah" homes, spread over a number of city blocks, were designed as single-family row homes. (The Nehemiah Houses initiative was launched in the Brownsville area of Brooklyn in 1982 by the East Brooklyn Coalition of Churches. The initiative combined city subsidies and mass-production techniques to provide homeownership opportunities for families with incomes as low as $16,000 to $20,000 [in 1982]. The houses were designed as stacks of two-story row houses with parking pads in the front and private backyards in the rear.) This project—again sponsored by a nonprofit developer and designed to accommodate low- and moderate-income families and directed toward creating homeownership opportunities—was a vast departure from what would have been required if either tower-in-the-park or contextual mandates had been carried out.

Both Nehemiah homes and Charlotte Street were a part of neighborhood-based community development strategies. In an era of drastically reduced federal resources and in a local political environment that was essentially hostile to neighborhood-driven development strategies, the proliferation of these alternate development entities was indeed wondrous. Vital to this approach was the recognition that community-based development required the direct participation and involvement of residents in all facets of the development process—not only in decision making but also in the production, management, and control of what is produced. These organizations actively sought the participation of other neighborhood residents and, with the help and support of foundations, attempted to rebuild their neighborhood in ways that met their needs better than did the design templates set out by zoning.[7]

ENVIRONMENTAL STANDARDS

The 1961 zoning revision incorporated several regulatory mechanisms (in particular, floor area ratios and open space requirements) that clearly linked new development with a consideration of the capacity of the environment and its infrastructure to absorb new and more intensive uses. In the late 1960s and early 1970s, federal and state environmental protection rules were enacted. These, coupled with new landmarks preservation requirements (passed in 1965) and the city's environmental quality regulations (instituted in the 1970s, these require consideration of the effects certain proposals would have on existing patterns of population concentration, distribution, or growth and existing community or neighborhood character), are the foundation of an ever-growing body of laws, rules, and procedures designed to require that all environmental effects of development and other planning proposals are reviewed and analyzed, and if there are negative impacts or consequences, that those impacts be adequately addressed prior to the approval of the proposal.[8]

The application of these various standards absolutely affected the placement, density, design, and function of those proposed developments that were judged to have negative impacts on the environment or landmarks. The more diligently applied environmental standards, coupled with a vastly more sophisticated advocacy community, demanded high standards of performance and remediation, sometimes stalling projects through legal suits for years. The quintessential examples of this are the Westway/West Side highway controversy and, more recently, the proposed development at Columbus Circle. In both cases, public advocates effectively used the regulations, the review processes, and the political machinery to force their arguments to be heard and to delay or defeat the proposals.

Looking at other examples, however, one must question whether the environmental standards themselves are the compelling factor in the outcome of these battles or whether it is the power of the advocates that chose to take sides. During the same period that the environmental activities were focused on primarily Manhattan (and primarily high-value) land use decisions, the city's poorer communities were being inundated with all manner of negative environmental impacts: jails, drug treatment facilities, waste disposal facilities, and homeless shelters, all generally considered "noxious" uses. For the most part, these facilities were developed on city-owned property using the extra bulk that the 1961 zoning revision allowed for "community facilities." Even though neighborhood advocates often came out in the hundreds to protest at the required ULURP public hearings, and even though their advocates filed the requisite legal actions and pressured the politicians, these projects often went forward in low-income, primarily nonwhite, areas of the city.

Today, the results of the negative environmental impacts of clustering "noxious" uses in neighborhoods whose physical, social, and economic infrastructure can least afford them are unavoidably obvious. The cluster of homeless shelters, jails, detention centers, and other facilities in central Brooklyn is an example. It is no coincidence that those neighborhoods that are poor are generally those neighborhoods that have a high concentration of nonwhite residents: African-American, Hispanic, and nonwhite immigrants, spawning the term "environmental racism" as a description of the effects of such decisions.[9]

"Tough but fair" might describe the city's environmental standards in theory, but the actual results have not been fair or equitable. The city's planning process, despite its requirement for environmental studies and for community public hearings, does not empower the city's low-income, primarily nonwhite neighborhoods to the same extent that it empowers well-heeled Manhattan neighborhoods. To the extent that the siting of noxious uses represents a consensus about the future of the city, people in these communities have not been involved in forging that consensus. It is not surprising that people in these communities, unhappy with the outcome of decisions that affect the quality of the places where they live, feel disconnected from the process of governing, of planning, and of determining the future of New York City.

INCENTIVE/MARKET-DRIVEN APPROACHES

Without question, the development of commercial buildings, accelerated by incentive zoning criteria set forth in the 1961 zoning revision and subsequent amendments, has flourished during the past thirty years. The value of real estate, especially in Manhattan, continued to rise, and denser, more efficient buildings became popular with investors.[10] Environmental issues, though important, were secondary; mitigating actions, such as the provision of open space, subway improvements, or pedestrian circulation improvements, were treated as bargaining chips in the review and approval process. The city's official policy was that commercial development was critical: it produced income for the city and enhanced New York City's reputation as the capital of development, especially as it became the center of the profitable finance and service industries.

In response to these pressures, the city planning department initiated studies that culminated in the commission's designation of special districts, such as the Special Midtown District,[11] whose purpose was to capture this development energy and to channel the economic market so as to reshape and expand the city's commercial core. Although the city experienced a prolonged recession in the early 1970s, by 1986 commercial real estate development was robust, land values were high, and the zoning encouraged densities that all but guaranteed a sizable profit. The various special districts, bonus programs, and negotiated agreements produced results as varied as subway improvements, plazas and arcades, theater preservation, and creative street improvements.

Had the economy continued to expand at the pace it did in the 1980s, development would have moved to the western edge of Midtown, a direction clearly encouraged by the underlying zoning and special development incentives, including generous tax abatements. Instead, the New York City market began to slide in mid-1987 and the national financial markets dropped precipitously in October of that year. New York City's real estate markets are still weak, and today there is little incentive to develop new commercial space.

On the other hand, even in good times, commercial and industrial development in low-income areas generally occurred, if at all, by extramarket means—often sponsored by nonprofit or public developers and also assisted with government subsidies. One example is the struggle with financing and developing the commercial center in Jamaica, Queens, a long-standing city urban renewal effort. Another is the almost legendary effort to encourage new industrial activity in the South Bronx, which several public economic development agencies have assisted.

Even during the years of economic prosperity, the real estate market did not operate in ways that encouraged the production or maintenance of housing affordable to low- and moderate-income New Yorkers. Properties in high-value areas that housed poor people were often regarded as having a "higher and better" use and were replaced with other uses for other populations. For this reason, and because of the decrease in federal funds for housing rehabilitation and new housing production, the absolute numbers of housing units available for low- and moderate-income residents declined. Housing vacancy rates hovered below 3 percent during the late 1970s and 1980s, contributing to the most prolonged crisis of homelessness New York City has ever known.

Market-driven development approaches and density incentives do not work efficiently, or barely at all, when the financial markets decline or in markets that appear to have little economic value. Neither planning that is based primarily on market forces nor zoning that is designed to support and encourage market-driven strategies has, during the past thirty years, proved to produce results that can be described as equitable. In good times and bad, government control and direction are needed to ensure that market forces provide benefits to the public. What matters most is the process by which decisions are made about what those benefits should be.

THE UNIFORM LAND USE REVIEW PROCEDURE

The New York City Charter requires that ULURP be used to review and decide upon certain land use actions, such as the rezonings, special permits, and special approvals often needed for the largest, most complex (and most profitable) projects. This review procedure, which prescribes a limited time for public review, in many ways shapes the exact nature of actions that are proposed. The requirements of environmental reviews, the requirements of public review, and the inherent discretionary nature of requests for changes often led the city and its planners to extend incentives or require remedial actions that attempt to appease the public and politicians.

Consequently, in the past thirty years, there has been a proliferation of "restrictive declarations," special agreements that are crafted specifically for each project approval and that pertain to issues not included in zoning. The agreements are made between the project sponsor and the city government and are recorded with the deed of the property (for this reason, the restrictive declaration does not disappear when the property changes hands). Clearly, ULURP, though well-intentioned, has encouraged the exercise of discretion and developed political expediency to an art form in order to move projects through the approval process. Each project becomes its own battle, and each result is limited and specific.

By the mid-1980s, it was evident that the structure of governance in New York City had to be changed; a court ruling had found that the city's Board of Estimate, a hybrid legislative-executive body, violated the U.S. Constitution's "one-person-one-vote" principle. The resulting revision of the city's charter—whose main purpose was to transfer much of the Board of Estimate's power to an expanded, popularly elected city council—affected every level of government and had a profound effect on the procedure by which the city government made land use decisions and in the way the city was planned. The new charter expanded the New York City Planning Commission from seven members to thirteen, encouraged broader creation of community-based plans,[12] dismantled the Board of Estimate, and shifted the responsibility for many land use decisions to the expanded city council.

In addition, the charter mandated that the City Planning Commission undertake a number of important rule makings. These rules were intended to increase public participation in planning and land use review, to reform the environmental review process, and to promote the more equitable siting of city facilities.[13] The "Fair Share" regulations for siting community facilities specifically call for "equitable balancing consideration" and basing decisions on "the city's long range policies and strategies," "expanding participation [in the decision making]," and "fostering consensus."[14] It is clear, for example, from recent attempts to find locations for homeless shelters, that fair share has not convinced middle-class and upper-class communities that they have to take any share of facilities with potentially unpleasant side effects. Moreover, if fair share criteria are applied only to land uses considered undesirable, it is unlikely that they can be effective, in either the long run or the short run, and that issues of equity may never be fully explored.

The section 197-a provisions, which enable community boards (as well as other units of government) to submit plans for consideration by the City Planning Commission, suggest a possible mechanism for building community consensus. However, they are localized in scale, and, as of yet, these plans seem to have no legal standing. Of course, there are still very few of these plans approved, which says something in and of itself.

So far, New York City has had little experience that we can use to judge the impact of the charter revisions that were approved in 1989. It is not clear whether the new charter's good intentions will be fulfilled, and it is not certain whether those good intentions—even if they are fulfilled—will be enough to create an equitable city.

THE QUESTIONS OF EQUITY

The 1961 zoning revision and subsequent reforms to the zoning text and map and to the land use approval process have not provided a clear, overarching, or comprehensive strategy for land use planning. Therefore, they also have not contemplated a means of assessing whether the application of the zoning resolution is moving the city as a whole closer to any particular planning or development objectives. There are several obvious reasons why this lapse is particularly critical.

First, the emergence of an overarching set of objectives would provide one of the few opportunities to establish some commonality of agreement among the various and wide-ranging communities of interest within the city—an agreement that is especially important in a politicized environment. In the absence of such a commonality, it is unlikely that civic spirit or the public will can be mobilized in constructive ways for the long term.[15]

Second, establishing an overarching set of objectives also means establishing a sense of priorities. Every issue is vitally important to some interest, and, without clearly established priorities, the competition among various interests is resolved through a win-lose process, in which blocking another issue may be as important as supporting one's own. Finally, the inability to assess the overall effectiveness of a planning implementation mechanism, such as zoning, virtually condemns any planning strategy to random success and severely limits our ability to learn from our experience and plan for the future.

New York City can ill afford to concede the uniqueness of its parts, its neighborhoods, that together make up the tone and texture of this city to any one design template. A predetermined design format cannot dictate development without great sacrifice to diversity and interest. Whether "tower in the park" or "contextual," a design template assumes an aesthetic, functions, and values that are neither universally held nor always appropriate. Nor can New York City entrust its vitality and its future solely to the cycles of the economic markets. Its economic engine, whether powerful when productive or weak and dysfunctional when depressed, cannot be controlled or long influenced by a set of zoning regulations that has proven to be malleable at best, and environmental standards, no matter how correct, cannot be judged as fair and equitable if their application consistently produces unfair results.

We are left with a paradox: Many well-intentioned efforts to enhance the legitimacy of social issues and quality of life issues through governmental processes have, in fact, undermined the desired consequences, efforts, or effectiveness. In the absence of an overarching set of planning policies, it is not clear what we are trying to achieve. How do we know if we are fair? Fair to whom? How do we know if we are moving the city as a whole forward?

We must begin anew. Fiddling with the zoning resolution will not get us there. We must plan in ways that acknowledge and respect diversity and build a common vision. However, to prevent diversity from destroying wholeness, there must be some commonly agreed on ways to resolve disputes, build coalitions, and mediate results. New York City's planning process must accomplish all of this if the city is to continue as a thriving metropolis in the twenty-first century.

WHERE WE WANT TO BE

New York City is a very different place now than it was when the 1961 zoning revision was introduced. Its population, the distribution of wealth, investment and locational choices, the uses to which land is put in support of production, and national and global contexts all have changed drastically. For example, recent data show that "for the first time in the city's recorded history, there is no single race or ethnic group that is in the majority."[16] As a result of these changes, New York City today is a turbulent environment in which there are few, if any, commonly held values or assumptions. This is the problem with which New York City's planning process must cope first: Planning should be based on an effective process for forging agreements that recognize there will be differences in values; planning should not impose a set of values.

There are, in fact, concrete and positive examples of effective decision-making and problem-solving strategies to which New York City can turn. Effective neighborhood development strategies recognize that physical, economic, and social factors are interdependent, for example, that housing development requires financial investment that produces a physical structure and often frames the social interactions of the people who reside in the housing. This is true not only in "disadvantaged" communities but also in communities of all types.[17]

Educational strategies and social service and transfer payment delivery system innovations have all triggered a fundamental rethinking about strategies that might engender long-term and substantial improvements in neighborhoods that are now poor. For instance, the Head Start program set an example of how parents can be involved in the education of their children and also participate in the process of running a school. As their children progress through public school education, parents demand the same sort of interaction.

Even in the corporate sphere, "innovation" and "flexibility" are the new watchwords; whether businesses are trying to cope with maintaining competitiveness, organizational structure, management style, or technological and informational advances, they are rethinking their strategies. After years of competing head-to-head, IBM and Apple have decided to join forces in developing complementary rather than competitive production and marketing strategies.

In the international, corporate, and community development sectors alike, there is a fundamental reordering of assumptions. There seems to be a renewed respect for using the structure of the decision-making process as a gauge for measuring the equity of the outcome, as evidenced in this statement by an agency involved in funding community improvement programs: "A developing consensus among experts, providers and funders is that successful programs emerge from empowered communities that participate proactively in all phases of program planning, implementation and planning."[18]

Collaboration is, I believe, the best process through which consensus can be built and will provide opportunities for solving complex multiparty problems. Collaboration is a process through which parties with differing perspectives on complex and difficult problems come together to forge solutions that are beyond the capacity of single limited visions of what is desirable and what is possible. The primary objective of collaboration is to create an environment in which conflict and adversity can be overcome for the common good of the whole, so that individual and institutional self-interests can be met in a way that also promotes mutual benefit.[19] The measurement of effective consensus is whether it offers "the wisest, fairest, most efficient and most stable outcome possible."[20]

Collaboration is a process, not a prescribed state of organization and not a prescribed outcome. It requires that power balances shift to reflect the nature of the process. Effective collaboration may require a change in the definition of both leadership and responsible citizenship.[21] Being a responsible citizen no longer means marching lockstep behind a leader, it means being willing to face up to and tackle the problems in our communities. Collaboration is a dynamic and interdependent process that recognizes the interrelationships among issues and can provide maximum flexibility without sacrificing a comprehensive scope. Critics of collaboration often assail it as "idealistic and naive."[22] There are innumerable arguments against putting forward such a process, but it is a better process for moving us forward equitably than our current approaches to land use and resource planning.

How can collaboration help us reach our goal of planning and shaping a more equitable city? The collaborative process allows us to break down complex problems into a series of mutually agreed upon elements so that the outcome is more beneficial for all interests and parties. Although there is probably no single indicator of fairness that would be universally accepted, the premise here is that it is more important that the perceptions of those who participate in the problem solving, that is, those who are directly affected by its outcome, view it as fair. If the involved parties think a given process has been fair, they are more likely to abide by its outcome; if they do not, they will seek to undermine it.[23]

A more equitable city requires collaboration that can provide a mechanism for managing differences constructively, both from the viewpoint of defining the problems and proposing solutions.[24] A process that respects and encourages the establishment of mutual relationships based on the acknowledgment of interdependence, as collaboration requires, is more likely to result in stability and endure over time. "With a collaborative approach, the final agreement defining the common good is not the proclamation of a ruling elite or the result of political logrolling and majority rule, but rather a consensus agreement among those chiefly involved. Even when a collaborative agreement serves as input to a traditional legislative or administrative body [and thus becomes subject to pluralistic bargaining in that arena], opposition to the collaborative consensus should be minimal if a wide enough set of stakeholders participated in its development."[25]

Relying more on collaboration might mean scrapping or transforming ULURP or it might not. What is more important is that a new zoning resolution for the city should embody a set of overarching goals that New Yorkers can come to agree upon. The next zoning resolution should not just be a revision of land use rules, it should evolve from a process that allows the many interests that comprise the city of New York to come together in a consensus about what the city's development and resource allocation priorities should be.

CONCLUSION

Land use planning and zoning are relatively small elements of a much larger set of elements that contribute to New York City being a healthy, vibrant, economically stable city that meets the needs of each of its unique neighborhoods and builds on the strengths of its people and institutions. Nevertheless, they provide an opportunity to critically examine and analyze the current state of the city and to shape the course of its future: How it goes about making decisions and resolving problems defines that course, and how it goes about developing its plans as well as who participates in the planning process are critical to achieving equitable plans that create and encourage New York City at its best.

The people and institutions of New York City express strongly held assumptions and values and can, when motivated, garner powerful commitments to transform any element of the city, but these commitments are rarely widely shared; in fact, they often conflict with one another, to the detriment of the city as a whole. Since 1961, many of the city's experiences in planning and zoning have demonstrated that unless the city has established commonly held or overarching goals, even the most well-intentioned plans and land use actions can have disastrous side effects. Equity, or seeking fair solutions, would recognize these different interests and seek a means for them to be met—it seems like an impossible dream. In fact, many people, particularly those who feel their interests are not heard, have given up on the city.

Still, the situations facing New York City are not unlike other serious and heretofore intractable problems facing us as we venture toward the twenty-first century. These problems are characterized by dramatic changes in public expectations; dwindling or unpredictable resources and upheavals in the international, national, state, and local economies; demographic and political uncertainties; and anxiety about the complexities, both technological and social, that intertwine issues.

There are, however, concrete and positive examples of effective decision-making and problem-solving strategies in international diplomacy, corporate restructuring, and inner-city neighborhood redevelopment. Common characteristics include: comprehensive and integrative planning; collaboration among stakeholders rather than the imposition of solutions; acceptance of interdependence rather than either crippling dependence or independence as the basis of long-term relationships; and the encouragement of leadership development at all levels.

So how do we get there from here? We start by putting one foot in front of the other. We start by listening. We start by agreeing to respect different perspectives. We start by insisting that our political leaders and our public agencies take more responsibility for building consensus. We start with the commission; planning is what it is supposed to do. The commission provides an arena within which citizens, public interest groups, business leaders, and other city agencies and entities might willingly participate.

Long-term and substantial improvement in this city requires that we think about urban planning and zoning in different ways. It requires that we think about problem solving and decision making in radically different ways. The role of economic markets, assumptions of good design, environmental quality, and social parity all have to be recast so that the complex and many times uncontrollable elements that shape and influence the health and vitality of New York City can be commandeered.

It is not the absence of problems or differences that will mark our success; that is unrealistic. Differences are bound to arise. How we resolve our differences in making New York City the best that it can be is the critical question. Recognizing that we will not get any of what we want unless we can effectively handle those differences is the key. Collaboration that leads to consensus building is the art of managing differences. If we can institute processes in land use planning that result in the belief that an agreed upon resolution is the best possible, then we will have begun to fulfill our vision of planning for the equitable city.

NOTES

1. David Sills, ed., *International Encyclopedia of the Social Sciences,* Vol. 12: *Regional and Urban Planning* (New York: Macmillan and the Free Press, 1968). See the article on "Social Planning," pages 129 to 137.

2. *Annual Report on Social Indicators* and *Graphic Summary of 1991 Annual Report on Social Indicators and Citywide Industrial Trends* (New York: New York City Department of City Planning, October 1991).

3. Although ULURP has been modified since it was first instituted, the basic process remains the same. After an application for a land use action (including zoning changes, special permits, street closings or openings, park mappings, sale of public land, and so on) and its accompanying environmental studies are certified as complete by the New York City Department of City Planning, then the affected local community board(s), the affected borough board or borough president, and the New York City Planning Commission all review and comment on the proposal within a specified time period. Before the recent charter revision, all proposals were sent to the Board of Estimate for a final decision. Now the City Planning Commission is empowered to make the final decision in some cases; in other cases, the city council makes the final decision, subject to mayoral veto.

4. Lawrence Susskind and Jeffrey Cruikshank, *Breaking the Impasse. Consensual Approaches to Resolving Public Disputes* (New York: Basic Books, 1987).

5. "Wedding cake" towers, characterized by intricate setbacks, required complicated architectural planning. Much of the space in their towers, which could cover only 25 percent of the lot, had to be used for nonincome-producing services, such as elevator shafts. The taller, rectangular slabs favored by the 1961 resolution allowed architects to design one floor plan and repeat it for the entire height of the building; the rule that towers could cover 40 percent of a lot meant that upper stories would have more rentable floor space.

6. As Roy Strickland notes in his paper in this book, "The 1961 Zoning Resolution and the Template of the Ideal City," the New York City urban renewal program and the city's housing authority had been using this architectural form for more than a decade before the zoning revision.

7. Planning and development processes such as these also can lead to what John McKnight, the director of the Center for Urban Affairs and Policy Research at Northwestern University in Evanston, Illinois, refers to as a "productive" economy. In this sense, "productive" is defined "not only as the generation of goods and services but [also] the capacity for [providing] mutual support, care, and effective problem solving." See R. Susan Motley and Ronald Shiffman, *Comprehensive and Integrative Planning for Community Development* (New York: New School for Social Research Community Development Research Center, 1990).

8. *Rules and Procedure for City Environmental Quality Review* (New York: New York City Planning Department, September 1991).

9. *Toxic Waste and Race in the U.S.: A National Report on Racial and Socioeconomic Characteristics in Communities with Hazardous Sites* (United Church of Christ, Commission on Racial Justice, 1987).

10. Federal income tax and city property tax policies also influenced the amount and location of capital investment in the city.

11. For example, the Special Midtown District. See the New York City Zoning Resolution, Section 81–00 Special Midtown District, added 13 May 1982, N820253AZRM.

12. Section 197-a of the New York City Charter establishes provisions for plans that are created by agencies of the government other than the Department of City Planning and outlines the ULURP procedure by which those plans would be reviewed. Among the agencies empowered to develop and submit plans are the city's fifty-nine community-based planning boards. As a result of the charter revision, the City Planning Commission and department were required to develop rules by which they would review 197-a plans.

13. *Planning New York City 1991–1992* (New York: New York City Department of City Planning, October 1991).

14. *Criteria for the Location of City Facilities* (New York: New York City Department of City Planning, December 1990).

15. Roger Fisher and William Ury, *Getting to Yes* (Boston: Houghton Mifflin, 1981).

16. *Annual Report on Social Indicators* and *Graphic Summary of 1991 Annual Report*.

17. William Julius Wilson, *The Truly Disadvantaged* (Chicago: University of Chicago Press, 1987), p. 163.

18. "Call for Evaluation Proposals" (Oakland, CA: East Bay Funders, 1991).

19. Barbara Gray, *Collaborating: Finding Common Ground for Multiparty Problems* (San Francisco: Jossey-Bass, 1989).

20. Susskind and Cruikshank, *Breaking the Impasse*, p. 21.

21. Ibid., p. 19.

22. Gray, *Collaborating*, p. 246.

23. Susskind and Cruikshank, *Breaking the Impasse*, p. 25; and Robert Chaskin, *The Ford Foundation's Neighborhood and Family Initiative: Toward a Model of Comprehensive Neighborhood-Based Development* (Chicago: Chapin Hall Center for Children, University of Chicago, 1992).

24. Susskind and Cruikshank, *Breaking the Impasse*, p. 119.

25. Gray, *Collaborating*, p. 118.

COMMENTARY

This Commentary is edited from a panel discussion that took place after the presentation of the previous four papers at the "Planning and Zoning New York City: Yesterday, Today, and Tomorrow" symposium in New York City on January 30, 1992. Jonathan Barnett served as moderator.

JONATHAN BARNETT: I will not pose the paralyzing questions mentioned in the panel discussion about the first group of papers in this book: What is a good city and how can it be embodied in zoning? Those questions, like the questions, "What is the meaning of life?" or "Why are we here?", are too difficult to try to answer in this kind of a format. Instead, the question for our discussion will be: Given the current state of New York City's development regulations—whose evolution we followed this morning—and the current state of the city, where do we go from here?

The impressive attendance at this symposium is evidence that the power of zoning is appreciated—the details of zoning may be arcane but the power of zoning is pervasive. There was quite a bit of discussion in the previous set of papers, and among the respondents, about how little planning has been done in New York City and, thus, how little zoning has to do with planning. Actually, I find it hard to agree. Consider these examples:

- The Lower Manhattan Plan, prepared just before John Lindsay became mayor, probably was regarded, at the time, as a hopelessly visionary document, but more than half of it has been implemented.
- The transformation of Times Square—there was a plan, embodied in the Special Midtown District and in ordinances for signs. There are investors out there, I am sure, who wish today they had never heard of Times

Square, but the fact is, the city produced a plan in the form of zoning and got what it asked for.
- The transformation of SoHo and Tribeca—the private market provided the initiative, but the amazing changes in those areas have been managed by the tools of zoning and historic preservation.
- Finally, there was a seemingly trivial change in the regulations governing the merging of zoning lots, which had the most amazing effects.

Our discussion this afternoon seems to me to center around three sets of issues. One issue that is clearly before us is how much of the current zoning resolution must be changed. The spectrum of opinion runs from all of it, to none of it, to somewhere in between. The city's ability to revise zoning is affected by the fact that zoning now interacts with environmental review processes. There are two ways of dealing with the process by which projects are reviewed on the basis of their impacts on the environment: one is wholesale, the other is retail. An example of wholesale would be the downtown plan of San Francisco, which provides that any building that is built in accordance with the zoning and the plan has satisfied the requirements for an environmental impact statement. Retail you all know about; that is what we do in New York City. Any sponsor of a proposal that comes before the New York City Planning Commission, and that would include proposals seeking rezoning, special permits, and other discretionary actions, must also evaluate the effect of that proposal on the environment.

The second set of issues is defined by the polarities Jerold Kayden described in the earlier panel discussion. Should zoning rules be performance-based or prescriptive, general or detailed? Do we have a "Model-T" ordinance or a "Cadillac Seville"?

Finally, there is the approach toward property rights. One is that zoning is an abridgment of individual rights by a society that is acting in the interest of public health and safety. Otherwise, a property owner would have an infinite series of development possibilities, from digging to the center of the earth to building to the top of the sky. On the other hand, some people assume that development rights are a privilege conferred upon property owners by society, which has created the support system that makes development possible. Those are two very different views and they almost certainly will be the subject of debate, not just by our panel but in the courts during the coming years.

MARILYN TAYLOR: I come as an architect, sometimes a strategist, and almost never a theorist, so my comments are probably going to sound simple and straightforward. That is what I intend them to be because I hope, and I firmly believe, that there is a straightforward and wonderful way out of the dilemmas that we face at this moment.

COMMENTARY

Like the city itself, New York City's zoning ordinance is beloved in a few corners, besieged in many others. It has, to its credit, allowed the emergence of a profoundly complex city, with a diversity, both human and physical, that we love, but it is also confoundingly complex and no longer implemented with predictability or without considerable cost, especially as its City Environmental Quality Review (CEQR) entanglements confound us all.

In the face of the extraordinary web of ideas that have been presented in this collection of papers, I found that the most compelling statement about zoning for the city is at the beginning of Carol Willis's paper. That is, with just a slight restatement, that zoning is an assertion of public prerogative over private initiative, and even sometimes over private lack of initiative. The most fundamental question before us is what public prerogatives do we wish to assert in the zoning resolution?

As for the actual mechanisms that are used to implement zoning, if the 1961 zoning ordinance rested upon a trinity of three hierarchical definitions of allowable use, perhaps the analog for the future lies in three hierarchical definitions of change. The resolution should encourage change in places that are changing, allow change in places that are stabilizing, and discourage change in places that are to be preserved. These degrees of change, which would precede all other zoning designations, are recognizable from their success in the Special Midtown District and from Michael Kwartler's paper.

Why is change such an important parameter, the most important, perhaps, in considering how to organize our zoning ordinance? Because it is this planning distinction that gives us a basis for choosing between fine- and coarse-grained zoning approaches, between market-based and government-sponsored development strategies, and between equity-oriented and self-regulating activities.

Let's step back for a moment to consider where our fabulous city ought to be going. We must assert a vision, as well as a sense of confidence that we can move toward that vision. I believe that our physical planning strategies for the next decades, not forever, should address the following six challenges:

- We should promote the population diversity that has long distinguished New York City from other American cities. For all segments of this population, jobs, schools, and personal safety should be available.
- We should make and maintain that essential characteristic of cities, beloved public spaces.
- We should create an animated, accessible waterfront and allow it to be a working waterfront wherever possible.
- We should maintain and encourage even more the ability and the desire to get around without a car.

- We must update and renew what we have before we build anew—a goal that reflects concern with energy consciousness and resource conservation.
- We must catalyze change where it should occur.

Obviously, many tools are required to accomplish these objectives or other objectives that are identified and agreed upon through a thorough, equitable process for reevaluating the zoning ordinance, but, with regard to zoning, the primary definitions of categories should be couched in terms of degrees of desired change. These categories could be generalized or specialized, depending upon how likely it is that places within a particular category will be affected by market forces.

For example, in a neighborhood that is to be preserved, the emphasis would be on prescription, staying within the norm; in a stabilizing neighborhood, the emphasis would be on maintaining a balance, meeting the average; in a changing neighborhood, the emphasis would be on requiring direct responses to specifically articulated public objectives and to specifically planned public investments.

I would not be true to my colors as an architect if I did not echo the sentiment that all zoning tools, once articulated through a public process, should emphasize as-of-right development. There should be little discretionary review and no incentive bonuses. There could, however, be both a prescribed standard and a performance standard, as at least one current proposal suggests on the model of Midtown. I think we are sophisticated enough to do fairly well with an arrangement like that.

So, I would reiterate my support for a minimalist approach with generalized rules that are structured to promote various degrees of desired change, not particular land uses. In regard to fine-grained zoning regulations, I would choose the places where it is appropriate to devote the extraordinary resources required to prepare this level of regulation. There could be places in which change is occurring and bringing great density or places in which public objectives and the cost of meeting them are not easily anticipated.

I worry about whether our planning process can be more equitable or provide more equitable results. I worry that the habit of argument, not to say the love of argument, in this city is too ingrained to allow us to come to consensus. Collaboration requires trust, if not before the fact, at least during and after. Perhaps, too, the definition of equity is too elusive or transient to be embodied in regulations.

Susan Motley is right in saying that our best chance, therefore, is to embody our concerns for equity in the planning process. There are citywide responsibilities; they must be translated into plans at a community level for balanced allocation that serves not only the needs and interests of each city neighborhood but also its residents.

COMMENTARY

To assert that New York City is a city that is planned, zoning must be the glove to the strong right hand of public action. The private sector must do what it does best, sense the market and seize the opportunity. For this to happen in a manner even coarsely consistent with public goals, the public sector must do what only it can do, direct the private initiatives to a greater future. We must find the money so the city planning department can make progress in its efforts to do this.

Lest these challenges seem too daunting, I offer in closing a paragraph from the essay "Metropolis and Her Children," one of the articles the Federal Writers Project generated about New York City:

> There are those who consider that it is impossible to find any unity in the chaotic pattern of New York; or that, romantically enough, the emergence of unity would cancel its major charm. But the uneconomic and antisocial nature of many of the city's living ways demand[s] a clear reorientation. The potential unity necessary to such reorientation already exists in the New Yorker's own concept of his city. In this shared consciousness—generated by a look, a grin, an anecdote as cabalistic to outsiders as the shop talk of mathematicians—the complex of the metropolis finds its organizing principle, deeper than civic pride and more basic than the domination of mass or power. To the degree that this principle...can be instrumented by the forms and processes appropriate to it, New York will emerge in greatness from the paradox of its confusions.[1]

ROBERT F. WAGNER, JR.: I will talk less about zoning and more about planning. Since there is so little development taking place in the city right now, it is probably a terrific time to redo the zoning ordinance, and it is probably possible to have a resolution that is far less complicated than the one we have now, that does promote the as-of-right development and that does seek contextual planning; it is less likely, however, that we can have a zoning ordinance that deals effectively with issues of equity.

But focusing on the zoning resolution, important as it is to the shape of neighborhoods and, ultimately, of the city, misses, to some extent, the urgency of the data that are summarized in the Appendix. The city truly is at a point of crisis. We must be concerned about the nature of the poverty that this city faces, as well as its extent. We must be concerned that during the economic boom of the 1980s, years in which the city recorded the largest increase in the number of jobs ever recorded by the Bureau of Labor Statistics, the proportion of people living below the poverty line increased from one out of every seven New Yorkers to one out of every four. Most of the problems in this city relate to poverty, whether they be the problems of the school system, criminal justice, health, and the like. There is a host of key issues upon which planners must focus; they are issues of equity, as Susan Motley said, but issues that have social dimensions.

One could make the argument that today we are better off than we were a century ago. Jacob Riis's landmark book, *How the Other Half Lives*,[2] reported that essentially half the city's population was living in substandard housing. Robert Hunter, in his classic 1904 study of poverty,[3] pointed out that better than half the population was living in poverty. You could say that the numbers today are not nearly as bad, but the truth is, we are a city more divided than we ever have been, with a real danger of a permanent underclass, a real danger of being two cities.

In terms of physical development, it is important for the City Planning Commission not only to spearhead efforts to develop a new zoning resolution but also not to be reactive. There is a tendency to look at development on a project-by-project basis, to react as individual issues come forward and not to think through what an overall strategy should be; this certainly was true of the commission when I was chair. To some extent, this focus results from the mandates of the city charter, probably even more so as a result of the new charter and the cuts to the budget of the city planning department.

This is a critical time to consider the issue of housing again, as well as the kind of investment we should be making in infrastructure. One of the great concerns I have is seeing the city's capital program reduced from $57 billion for a ten-year program to about $45 billion. The truth is, the $57 billion program in no way came close to meeting the real needs of the city in terms of the schools that should be constructed, the hospitals that should be rehabilitated, the housing that should be built, or a whole host of other infrastructure issues, ranging from resource recovery to the water supply system. It is as important for planners to deal with those kinds of issues as it is to take a new look at zoning.

Yes, make the system more as-of-right; yes, do it in a way that builds in design guidelines and contextual zoning, but do not neglect the larger planning issues, the strategic issues that are going to define the kind of city New York City is going to be in the next century. In particular, do not neglect the human side of what is happening in New York City right now.

BARNETT: I thought I might ask you, Ms. Motley, whether you think Peter Salins's proposal could, in fact, be a basis for equitable planning.

R. SUSAN MOTLEY: There are some things that Peter Salins said with which I agree. We do need to reinvent the art and science of planning and zoning in New York City, and I do not argue with his definitions of a market-driven economy, although I caution that the market-driven economy has not been beneficial for New York City as a whole. When we talk about the market-driven economy, we frequently talk about a model that assumes an ever-expanding demand for development, and that assumes that condition to be good. Perhaps we should ask how the market economy can meet the needs of the city as a whole, not just an ever-expanding development mode. How can it work in ways that help to diminish or to remedy problems, the serious problems that exist, like large pockets of poverty?

We are a capitalist country, but we have a choice about how we use our capital to address our problems. My argument is that the people in the city are more important than the buildings. The ways in which we think about economics or our market-driven economy ought to be shaped as much by the needs of the people as it is with the traditional notion of how it might drive the building of buildings.

BARNETT: Peter, is Susan Motley's description of equity compatible with what you are proposing for zoning?

PETER D. SALINS: Let me point out two areas in which there is a connection between some of my ideas and some of Susan's concerns, and probably the concerns of Robert Wagner and everyone else here. First, the kind of regulatory scheme I envision would promote economic growth. The issue is not whether the market development of the 1980s helped the poor but that economic growth will help all classes. For example, development regulation can be a constraint on housing construction and on the rebuilding of the older housing stock. Clearly, any increase in the amount of housing development would benefit all social classes. Second, the development regulation of residential neighborhoods throughout the city should be left, in large part, to the residents of those areas.

BARNETT: That theme also can be found in Michael Kwartler's discussion of how planning should be done. John, it seems to me that you're the only person, in fact, on this panel who proposes working with the existing resolution. Everybody else is saying start over. Am I correct?

JOHN SHAPIRO: Only in a matter of degree. I suggest that we do not yet have a mandate, although maybe we have more of one after today, to scrap the zoning ordinance and say "starting today we're going to write a whole new one."

Yet the cost of keeping the basic framework we have now, and changing it a bit here and a bit there, is very high in terms of the city's economy and in terms of implementing a vision of the city. We should at least take the zoning ordinance and look at it thoroughly, at least land use by land use, asking how we might change it. I'd start with industrial districts because that is the most out-of-date section of the ordinance.

BARNETT: Does that seem a practical alternative?

MICHAEL KWARTLER: No, I don't think so. The problem with the approach John is suggesting is that while it may clean up the zoning ordinance—which is not so complex, it's just very confusing and contradictory—the ordinance will not necessarily be tied to any planning notion.

If we are looking to build the future of this city, and for New York City to be a world-class city and attract foreign investment, there must be some predictability, in part because other cities around the world are much more predictable in terms of where they're going and how values are socialized. The free-market approach that Peter and, to some degree, John advocate is antithetical to that kind of investment. It is inappropriate, at this point, to suggest that a city of this size in a region of this size should continue to bungle along piece by piece.

BARNETT: One of the issues the city might confront if it were to develop a zoning ordinance from scratch would be historic landmarks. We had a question from the audience for Peter Salins: How could you support the destruction of Grand Central Terminal when such a public outcry developed around the destruction of Penn Station in the 1960s?

SALINS: I am not against preserving historic structures. What I said is that I do not think the city should regulate the preservation of historic structures. Essentially, what the city should have done in the case of Penn Station, and should do in the case of Grand Central if it really were threatened, would be to buy the preservation, in effect. There is an economic value attached to preserving individual structures. If it is valuable to the general public to preserve these structures, the general public, through taxation, should pay for that preservation.

For the purposes of my paper, I was asked to carry my opinions to a logical extreme. Were I in a planning commissioner's shoes, I might not go as far as the paper implied. Certainly, in terms of truly eminent and widely agreed upon individual structures, such as Grand Central and Penn Station, I would be willing to have a limited degree of regulatory protection.

What I think is outrageous is the use of landmark designation to sweep across entire neighborhoods. Buildings that are historically interesting or not, old or new, architecturally significant or not, all come under the same protective rubric.

KWARTLER: To some degree, Peter's point about historic districts is well taken. The reason why historic districts have proliferated and for the sheer size of some of them is that landmark designation is a way of planning without preparing an environmental impact study. The current environmental impact statement process virtually, in a kind of ironic way, really prevents the kind of planning that would lead to the appropriate kind of zoning, either Marilyn's form of it or my version of it, which would be a very tight-fit kit of parts.

I would tend to agree that limiting the extraordinary control the Landmarks Preservation Commission may exercise in some of these areas might unburden the commission to focus on other issues. This could be accomplished by taking the kinds of design controls that many other preservation commissions in the United States are writing into historic district guidelines and instituting them as part of the zoning regulations.

TAYLOR: I would like to observe that Peter is probably as correct with his comments on environmental review as he is wrong with his comments about landmarking.

SHAPIRO: There is another reason besides avoiding the CEQR process that prompts communities to seek landmark designation: Historic districts are better understood by and more predictable to residents than zoning.

This is why: If you own a vacant lot on a block of row houses in a historic district and want to build something on it, you must appear before the Landmarks Preservation Commission. The commission has the ability to recommend waiving all sorts of zoning requirements, including use, bulk, and density provisions, but residents know that the commission will almost certainly require you to replace the block's missing tooth with another row house or, at least, a look-alike row house. This is the same sort of protection that Michael and Peter are advocating for very stable residential neighborhoods. The difference is that in historic districts, such protection takes place through discretionary review, as opposed to an as-of-right formula.

By the way, developers also know what to expect when they go before the Landmarks Preservation Commission; they know what the commission's concerns will be. So the great irony is that historic districts function as a very predictable form of zoning, albeit involving discretionary review.

KWARTLER: There is also confusion between what you're calling fine-grained zoning and what currently exists. What we have now is what I would call typologically based zoning, which means that the zoning resolution is legislating a particular building type. This is exactly what was done in the 1961 revision, which promoted tall buildings surrounded by open space that we now call the "tower in the park," and it is what the city is doing with contextual zoning, which legislates what is called a perimeter block building. Either of these may be appropriate or inappropriate in certain situations, but what could be done in a historic district is to legislate the unique characteristics of that district. In combination, these characteristics would produce places rather than legislating building types.

BARNETT: It sounds as if we now have consensus, almost, that we should dump the zoning resolution and start over again. I would like to ask Robert Wagner, as our resident expert on how things really happen in New York City, is this a realistic idea?

WAGNER: It is easy for us to sit up here and give all sorts of instructions about what should be done. It is much harder to do what should be done, particularly in the kind of context in which we are all working right now. I remember when I became chair of the planning commission I had a tremendous sense of power. Here I was with a good-sized agency of some four hundred people; I thought I had power and control. Then the inspector general told me the department had thirteen telephones that were not accountable to anybody and calls were being made to Tokyo, Paris, and London and all over the country. So I said get rid of them. Three weeks later, only one phone had been removed; it was my private line. So there are real limits in government as to what you can get done.

In terms of how the City Planning Commission and Landmarks Preservation Commission interact, how the planning commission and Board of Standards and Appeals interact, how the Public Development Corporation and the planning commission interact, my own view would be to move many of the powers that those other agencies have into the planning commission and department to give them a greater ability to plan.

Is this a time at which one might begin a major reexamination of the zoning resolution? I think yes. I think the fact that there has been an enormous turnout at today's symposium is a reflection of that. That there is only limited development pressure also probably makes this a very good time to start. I think Susan's points about how the process should be reexamined, about involving the communities of the city, are very important.

It is clear that there is a desire to come up with a plan that reflects a vision for the city's future and that there is a sense that the existing system—while not as terrible as many people think—is enormously cumbersome and very difficult and works against both good planning and necessary development.

BARNETT: If we really are talking about changing the zoning resolution, at least to some extent, we have to face the issue of equity. The audience posed a number of questions regarding this. One is, how do we create an enabling vision of our city that is inclusive rather than exclusive? And if we have as-of-right benefits to property owners, can we also have as-of-right obligations?

MOTLEY: When I am sitting at a table like this and looking at an audience like this and know that it really is not representative of the people that live in New York City, I almost cannot say anything. We must be aware of the mind-set that allows us, a very narrow group of people with wonderful ideas, to sit up here arrogantly and talk about planning and zoning for New York City. It horrifies me to hear a conversation about the "free market" when I know that the larger developments in Manhattan are subsidized. They're subsidized very heavily by the city and by taxpayers.

When we talk about being inclusive, we assume that there is a private club and that we must generously open it up. Rather, we should assume that we must serve the interests of the city and the people of the city, who include not only the developers and bankers and architects and the academicians but also the 43 percent or so of the population that is not represented here, that works, sometimes does not work, that struggles and tries to solve those problems.

So the first thing we must do is question our assumptions about who is at the table and what the issues are because the assumptions that have been put forth here are not assumptions that are accepted throughout most of the city. So one of them is just to stop and open up those assumptions. If we're here, then we do it here. The City Planning Commission has the power to open the discussion up.

SALINS: If we were to adopt my zoning proposal, the inclusionary zoning question, which means allowing multifamily housing and inexpensive housing, would be moot. The basic zoning would not exclude those types of structures. The scale of the housing, to some extent, would be regulated, but otherwise you could build any kind of housing that you wanted, with respect to the type of dwelling unit, configuration, and quality. Inclusionary zoning is an issue primarily in the suburbs.

KWARTLER: I am not quite so sure that is the case with your scheme, Peter. There is a contradiction that is built into it, which is that local communities would be empowered without any other controls superimposed on them to determine their own basic zoning regulations. Since we are trying to look at zoning in the framework of planning, that raises the "not-in-my-backyard"—NIMBY—question, which causes us to ask who is empowered and how power is distributed. If the planning mechanism does not include a connection back to the whole, and I did not really understand how in your proposal there was such a connection, then I am not sure how the location of those kinds of services that are essential to the city's infrastructure would be determined. There has to be a balance between community planning and broad-based city planning to determine the allocation of these facilities.

What is really at the core of this is having a notion that we are all in this together. The fragmentation that seems to have been created under the current charter will further fragment the city into distinct places that do not see themselves as part of a whole. There should be some sort of centralization that allows everybody to participate in an equitable fashion, to see a reciprocity of the benefits. Right now, there is no context for that.

SALINS: I am not convinced that NIMBY issues are nonneighborhood issues nor am I convinced that we should necessarily inflict guilt on local communities that reject unpopular kinds of developments. It is wrong to assume that a central planning authority or a central guidance system would be all that benign. We assume automatically that a central guidance mechanism and centrally established organizations and structures are always working for the general public good.

I came to Hunter College when Paul Davidoff had just started the planning program, and, as I understood Paul's basic message, it was that there is no such thing as the general public good. There are a whole series of local goods. Paul was very much identified with the local goods of poor communities, but the principle can really be applied to the local goods for all communities. New York City is simply too big for any central agency or central

FUTURE SCENARIOS

planning mechanism to decide what's good for everybody, and I will not accept that local communities should be made to feel guilty for rejecting facilities that they think will be harmful to their welfare. Some of the things that local communities oppose need not be built anywhere, perhaps. I am not certain that we need garbage incinerators anywhere in the city. If no neighborhood in the city wants a garbage incinerator, then we'll have no garbage incinerators in New York City and figure out some other way of disposing of garbage.

WAGNER: It strikes me that the zoning resolution, and reexamining the zoning resolution, can address issues of equity. In many ways, we have abandoned the braver planning that took place in the 1960s and 1970s.

Nevertheless, the truth is, no zoning resolution will be able to deal with the root problems that exist, and that is why I was talking earlier about a broader definition of planning. You could create whatever kind of zoning you wanted for Harlem, but it could not deal with the fact that 82 percent of all births in Harlem are to single mothers. It could not deal with the concentrations of poverty in the South Bronx, central Harlem, East Harlem, and central Brooklyn.

I agree that we should have a vision of integrated communities; I agree that we should have some concept of how the benefits of development in Midtown and downtown, assuming we ever get development in Midtown and downtown again, could be spun off to the poorer neighborhoods in the city, but the zoning resolution can play only a limited role in shaping the kind of city New York City will be in the next century, particularly in dealing with what I believe is the central issue of poverty in the city.

MOTLEY: I do not really disagree with you, Mr. Wagner, except that my instincts tell me that we are still not quite getting to the real issue. If there is a plan for the city, an overarching planning policy, that assumes certain things. For example, if the city establishes an overarching planning policy that assumes and encourages investment in buildings, then the result will be that investment in buildings is more likely to occur. If you have a planning policy that presumes and encourages, for example, job development, then it is more likely that jobs will result.

Zoning plays a small part in that, but the fact is that if the city does not have a goal for which it is aiming, then the city will never attain any of its goals, and to just shrug our shoulders and say, well, zoning cannot do it, means that we really will miss the target.

SALINS: I like vision. I think vision is terrific. [City Beautiful–era architect and planner] Daniel Burnham, with his talk about making no little plans, inspired me to say some of the outrageous things that I said, but vision does not mean a static endpoint. The real difference that I have with some people is that they think of vision in terms of a perfected place, and there can be no perfected New York City, equitable or not.

All we can talk about is putting in place certain kinds of processes, rules, and opportunities and work through those. So the vision really is not how we frame or describe the basic things that the public sector and the community as a whole must do. We must let nature take its course and let the lives of seven and a half million people and millions of firms and businesses and so forth operate filling this vision out. There is no physically perfect picture that we can draw for the city.

NOTES

1. Federal Writers Project, "Metropolis and Her Children," in *New York Panorama* (New York: Random House, 1938).
2. Jacob Riis, *How the Other Half Lives* (New York: Scribner, 1890).
3. Robert Hunter, *Poverty* (New York: Macmillan, 1904).

PART III

IMPLICATIONS

REFLECTIONS ON PLANNING AND ZONING NEW YORK CITY

RICHARD L. SCHAFFER

The papers in this book and the panel discussions that follow them offer perspectives on planning and zoning New York City. Some authors are concerned about the planning process, or the manner in which planning decisions are made—or not made—in New York City. Others are concerned about social, economic, and demographic trends that will affect the way people live, the use of existing buildings, and the types of new buildings and new neighborhoods that will be developed. Others are concerned that the current zoning resolution and planning process are too unwieldy and unpredictable.

The authors recognize that meaningful consideration of New York City's zoning resolution begins with the planning challenges the city faces. Zoning is a tool that helps the city address broader public policy issues—such as the size, location, and nature of its business districts, environmental protection and infrastructure provision, the maintenance of a neighborhood's physical character and quality of life, and the reclamation of the long-neglected waterfront edge.

New York City must accommodate change and guide development through planning and zoning policies that acknowledge the existing built fabric and foster a more efficient, equitable, and environmentally sustainable city. The planning responses that the city is seeking—whether through zoning or other policies—must recognize that New York City in 1992 is built out to a much greater extent than it was in 1916 or in 1961, when comprehensive zoning ordinances were implemented. We live in a mature city where new development will incrementally replace only a small portion of the built environment.

COMPREHENSIVE OR PIECEMEAL REVISION?

Does our zoning resolution need to be revised to meet our planning goals? Of course it does. Any zoning ordinance needs constant review and revision. Our zoning resolution needs a major overhaul. We need to reconsider both the zoning text—the regulatory tools and districts—and the zoning map, which distributes districts throughout the city. It has been more than thirty years since the original districts were created and many areas in the city were last remapped. There are numerous areas in which the zoning map no longer makes sense, particularly in some manufacturing zones. There are also many residential neighborhoods that have not been reevaluated for decades.

Should we scrap the resolution and start all over again, as suggested by several of the authors and commentators in this book? Proponents for starting over are often vague about the planning policies that they want new zoning to accomplish. Zoning is only a tool, albeit a powerful one, and one must define both the policies that it is meant to realize and its limitations.

Before we scrap the current resolution and begin anew, we must achieve a consensus on planning policies. The diverse opinions of the authors and commentators suggest that such a consensus remains elusive. Peter D. Salins sets forth a provocative argument on the need for a zoning resolution with greatly enhanced flexibility. However, the comments of the other authors and commentators indicate that the level of flexibility he suggests is more than many are willing to accept.

I do not think we need to start from scratch. Rather, we would be better served by rewriting the zoning text one major component at a time, along the lines suggested by Brian Kintish and John Shapiro, and by undertaking significant remapping actions. This course of action is the most reasonable way to proceed, given the city's limited resources and other constraints to drafting a new resolution. It permits the city to concentrate its resources on specific strategic planning and zoning issues, to present those issues to the public in discrete, understandable packages, and to complete timely environmental evaluations.

During the past decade, the New York City Planning Commission and the New York City Department of City Planning started this overhaul. Most significantly, the addition of contextual zones has provided a new set of tools for responding to land use concerns in residential neighborhoods. Also, we recently started to write an entirely new section of the zoning resolution that will address the unique characteristics of the waterfront. The community facilities provisions of the ordinance are also being reconsidered, and we will have to explore increasing the number of commercial zones and the areas in which they are mapped.

CONTEXTUAL ZONING IN RESIDENTIAL DISTRICTS

The general approach to the residential areas of the city has been to create new zones that will ensure that future development will be more sensitive to the built fabric, or context, of established neighborhoods. In the last decade, seventeen contextual zones have been added to the palette of zones that can be mapped in residential areas. This more than doubled the number of residential zoning districts and provided the planning commission with the tools for a more fine-grained zoning system that resembles, to some extent, the approach suggested by Michael Kwartler.

We are now applying these new tools in residential areas where they are appropriate. In neighborhoods with an established, consistent physical character, we are moving away from the zones mapped in 1961, which encouraged buildings that are often described as towers in the park. By providing suitable building envelopes, the new contextual zones correct mismatches between zoning and the built fabric and provide balanced opportunities to reinvest in neighborhoods. In some cases, these contextual zones enable existing homeowners to expand their homes in appropriate ways that were prohibited under the 1961 zoning text. While we study neighborhoods for potential contextual rezonings, we are also looking for locations in which development would be most environmentally benign, like along wide streets or near transit nodes.

In creating contextual zoning, the commission did not eliminate the basic zones established by the 1961 ordinance. There has been some criticism that the contextual zones add an extra layer of complexity to the zoning resolution. However, there are some neighborhoods in which contextual zones are not appropriate. These are neighborhoods with a diverse array of building types, where an argument cannot be made that there is a consistent built fabric. In these neighborhoods, it may be more appropriate to map more permissive zones like those adopted in the 1961 zoning. We must analyze whether the 1961 residential zoning is the best approach for these neighborhoods of if it should be revised or replaced.

Low-income residential neighborhoods require additional planning approaches. Zoning regulations are a much less powerful tool for implementing planning policies in these neighborhoods because there is little active private market development. Developers of housing in these neighborhoods—virtually all of it with public subsidies—rarely build inappropriately large buildings; in fact, sites are frequently underbuilt. Because a large proportion of the land in low-income neighborhoods is city-owned, the major determinants of redevelopment are policies for the assemblage and disposition of city-owned buildings and land, for capital budget expenditures on infrastructure, and for the provision of public services. These factors shape low-income residential areas and require the commission's continued attention.

RECLAIMING THE WATERFRONT

The possibility of significant change along the waterfront, a valuable but vastly underutilized resource, was for all intents and purposes ignored in the 1961 zoning amendment. The resolution did not recognize the special character of the waterfront; it simply mapped manufacturing zones to the water's edge and beyond. This may have made sense in 1961, when much of the waterfront was devoted to waterfront shipping. Today, however, shipping and other industrial uses occupy much less of the waterfront while residential and commercial uses compete for relatively scarce space inland. The reuse of portions of the waterfront offers a major opportunity to provide enhanced public amenities and economic value. It is time to reclaim this derelict edge of the city.

We are currently working to create planning policies and a comprehensive waterfront plan that will allow appropriate development along portions of the waterfront. Our work is based on four fundamental waterfront planning principles: preserving the sensitive coastal ecosystems of the natural waterfront, reestablishing public access and enhanced recreational opportunities, promoting a viable working waterfront, and redeveloping new land uses in appropriate areas. Zoning is one of the primary tools necessary to implement our vision of the waterfront. Other tools will include the Waterfront Revitalization Program, capital investments, and a policy for the disposition of publicly owned land.

As with residential districts, determining how and where to implement these mechanisms remains an issue. For instance, to encourage housing on a particular stretch of waterfront, we might not want simply to remap from a manufacturing to a residential zone. A basic residential zone may work appropriately upland, but development on the waterfront raises issues of view corridors, public access, and scale that demand special building envelope controls.

We are writing a new waterfront zoning text that will address such issues as the exact boundaries of waterfront lots, the ability of land underwater to generate floor area, building bulk controls, standards for ensuring appropriate visual and physical access, the definition of floating structures, and parking requirements. We must also determine what uses and what combinations of uses will be allowed and what types of uses and bulk will be allowed on piers and platforms. We will propose adding a new chapter to the zoning resolution with supplemental regulations for waterfront development that would apply, to the maximum extent feasible, on an as-of-right basis.

REINVENTING COMMERCIAL DISTRICTS

New York City is one of the nerve centers—command posts—of an increasingly integrated global economy in which major cities compete for economic advantage. To produce and export goods and services successfully to the region, nation, and world, the city's business districts must constantly reinvent themselves. One of the long-term issues facing the city's economy is the demand for space to accommodate changing needs. This is true of business districts in lower Manhattan and Midtown and of areas like Long Island City and downtown Brooklyn. During the past twenty years, the demand for commercial space has been more a function of the evolving nature of economic activity, employment, and space use than of dramatic changes in the total job base of the city.

Addressing the need for modern office space will require both new commercial zoning tools and significant remapping actions. For example, to facilitate the expansion of the Midtown and lower Manhattan office districts, it may be necessary to add contextual commercial zones to better integrate these districts with adjoining areas. Portions of Long Island City and downtown Flushing also will need to be remapped for commercial development. Appropriate zoning is only one of the issues confronting the planning for commercial areas. The department has undertaken comprehensive plans for lower Manhattan, Long Island City, and downtown Flushing that address the current pattern of development, future growth opportunities, zoning and urban design, infrastructure requirements, and improvement of the public environment.

It is essential that the zoning resolution adapt to New York City's changing commercial needs. Certain uses that were considered to be too noxious for commercial zones in 1961 are being thought of differently today, especially as the nature and extent of manufacturing changes. High-technology research and production are much cleaner and better neighbors than were traditional industries. Business establishments that combine production operations, wholesaling, and retailing have created hybrid uses that did not exist in 1961 and are not easily accommodated under the relatively rigid separation of use regulations now in effect. More mixed-use commercial and manufacturing districts will have to be considered.

REVISING PROVISIONS FOR COMMUNITY FACILITIES

We must reconsider the way in which the zoning resolution treats community facilities—a wide range of uses, such as schools, churches, hospitals, drug clinics, and homeless shelters. The issues stem from not only the way the 1961 zoning revision was written but also the changing character of community facilities.

The 1961 zoning revision gave New York City what are now the most liberal community facilities regulations in the country; in many residential neighborhoods, buildings devoted to such uses are permitted twice as much bulk as residential buildings. The nature of community facilities, however, is different than it was thirty years ago. For example, in the past, hospitals were typically of modest size and relatively nonintrusive in neighborhoods. Today, hospitals often generate the most intensive pedestrian and vehicular activity in communities and many sponsor research and teaching programs. Hospitals provide New Yorkers with more than health care—they are an important element in the growth of the city's economy and employment base.

Houses of worship are another example of the continuing evolution of community facilities. In the past, most houses of worship served a local population; now they often serve a regional one. This changes the relationship of houses of worship to communities. A church, synagogue, or mosque and its ancillary buildings can be the largest structures in a neighborhood. Public tolerance of the extra bulk of these buildings declines when their users come from outside the community, particularly when they create extra traffic and parking problems.

Planners must focus on the built fabric and the quality of life in neighborhoods, but these concerns must be balanced against the economic, cultural, and social importance of community facilities and their need for adequate space. Striking this balance does not require that we toss out the entire zoning ordinance and start over. The community facilities provisions of the current ordinance must be carefully reviewed and modified.

UPDATING THE ZONING

Zoning text reform must be accompanied by remappings that apply particular zones to specific geographic areas. As discrete sections of the resolution are revised, the new zones must be mapped to help shape market forces and guide the city's orderly growth and development.

Clearly, there are areas of the city that should be rezoned. In the past few years, numerous rezoning actions have been undertaken, but they have too often been on a site-by-site basis or have covered only a few blocks. Planning and rezoning must be done on a broader scale; therefore, the department has undertaken several planning initiatives that will inform future larger scale rezonings. These include the comprehensive waterfront plan, the citywide industrial study, the comprehensive recreation and open space plan, three comprehensive business district plans, several infrastructure analyses, neighborhood redevelopment plans, and the lower density contextual rezoning studies. There are also more targeted borough plans and studies that will propose rezonings for substantial areas of the city.

The zoning map is the city's geographic policy statement for growth and development, indicating the location and magnitude of appropriate investment. Planners must produce balanced, economically realistic rules of the game for developers and residents alike. This requires a constantly updated zoning map and text. Outdated zoning forces developers to seek rezonings that take an extraordinary amount of their—and of the city's—time, effort, and expense.

IS ZONING TOO COMPLICATED?

Some of the authors argue that the original 1961 zoning districts, combined with subsequent special districts, contextual districts, and a range of other special provisions, have made the ordinance so large and complicated that it is nearly unworkable. However, there is nothing inherently good or bad about a resolution that consists of 835 pages. I am not troubled that our resolution offers a palette of thirty contextual and noncontextual residential zones from which to choose when mapping residential districts. Quite frankly, I do not think it troubles most New Yorkers either, even those who follow these matters closely. We are planning for a very large, complex city with a diverse array of neighborhoods. The issue should be how well the zoning resolution provides for the orderly growth and development of the city, not how many pages, zones, or special districts are in it.

Sections of the resolution certainly should be pared down. For example, do we really need three slightly different versions of the subway bonus? Furthermore, close to four hundred pages of the resolution are text for special districts. Some of these districts could be replaced by mapping the contextual residential zones we have developed in recent years.

It is true, as several of the papers and commentators state, that the department and the commission have been far better at drafting new zoning text than they have been at eliminating existing text. However, it is important to remember that all of the text in the resolution was put there for a reason. For instance, having nearly parallel sets of residential zones—the original 1961 zones and the contextual zones, which were added later—makes the zoning ordinance more complicated. This approach was intentional; the department and the commission knew that contextual zones, while necessary, were not appropriate responses to all situations. There are undeveloped areas in our city, as well as existing neighborhoods, with no consistent built fabric.

City residents' increasing demands on zoning account for some of the growing complexity of the zoning ordinance. As the city has been built out during the past seventy-five years and as the standard of living has improved, people's expectations have grown about the quality of their lives and their environment. The demands on zoning in 1916 were primitive compared to what we currently ask of the zoning ordinance or even what we asked of it in 1961.

Today, zoning tackles issues that were unthinkable, legally or politically, in 1916 or 1961. Zoning has evolved from a regulatory system whose purpose was to prevent a harm—limit extreme densities, prevent excessive loss of light and air, and segregate noxious uses—to one that also seeks to confer a good. The shift started in the 1961 comprehensive amendment to the zoning resolution, which offered density bonuses to developers for providing certain types of public open space. Incentive zoning has since been expanded to encourage the provision of other amenities, such as low-income housing, subway station improvements, and covered pedestrian spaces.

Some of the traditional concerns of zoning have also taken on new manifestations. For example, though separating noxious uses from other activities has always been a fundamental concern of zoning, the framers of the 1916 and 1961 ordinances could not have anticipated the problems posed by the proliferation of waste transfer stations. These are places where garbage collection trucks dump waste for sorting or shipment on larger trucks to recycling facilities or distant landfills. In 1961, most waste went directly from collection trucks to landfills or incinerators in the city. Today, as most of the landfills and some of the incinerators have closed, a substantial portion of the city's waste stream passes through these transfer stations, much to the annoyance of nearby residences.

Zoning must evolve to meet the changing needs and aspirations of an increasingly complex city; however, it is only one of the public policy tools available to promote the general welfare. Depending on the particular issue or circumstance, there may be other measures that are more effective than zoning. For instance, the 1961 zoning revision introduced noise regulations for manufacturing zones. Since then, the city's administrative code has adopted noise provisions that are more restrictive than those in the zoning. It may be that noise provisions are no longer needed in zoning. Similarly, when the Quality Housing provisions for residential buildings were introduced into the zoning text in 1987, they included innovative requirements for storing recyclable materials. Now the Department of Sanitation is considering an amendment to the administrative code that would require similar storage for all types of housing. Zoning may have been the best tool available at the time to achieve these goals, but we must continually reassess whether other regulatory measures could be more effective.

There are limits on our ability to use zoning to achieve the broader goals of planning. First, the use of zoning to implement public policy relies on private market development. Revised zoning will not address the plight of low-income communities that do not have private market development. Second, zoning cannot be so complicated that it cannot be easily administered or enforced. The city has limited resources available to oversee implementation of its zoning and other regulations. Complex or discretionary rules require additional staff time and financial resources that often exceed the city's funding ability.

Finally, zoning may not be precise enough to achieve certain goals. The resolution outlines rules and standards for broad categories of uses; it cannot be responsive to specific situations. Zoning, for instance, can place general restrictions and enclosure requirements on waste transfer stations. To deal even more effectively with them, though, the Department of Sanitation has developed detailed, complementary regulations. These regulations will operate on a micro scale, considering where a particular waste transfer station should be located and how it should be maintained in an environmentally sensitive manner.

These general limitations of zoning, as well as particular shortcomings of the city's zoning resolution, are addressed in both Peter Salins's and Michael Kwartler's papers. Kwartler advocates an entirely new resolution consisting of an intricate "kit of parts" that can be combined in various permutations and combinations to respond with a high degree of specificity to local situations. This kit of parts would allow diverse, custom-tailored planning agendas to be carried out throughout the city. Older, established neighborhoods might be assigned detailed, almost shrink-wrapped zoning that would allow very limited change while areas slated for redevelopment might have permissive regulations that would permit a wide variety of uses and building configurations. Kwartler points out that his alternative kit-of-parts regulatory regime would require planners to make conscious decisions about how to manage change and its physical manifestations in every neighborhood.

How big should the kit of parts be and how fine-grained should we make the resolution? The current resolution has a basic residential kit of parts consisting of thirty zones. Kwartler's kit of parts would have hundreds, if not thousands, of permutations, which would be more than the people who write and administer zoning could efficiently manage; there would just be too many building blocks to juggle.

Conversely, Peter Salins recommends a new zoning resolution with a much simpler, coarser grained set of rules than today's ordinance. There is elegance in a simple resolution that could have the added benefit of being easily understood and administered. It could help to provide the regulatory flexibility that is necessary to respond to the constantly changing needs of a modern urban economy. But does his proposal have enough building blocks to serve the planning needs of the city? For example, Salins recognizes that low-density residential communities deserve relatively protective regulations. However, the residents of middle-density and higher density communities are just as concerned about the built form of their communities as residents of lower density areas. If the city were to implement the Salins proposal, many additional zones would probably have to be added. Furthermore, his approach does not specifically address unique areas, such as the waterfront. Would we want to see, or would the public permit, the waterfront to be developed without regard to its special character?

One of our zoning objectives is to balance Kwartler's fine-grained approach with the more coarse-grained one suggested by Salins. Both have their merits in a city as diverse as New York City. Flexible zoning can help the city to accommodate unpredictable future needs, especially in the commercial and manufacturing zones that must constantly adapt to changing economic realities. However, many people select particular neighborhoods in which to live based, at least in part, on the physical environments they offer. It is legitimate for residents to expect that zoning will provide a reasonable degree of predictability about the nature of future development.

CONSTRAINTS TO CHANGE

There are three constraints in the consideration of any rezoning, whether it is a comprehensive, citywide revision or a simple remapping of a district. First, sufficient consensus must be achieved among a diverse array of groups, including the community, the City Planning Commission, and the City Council and other elected officials. Second, the limited staff and resources of the Department of City Planning restrict the speed and scope of planning and zoning initiatives. Finally, the City Environmental Quality Review (CEQR) process can be a major obstacle to effective planning and zoning.

The sheer size, pace of change, and diversity of New York City make consensus-building on particular planning and zoning policies a daunting task. The zoning resolution is based on the premise, which I strongly support, of as-of-right zoning; however, many communities favor discretionary review of proposed developments. Outmoded zoning increases the likelihood of discretionary review because a developer seeking to undertake a substantial project will need a rezoning or a variance. This provides the community board and elected officials with the opportunity to review the proposal.

Interestingly enough, communities, in spite of their desire for site-by-site review, often want comprehensive plans for an entire neighborhood. Such larger scale plans and rezonings are certainly preferable to site-by-site rezonings. After an areawide rezoning, development would most likely take place as-of-right, with no discretionary review. This can make communities apprehensive and reluctant to pursue broad rezonings. A key element in allaying such fears is, as R. Susan Motley notes in her paper, an inclusive community planning process involving all of the relevant stakeholders. Planning is both product and process.

The second constraint to zoning reform is the department's limited staff and resources. Rezonings require extensive planning studies, environmental reviews, and a lengthy public review process, yet New York City has a relatively small planning department. With recent budget cuts, the number of staff is at its lowest level since 1970. In terms of planning department staff per 100,000 city residents, New York City ranks in the bottom fifth of the nation's one hundred largest cities.

Finally, CEQR, a disclosure process that injects environmental considerations directly into decision making, can be a major hurdle to good planning and zoning. When a discretionary action is submitted to the City Planning Commission, CEQR requires either a study of its environmental impacts or a finding that the action would have no significant adverse environmental impacts. Every special permit, every zoning text change, and every remapping is subject to this process.

Such studies could provide useful and meaningful analyses of probable environmental impacts and methods of mitigation, provided they ask and answer the pertinent planning questions. Unfortunately, CEQR has evolved into a rigid, litigation-driven system that frequently asks and answers questions that are not relevant to the issues at hand and that provides large amounts of quantitative data of dubious value.

Another problem with CEQR is that city agencies have come to rely on it as a tool to further their policy agendas and enforcement initiatives rather than as a process to disclose the impacts of regulatory actions and specific projects. Consequently, planners and project sponsors can be tied up for inordinately long periods of time analyzing issues that are of more concern to particular operating agencies than to the final decision makers in the zoning and land use action. Operating agencies should use other means to enforce citywide policy regulations. CEQR is not an effective, consistent policy enforcement tool because only a limited number of discretionary actions are subject to environmental review.

Finally, environmental impact statements (EISs) create a false impression of scientific accuracy. For example, a project sponsor could be required to estimate to the second or third decimal place the air quality impacts of a project or the volume-to-capacity ratio of traffic at a particular intersection. Can we really accurately measure and predict impacts to such a fine degree? Reasonable order of magnitude estimates of probable environmental impacts would be sufficient for the final decision makers.

To a significant degree, CEQR problems are a self-inflicted wound. The city has the authority under the state environmental quality review law to reform its own process. The City Planning Commission, which, under the new city charter has responsibility for setting the city's environmental review rules, has already unanimously approved a revision to the CEQR rules that eliminated the co-lead agency system under which each expert agency was responsible for reviewing every action. This should streamline the initial stages of the process. There are other much-needed managerial and methodological reforms under way, including developing the techniques to conduct meaningful environmental reviews of proposed areawide rezonings. Environmental review must inform good planning, not be an obstacle to it.

Many environmental issues would not have to be analyzed extensively in the CEQR process if the city's land use planning and zoning policies were better coordinated with infrastructure planning. CEQR is a disclosure process; it is no substitute for effective environmental planning and regulation. For instance, if the city were to address air quality by implementing a plan to control the flow of traffic, it would be much less likely that adverse impacts relating to air quality would be identified when a project sponsor had to prepare an EIS.

Some have suggested that if the city wanted to undertake a comprehensive revision of the zoning resolution, it should ask the state legislature for an exemption from CEQR. That is an idea with some initial appeal, but it avoids the real issues of CEQR reform and the need to integrate land use regulation with infrastructure and environmental planning.

THE LEGACY OF 1961

The 1961 comprehensive amendment to the zoning resolution, arguably the most ambitious citywide land use strategy ever adopted in New York City, was premised on a vision of a city that would be rebuilt in a form substantially different from the traditional city fabric. Based largely on architectural and urban redevelopment theories and concepts of the 1920s and 1930s that embraced Modernism's "tower in the park," the 1961 revision also responded to greatly increased automobile use, an expanded population, and new building technologies. The revised ordinance not only had relatively little respect for the existing built fabric of the city, it was purposefully in conflict with it. This was not a resolution designed to foster sympathetic infill solutions.

Fortunately, in recent years, planners have come to value much more of the existing built fabric and have made greater efforts to accommodate change more respectfully. We have learned that many of the approaches put forth in 1961 have not worked well. Places were built that people do not like, that do not function well, and that do not take advantage of the city's unique characteristics.

Today, we seek to shape a zoning resolution based on a different premise. Instead of using zoning to create a new city, we seek to knit new threads into the existing fabric of a mature city. Change will inevitably occur and is crucial for the city's future prosperity, but in a mature city, change will affect only a small portion of the built fabric. How do we fit the new amidst the old? Each of the authors seeks to find the most appropriate way to accommodate change and guide the orderly growth and development of New York City.

This is the task that confronts the City Planning Commission as it drafts the first charter-mandated *Planning and Zoning Report*. In this report, the commission will articulate its vision of New York City and a set of the planning and zoning policies to achieve it. By analyzing the relationships of earlier zoning initiatives to the development of New York City and by portraying alternative visions for a future zoning regime, the authors of these papers have played an important role in informing both the members of the City Planning Commission and the general public.

APPENDIX

A BRIEF PROFILE OF TODAY'S CITY AND TRENDS FOR THE FUTURE

COMPILED BY ERIC KOBER, WITH LARRY LITTLEFIELD

New York City's population peaked at nearly eight million in 1950 and 1970, declined sharply to approximately seven million in 1980, and has recovered somewhat in the last decade. Manhattan's share of the city's population has declined steadily since 1910. In the other boroughs, population first grew rapidly in Brooklyn, then in the Bronx, and then, particularly since World War II, in Queens and Staten Island.

For the first time in New York City's history, no racial or ethnic group is in the majority. The city's diversity reflects its large and growing immigrant population. About eighty-six thousand immigrants per year moved into the city in the 1980s and the yearly number has been increasing in the early 1990s.

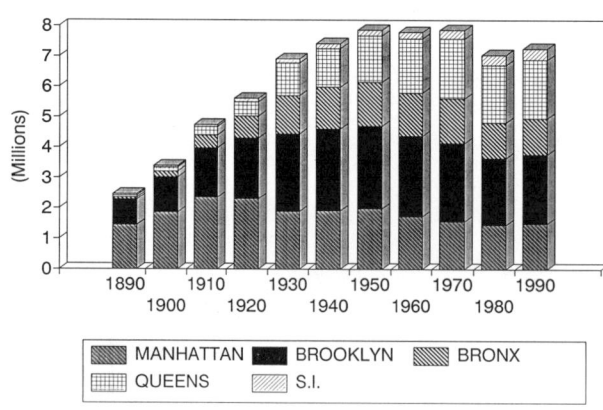

FIGURE 50
New York City Population, 1890 to 1990, by Borough

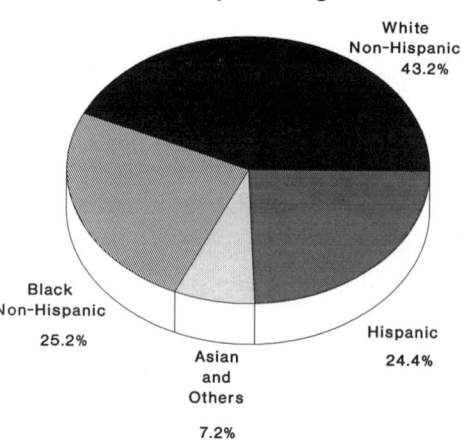

TODAY'S CITY AND TRENDS FOR THE FUTURE

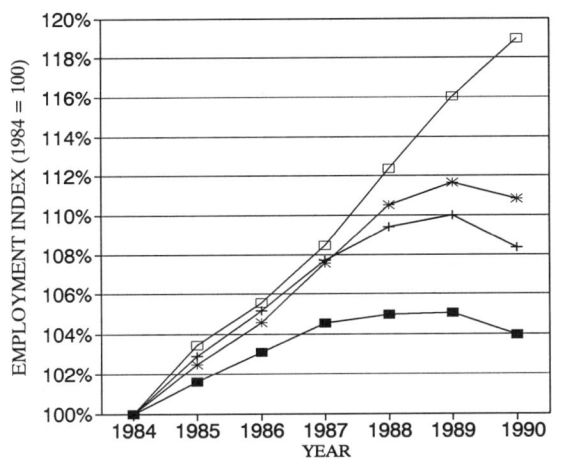
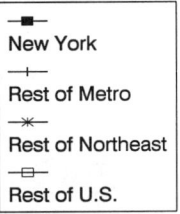

FIGURE 52
Total Employment Index: New York City and Other Areas, 1984–1990

SOURCE: Current Employment Survey data, New York State DOL

FIGURE 53
New York City Employment: 1958–1991

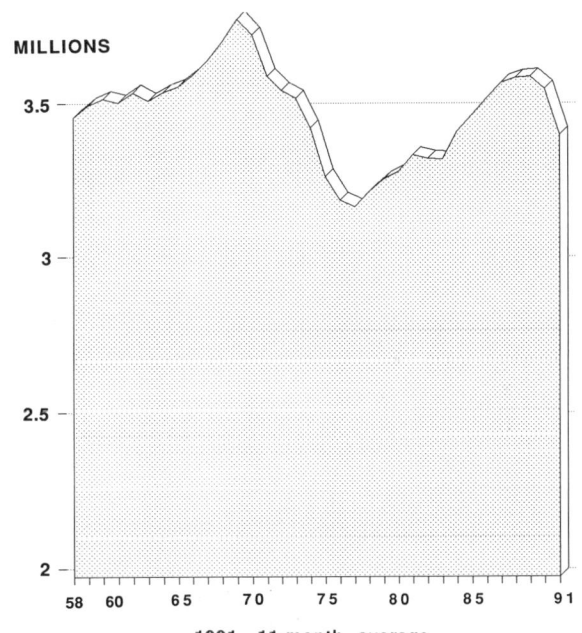

1991—11-month average

New York City's population is affected by the strength of its economy since jobs attract residents. After a steep fall during the 1970s fiscal crisis and a recovery during the 1980s, employment in the city is at about the same level as it was in 1961. The city's employment has fluctuated within a relatively narrow band, between 3.2 and 3.6 million jobs, during the past thirty years, although its manufacturing employment has declined steadily from 1954 to 1987. Most recently, employment has been falling, due to a regional recession that also affected surrounding suburbs. During 1991, the regional recession was worsened by a nationwide recession.

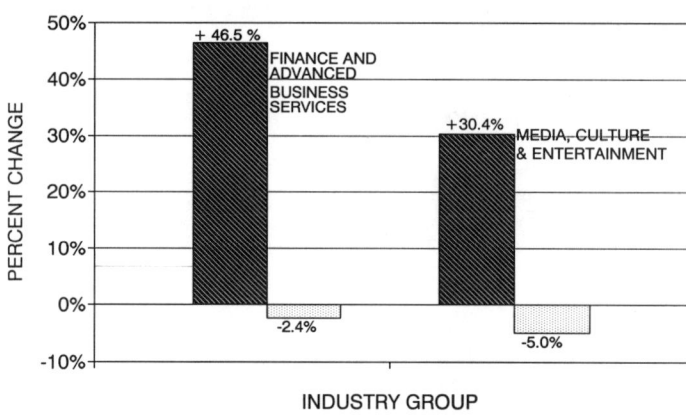

FIGURE 54
New York Key Industry Groups: Percent Change in Employment, 1977–1989

FIGURE 55
New York City Manufacturing Employment: Number of Production Workers, 1899–1987

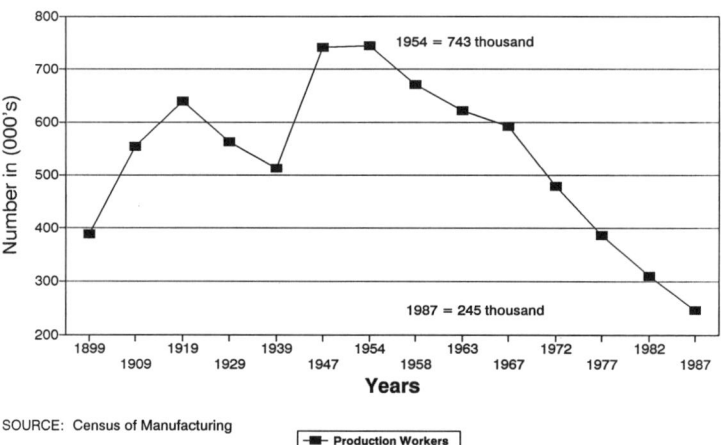

SOURCE: Census of Manufacturing

Despite this decline, the city still has an enormous job base. New York City's economic recovery in the 1980s was led primarily by financial and advanced business services. New York City also reinforced its preeminence as a center of media, culture, entertainment, and the arts. Since the 1987 stock market crash, however, these industries and others have been losing employment. The city is heavily dependent on its key service industries.

The strength of the economy influences the amount of revenue available to support city government. New York City spends more than the average U.S. city when expenditures are measured in relation to the income of its citizens. The city collects about the same amount as the average local government from revenue sources like federal and state aid; the additional revenues required by the city's higher spending levels must be collected from local taxpayers. As a result, New York City's income tax revenue, as a

TODAY'S CITY AND TRENDS FOR THE FUTURE

share of the income of city residents, is double the average for local government in the nation as a whole.

New York City spends more than other cities do for several types of public service—including social services, police/corrections/judicial, and interest/pensions. It spends less than average on education and about average on categories other than housing. The data shown in the bar graph include both operating and capital expenditures, but the city did not spend more than the national average on capital expenditures.

The services on which New York City spends more than average reflect the needs of the poor. Although these needs are a national problem, the city is forced to rely on higher local taxes to address them. New York City's low-income population is large. The city and state also provide more extensive services for the poor than do other parts of the country, and New York State mandates that the city pay a higher share for these services than is the case in other states.

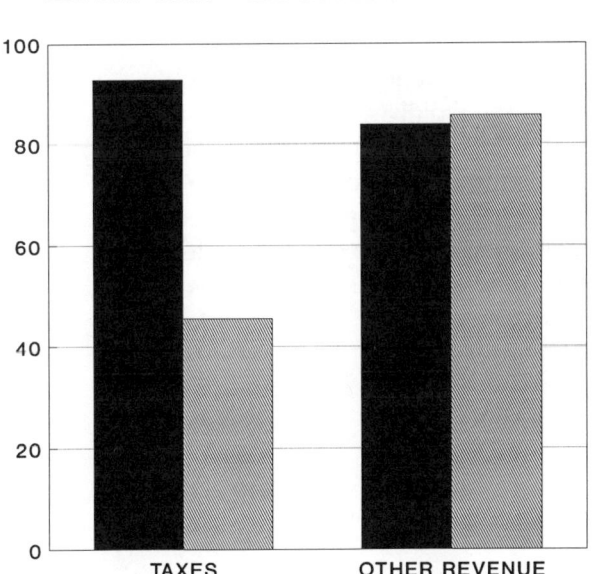

FIGURE 56
Local Government Revenue, New York City and U.S. Averages

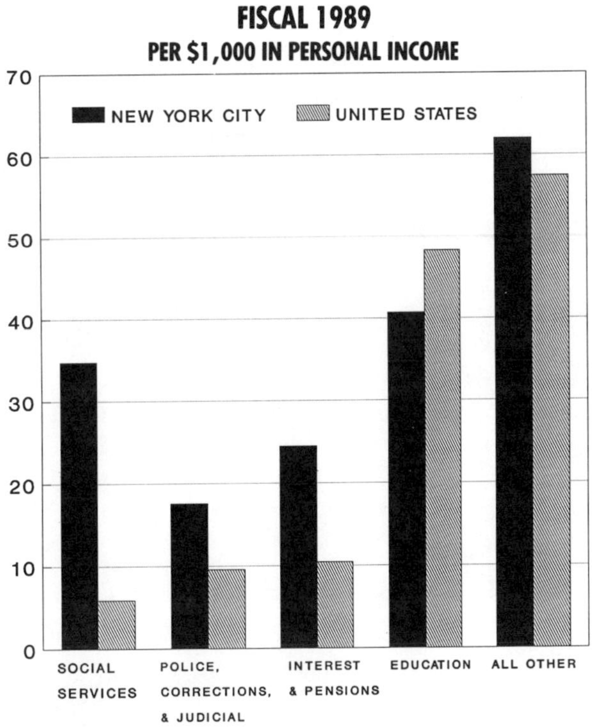

FIGURE 57
Local Government Expenditures, New York City and U.S. Averages

256
APPENDIX

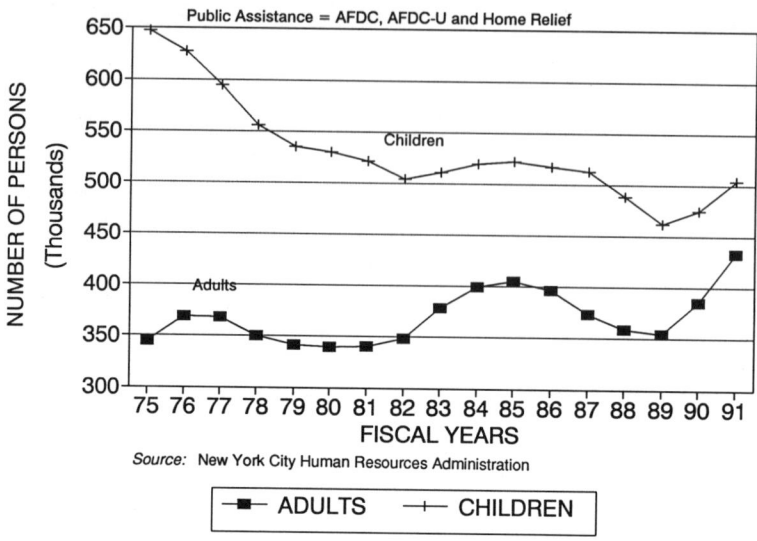

FIGURE 58
Public Assistance Recipients: Adults and Children, New York City, 1975–1991

The number of New York City residents on public assistance fell as the economy expanded in the 1980s but has risen rapidly since the onset of the recession. About 13 percent of the city's residents rely on public assistance, compared with about 5 percent of all residents in the northeast region and about 6 percent of all U.S. residents. Since 1975, the number of children on public assistance has fallen but the number of adults has risen. Even during the city's recent employment peak in 1989, more than 350,000 adults and 800,000 total persons relied on public assistance.

TODAY'S CITY AND TRENDS FOR THE FUTURE

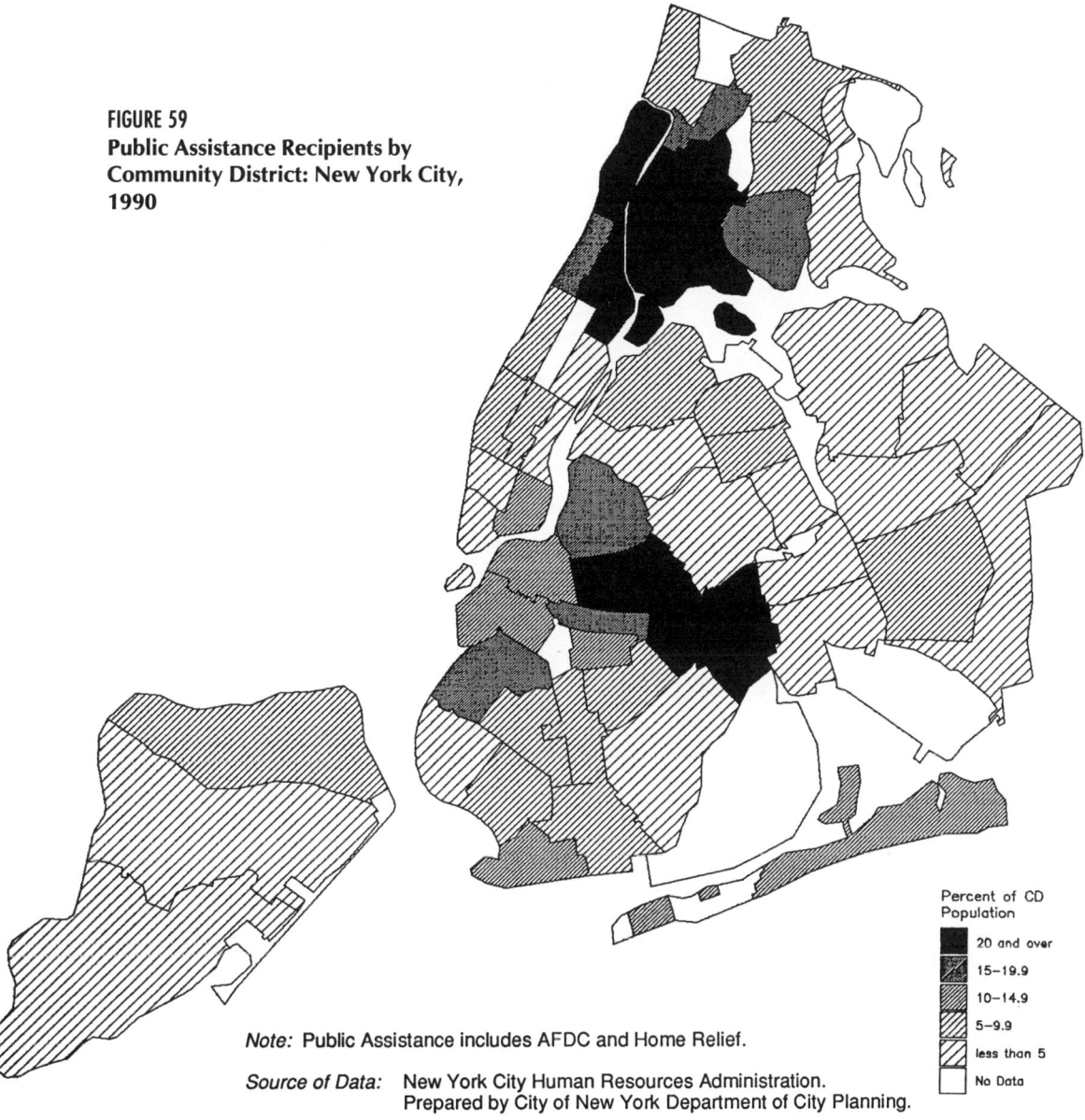

FIGURE 59
Public Assistance Recipients by Community District: New York City, 1990

Note: Public Assistance includes AFDC and Home Relief.

Source of Data: New York City Human Resources Administration. Prepared by City of New York Department of City Planning.

Percent of CD Population
- 20 and over
- 15–19.9
- 10–14.9
- 5–9.9
- less than 5
- No Data

New York City's poorest residents are concentrated in two broad bands of neighborhoods, which are shaded darkest on this map, in east and central Brooklyn, in northern Manhattan, and in the South Bronx. Many social problems, such as crime, infant mortality, and low educational achievement, also are concentrated in these neighborhoods.

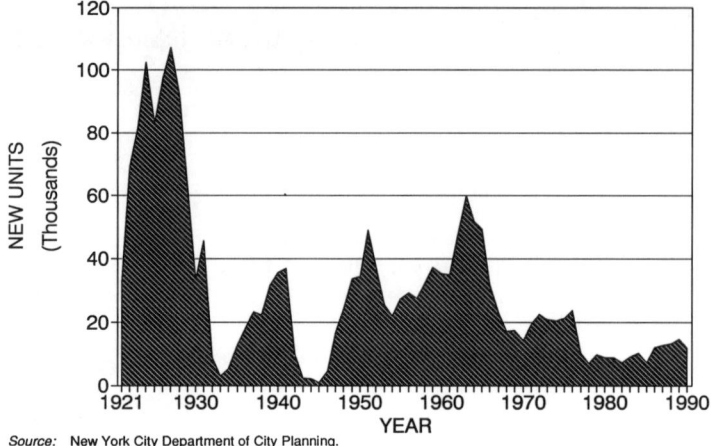

FIGURE 60
New Housing Completions,
New York City, 1921–1990

Source: New York City Department of City Planning.

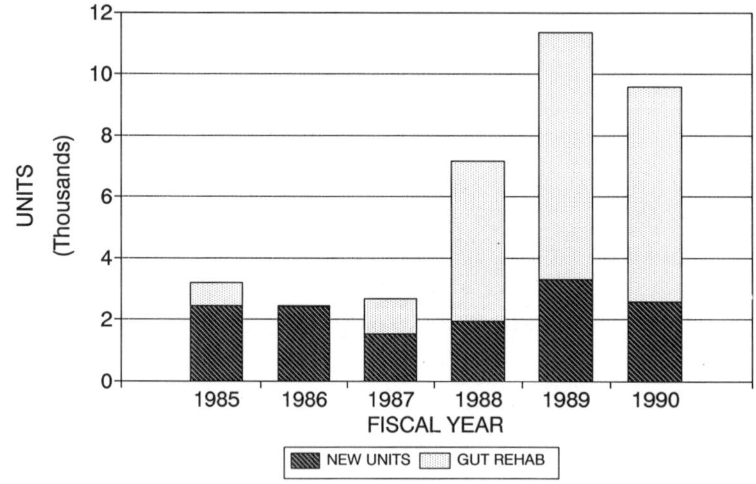

FIGURE 61
Housing Starts, Department
of Housing Preservation and
Development Subsidized
Housing, 1985–1990

Note: Does not include moderate rehabilitation.
Source: City of New York Department of Housing Preservation and Development.

The city's population and economy help shape land use patterns. New housing construction rose in New York City during the 1980s, but it remained far below the level of its peaks in the mid-1920s and its postwar peak in the early 1960s. These were periods of favorable credit conditions and, incidentally, coincided with grace periods established before more restrictive building regulations—the 1929 Multiple Dwelling Law and the 1961 zoning revision—were to take effect. The Multiple Dwelling Law established uniform design criteria for apartment buildings, regardless of the zoning district in which they were to be located.

Subsidized housing construction fell sharply after the cuts in federal assistance after the mid-1970s. The city's strong economy enabled it to undertake a major new housing program in the 1980s, but even this did not replace the lost federal support. From 1972 to 1976, for example, an average of 17,500 new subsidized units were completed each year in New York City, about double the city's recent production.

TODAY'S CITY AND TRENDS FOR THE FUTURE

The city of New York's built residential densities are the nation's highest. Even in the lowest density areas in New York City, which are shaded lightest on this map, in Staten Island and eastern Queens, residential density is at least eleven units per acre, high by national standards. In single-family areas of the suburbs, in contrast, the density of development might be eight units per acre or less. (In this map, density is measured as the number of units divided by the amount of developed residential land, not total land, which is why residential densities are high even in the central business district.)

The density of the city's neighborhoods reflects the availability of transit service, with the highest densities within a short subway ride of the central business district and the lowest densities in auto-dependent areas.

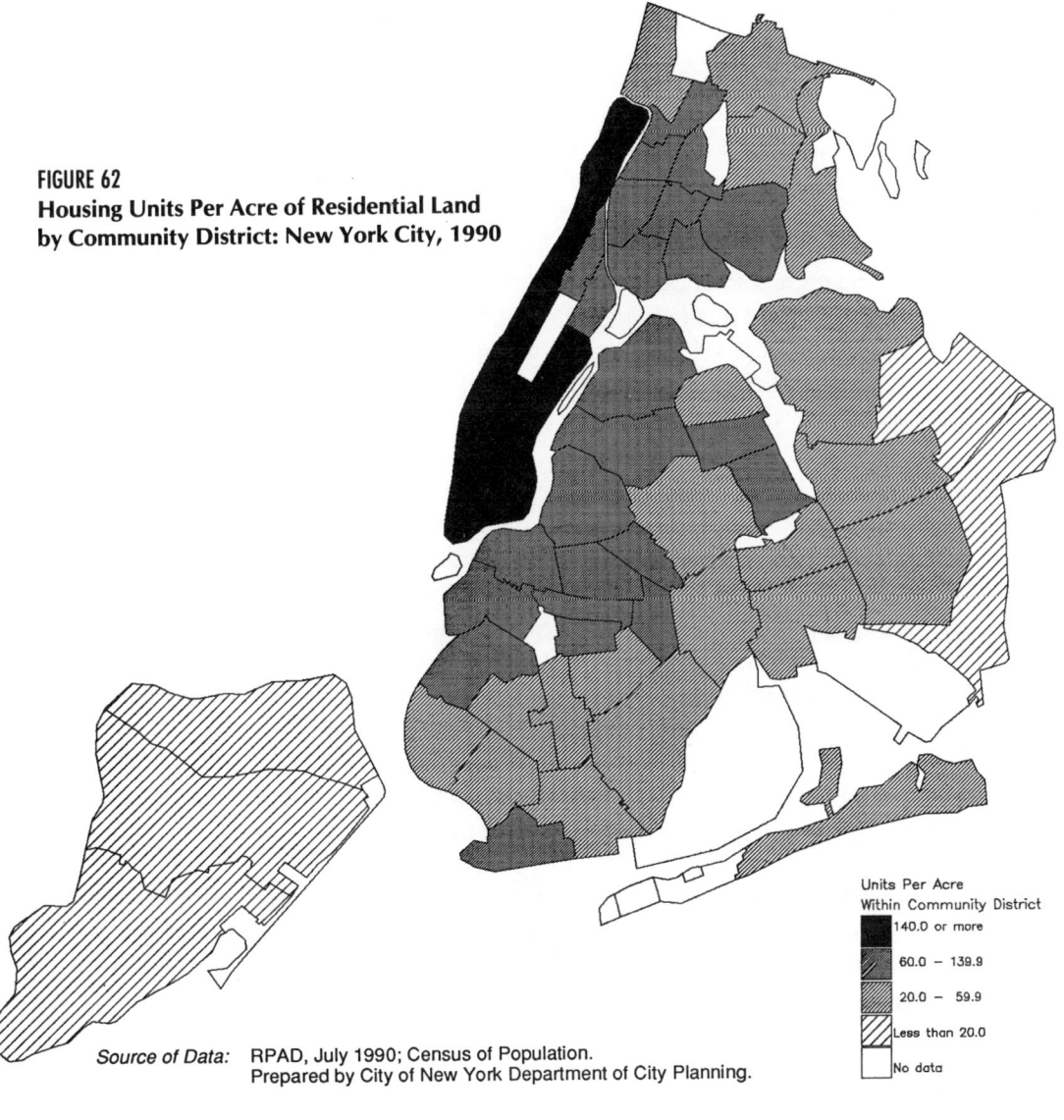

FIGURE 62
Housing Units Per Acre of Residential Land by Community District: New York City, 1990

Units Per Acre Within Community District
- 140.0 or more
- 60.0 – 139.9
- 20.0 – 59.9
- Less than 20.0
- No data

Source of Data: RPAD, July 1990; Census of Population.
Prepared by City of New York Department of City Planning.

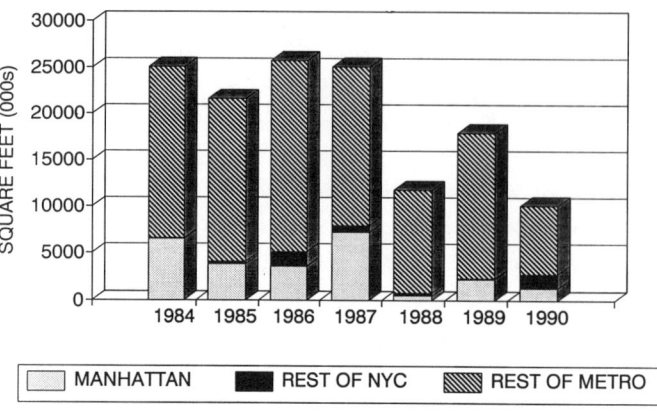

FIGURE 63
Metro Area Office Development,
Square Feet Receiving Permits,
1984–1990

Source: FW Dodge.

Increases in office-based employment during the 1980s spurred an office development boom in Manhattan's central business district. During that decade, fifty-five million square feet of office space was built in Manhattan's central business district, raising the inventory from under three hundred million square feet to about 350 million square feet. By the end of the 1980s, city government was helping spur office development in downtown areas of the other boroughs. However, the amount of new office development in the city was small compared to the boom in the surrounding suburbs.

New York City's ability to accommodate future development is constricted by the capacity of its infrastructure and the need to maintain and improve environmental quality. Although neither the city's population nor its employment has risen significantly over the long term, changing lifestyles, rising affluence, and the level of development required simply to replace obsolete buildings have placed pressure on infrastructure capacity.

The city's transportation network improved during the 1980s as a result of the rebuilding and repair of its highway, bridge, and transit infrastructure. This rebuilding was required to counteract the deterioration that occurred during years of deferred maintenance in the 1970s.

However, virtually all of the city's transportation network was completed more than thirty years ago and its capacity has not increased since then despite increased demand. For example, the city's key truck routes are chronically congested. Airport access and transit capacity into the central business district also are problems. Largely because of traffic congestion, New York City's air quality, although improving, still fails to meet federal standards for ozone and carbon monoxide.

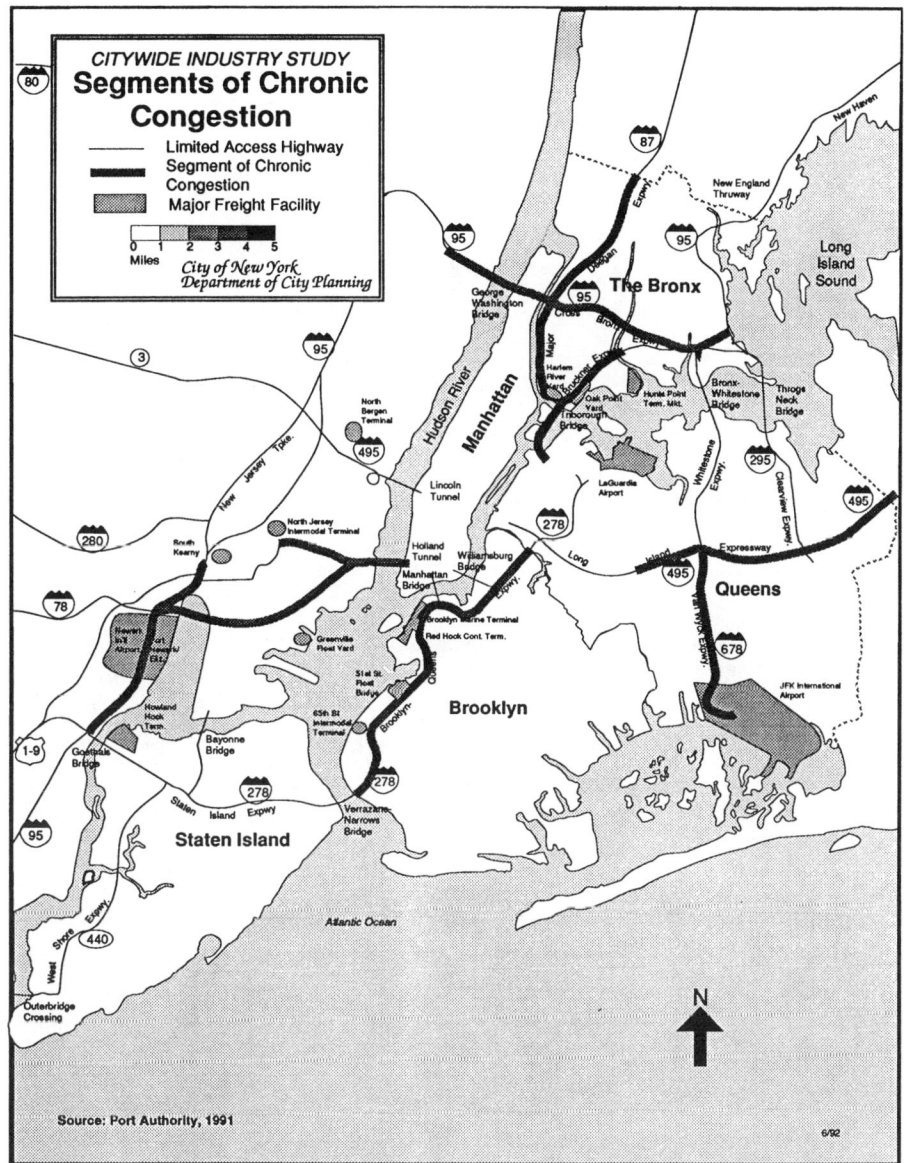

FIGURE 64
Segments of Chronic Traffic Congestion

NOTE

Much of the information presented in this Appendix is taken from the *1991 Annual Report on Social Indicators* (New York: New York City Department of City Planning, 1991), which provides far more information and detail.

CONTRIBUTORS

Jonathan Barnett is a professor of architecture at the City College of New York and is the director of the graduate program in urban design there. His urban design practice is based in Washington, D.C.

Todd W. Bressi writes and teaches about planning and urban design. He is the associate editor of the design journal *Places, A Quarterly Journal of Environmental Design.* Mr. Bressi is a visiting associate professor in Pratt Institute's urban design department and a lecturer in Hunter College's Department of Urban Affairs, both in New York City. For three years he edited *MetroPlanner,* published by the American Planning Association, New York Metro Chapter.

Sigurd Grava is a professor of urban planning at the Columbia University Graduate School of Architecture, Planning, and Preservation in New York City and is the director of the urban planning program there. He served as president of the American Planning Association, New York Metro Chapter, from 1990 to 1992.

Frances Halsband is the dean of Pratt Institute's School of Architecture in Brooklyn and is a principal in the architecture firm of R. M. Kliment and Frances Halsband in New York City.

Jerold Kayden, an attorney, is a Senior Fellow of the Lincoln Institute of Land Policy in Cambridge, Massachusetts.

Brian Kintish is an associate of Abeles Phillips Preiss and Shapiro, planning and real estate consultants, in New York City.

CONTRIBUTORS

Eric Kober is the director of the Housing, Economic, and Infrastructure Planning Division at the New York City Department of City Planning.

Michael Kwartler, FAIA, is an architect, an urban designer, and the director of the Environmental Simulation Center at the New School for Social Research in New York City.

Larry Littlefield is a planner in the Housing, Economic, and Infrastructure Planning Division at the New York City Department of City Planning. He specializes in regional economics.

Norman Marcus is counsel to the law firm of Bachner, Tally, Polevoy, Misher and Brinberg in New York City and was general counsel to the New York City Planning Commission and the Department of City Planning from 1963 to 1985.

R. Susan Motley is the president of RSM/Associates, a community development firm, and is a former member of the New York City Planning Commission.

Richard A. Plunz, an architectural historian, is a professor of architecture at the Columbia University Graduate School of Architecture, Planning, and Preservation in New York City.

Peter D. Salins, AICP, is a professor and the chairman of the Department of Urban Affairs and Planning at Hunter College in New York City and is a Senior Fellow of the Manhattan Institute for Policy Research.

Richard L. Schaffer is the chairman of the New York City Planning Commission.

John Shapiro is a principal of Abeles Phillips Preiss and Shapiro, planning and real estate consultants, in New York City.

Robert A. M. Stern is an architect and a professor at the Columbia University Graduate School of Architecture, Planning, and Preservation in New York City and is the coauthor of *New York 1900* (1983) and *New York 1930: Architecture and Urbanism Between the Two World Wars* (1987). His architectural practice is based in New York City.

Roy Strickland, an architect and historian, is an associate professor of architecture at the Massachusetts Institute of Technology in Cambridge and is a member of the Hudson Studio, Architects and Planners, in New York City.

Marilyn Taylor is an architect, planner, and partner at Skidmore, Owings and Merrill in New York City.

Robert F. Wagner, Jr., is vice chairman of L. H. Research, Inc. He is a former chairman of the New York City Planning Commission and was chairman of the Mayor's Commission on the Year 2000.

Carol Willis is an architectural historian and an assistant professor at the Columbia University Graduate School of Architecture, Planning, and Preservation in New York City.

CREDITS

FIGURE 1 J. Stubben, *Der Stadtebau*, Vol. 9 (Handbuches der Architektur, Entwerfen, Anlage, und Einrichtung der Gebaude) figure 574. Courtesy Avery Architectural and Fine Arts Library, Columbia University in the City of New York.

FIGURE 2 From Hugh Ferriss, *The Metropolis of Tomorrow* (New York: Ives Washburn, 1929; republished by Princeton Architectural Press, 1986). Collection of Carol Willis.

FIGURE 3 George B. Ford, *New York City Building Zone Resolution: Restricting the Height and Uses of Buildings and Prescribing the Minimum Sizes of Their Yards and Courts* (New York: New York Title and Mortgage Company).

FIGURE 4 Collection of Carol Willis.

FIGURE 5 Courtesy Avery Architectural and Fine Arts Library, Columbia University in the City of New York.

FIGURE 6 City Improvement Commission, 1907. Courtesy Avery Architectural and Fine Arts Library, Columbia University in the City of New York.

FIGURE 7 Courtesy the United States History, Local History and Geneaology Division, The New York Public Library, Astor, Lenox and Tilden Foundations.

FIGURE 8 Ford, *New York City Building Zone Resolution*.

FIGURE 9 Ford, *New York City Building Zone Resolution*.

FIGURE 10 Ford, *New York City Building Zone Resolution*.

FIGURE 11 Collection of Carol Willis.

FIGURE 12 Collection of Carol Willis.

FIGURE 13 Collection of Carol Willis.

FIGURE 14 Francisco Mujica, *The History of the Skyscraper* (Paris and New York: Architectural Press, 1929), Plate CXXIV. Courtesy Avery Architectural and Fine Arts Library, Columbia University in the City of New York.

FIGURE 15 Collection of Carol Willis.

FIGURE 16 *Final Report* (New York: New York City Commission on Building Districts and Restrictions, 1916). Courtesy Avery Architectural and Fine Arts Library, Columbia University in the City of New York.

CREDITS

FIGURE 17 *Final Report.* Courtesy Avery Architectural and Fine Arts Library, Columbia University in the City of New York.

FIGURE 18 *Final Report.* Courtesy Avery Architectural and Fine Arts Library, Columbia University in the City of New York.

FIGURE 19 *Development and Present Status of City Planning in New York City* (New York: New York City Board of Estimate and Apportionment, Committee on the City Plan, 1914). Courtesy Avery Architectural and Fine Arts Library, Columbia University in the City of New York.

FIGURE 20 Collection of Richard A. Plunz.

FIGURE 21 Walter I. Willis, *Queensboro, New York City: 1910–1920* (Long Island City: Queens Chamber of Commerce, 1920). Courtesy Queens Chamber of Commerce.

FIGURE 22 *Queensboro, New York City.* Courtesy Queens Chamber of Commerce.

FIGURE 23 George B. Ford, *Building Zones: A Handbook of Restrictions on the Height, Area and Use of Buildings* (New York: The Lawyers Mortgage Co., 1917). Courtesy Avery Architectural and Fine Arts Library, Columbia University in the City of New York.

FIGURE 24 Collection of Richard A. Plunz.

FIGURE 25 Collection of Richard A. Plunz.

FIGURE 26 Todd W. Bressi.

FIGURE 27 Todd W. Bressi.

FIGURE 28 New York City Department of City Planning.

FIGURE 29 Abeles Phillips Preiss and Shapiro.

FIGURE 30 New York City Department of City Planning.

FIGURE 31 Todd W. Bressi.

FIGURE 32 *The Zoning Handbook* (New York: New York City Department of City Planning, 1990), p. 84.

FIGURE 33 Todd W. Bressi.

FIGURE 34 New York City Zoning Resolution.

FIGURE 35 Sandy Hornick, New York City Department of City Planning.

FIGURE 36 Todd W. Bressi.

FIGURE 37 New York City Zoning Resolution.

FIGURE 38 New York City Zoning Resolution.

FIGURE 39 Dennis Ferris, New York City Department of City Planning.

FIGURE 40 Patrick Too, New York City Department of City Planning.

FIGURE 41 Abeles Phillips Preiss and Shapiro.

FIGURE 42 Elizabeth Mackintosh, New York City Department of City Planning.

FIGURE 43 Abeles Phillips Preiss and Shapiro.

FIGURE 44 New York City Department of City Planning.

FIGURE 45 Abeles Phillips Preiss and Shapiro.

FIGURE 46 Todd W. Bressi.

FIGURE 47 Sandy Hornick, New York City Department of City Planning.

CREDITS

FIGURE 48   Todd W. Bressi.

FIGURE 49   Abeles Phillips Preiss and Shapiro.

FIGURE 50   *1991 Annual Report on Social Indicators* (New York: New York City Department of City Planning, 1991; hereafter referred to as *Annual Report*.)

FIGURE 51   *Annual Report.*

FIGURE 52   *Annual Report.*

FIGURE 53   *Annual Report.*

FIGURE 54   *Annual Report.*

FIGURE 55   *Annual Report.*

FIGURE 56   *Annual Report.*

FIGURE 57   *Annual Report.*

FIGURE 58   *Annual Report.*

FIGURE 59   *Annual Report.*

FIGURE 60   *Annual Report.*

FIGURE 61   *Annual Report.*

FIGURE 62   *Annual Report.*

FIGURE 63   *Annual Report.*

FIGURE 64   New York City Department of City Planning.